Aug 2008

BBC ACTIVE

RUSSIAN

Phrase Book & Dictionary

Elena Filimonova

BBC Active, an imprint of Educational Publishers LLP, part of the Pearson Education Group, Edinburgh Gate, Harlow, Essex CM20 2JE, England

ISBN: 978-1-4066-1212-7

Cover design: Two Associates
Cover photograph: OJPHOTOS/Alamy
Insides design: Pentacor book design
Layout: Oxford Designers & Illustrators
Illustrations © Joanna Kerr, New Division
Development manager: Tara Dempsey
Series editor: Philippa Goodrich
Editor: Natasha Kurashova
Senior production controller: Man Fai Lau

Printed and bound in China. CTPSC/01

how to use this book

This book is divided into colour-coded sections to help you find the language you need as quickly as possible. You can also refer to the **contents** on pages 4–5, and the contents lists at the start of each section.

Along with travel and language tips, each section contains:

 YOU MAY WANT TO SAY...
language you'll need for every situation

 YOU MAY SEE...
words and phrases you'll see on signs or in print

 YOU MAY HEAR... questions, instructions or information people may ask or give you

On page 12 you'll find **essentials**, a list of basic, all-purpose phrases to help you start communicating straight away.

Many of the phrases can be adapted by simply using another word from the dictionary. For instance, take the question Где аэропо́рт? *gdye aerapórt* (Where is the airport?), if you want to know where the *station* is, just substitute вокза́л *vagzál* (station) for аэропо́рт *aerapórt* to give Где вокза́л? *gdye vagzál.*

The **pronunciation guide** is based on English sounds, and is explained on page 6. If you want some guidance on how the Russian language works, see **basic grammar** on page 145. The **dictionary** is separated into two sections: English–Russian (page 155) and Russian–English (page 197).

We welcome any comments or suggestions about this book, but in the meantime, have a good trip – Счастли́вого пути́! *schaslívava pootí*

contents

pronunciation guide

✳ the Russian alphabet

Russian is the most widespread of the Slavonic languages. It uses the Cyrillic alphabet, also used by some East and South Slavonic languages (e.g. Bulgarian, Serbian, Ukrainian), languages of the former USSR (some Caucasian, Uralic, Turkic languages), and Mongolian. Cyrillic is closely based on the Greek alphabet.

The Russian alphabet consists of 33 letters. The letters are best represented in three groups:

- those that look and sound similar to English: А, Е, К, М, О, Т.

- those that look similar but sound different to English letters: В, pronounced as English 'v', Н (n), Р (r), С (s), У (oo), Х (kh as ch in Scottish loch).

- those that look totally different from English, e.g. Ж, Ф, Ю, Я. Their sounds, however, are often quite similar to those we encounter in English.

LETTER	NAME OF LETTER	APPROX EQUIVALENT IN ENGLISH	SHOWN IN BOOK AS
А а	a	a as in 'father'	a
Б б	beh	b as in 'bad'	b
В в	veh	v as in 'voice'	v
Г г	geh	g as in 'good'	g
Д д	deh	d as in 'date'	d
Е е	yeh	ye as in 'yes'	ye

Ё ё	yo	yo as in 'yoghurt'	yo
Ж ж	zheh	s as in 'pleasure'	zh
З з	zeh	z as in 'zip'	z
И и	ee	ee as in 'eel'	i
Й й	ee krátkaye (lit. short ee)	short ee as y in 'boy'	ï *
К к	ka	k as in 'cat'	k
Л л	el	l as in 'love'	l
М м	em	m as in 'man'	m
Н н	en	n as in 'nail'	n
О о	o	o as in 'small'	o
П п	peh	p as in 'pan'	p
Р р	er	rolled 'r'	r
С с	es	s as in 'sad'	s
Т т	teh	t as in 'tap'	t
У у	oo	oo as in 'book'	oo
Ф ф	ef	f as in 'food'	f
Х х	kha	ch as in 'loch'	kh
Ц ц	tseh	ts as in 'toilets'	ts
Ч ч	cheh	ch as in 'cheap'	ch
Ш ш	sha	sh as in 'sheep'	sh
Щ щ	shcha	a long sh as in 'shock'	sch
ъ	tvyórdy znak (hard sign)	not pronounced, used to make a gap between syllables	(dash –)
ы	y	no equivalent in English. Start with i as in 'bit', then lower the middle part of	y

		the tongue and draw it backwards. No words start with this letter.	
ь	myákhki znak (soft sign)	not pronounced, softens the preceding consonant	no sign **
Э э	eh	e as in 'Mary'	e
Ю ю	yoo	u as in 'usual'	yoo
Я я	ya	ya as in 'yak'	ya

Notes:
* due to unclear pronunciation in colloquial Russian, masculine adjectives will have no *i* after *y* and *i* in the final position in the imitated pronunciation
** ь is not shown in the imitated pronunciation in this book

✱ vowels

Some vowels when pronounced do not correspond to what is written. Essential rules are: if unstressed *o* turns to *a*, and *e* turns to *i*.

Vowels in Russian are pronounced separately from each other, except for the combinations: *oo, ye, yi, yo, yoo, ya, aï, oï, yeï*. For example, the word for Russia Россия (*rasiya*) should be pronounced *ras-i-ya*, theatre театр (*tiatr*) is pronounced ti-á-tr, etc.

✳ stress

Russian pronunciation depends a lot on stress. In words with more than one syllable, one syllable will be more prominent, pronounced more strongly than the others. The stress may fall on any syllable in the word. In some cases the meaning of the word depends on what syllable is stressed, e.g. за ´мок 'castle' but замо ´к 'lock'. Some complex words may have a secondary stress. In this phrase book, we have indicated the stress by an accent on top of the corresponding vowel.

The letter ё (*yo*) is always stressed. You won't find a stress mark in the words with ё. Usually the two dots on top are not shown when written, Russians seem always to know whether it's е or ё. In this book, we have indicated the dots.

In the 'You may see…' sections, columns with Russian phrases lack the stress signs, since it is the way you'll indeed see them.

✳ intonation

Typically, in statements the intonation falls at the end of the sentence:

Вы хоти ´те ко ´фе. <u>You want coffee</u>.

Raising the intonation will transform a statement into a question, without changing the word order. In yes/no questions (where a 'yes' or 'no' answer is expected), the intonation rises towards the end of the most important word.

The examples below show how the meaning of the question depends on where the intonation is placed:

Вы хоти´те ко´фе? Is it <u>you</u> who wants coffee?

Вы хоти´те ко´фе? Do you <u>want</u> coffee?

Вы хоти´те ко´фе? Is it <u>coffee</u> you want?

the basics

*essentials

Hello.	Здра́вствуйте!	*zdrástvooïtye*
Goodbye.	До свида́ния.	*da svidániya*
Good morning.	До́брое у́тро.	*dóbraye óotra*
Good afternoon.	До́брый день.	*dóbry dyen*
Good evening.	До́брый ве́чер.	*dóbry vyéchir*
Good night.	Споко́йной но́чи.	*spakóinaï nóchi*
Yes.	Да.	*da*
No.	Нет.	*nyet*
Please.	Пожа́луйста.	*pazhálsta*
Thank you (very much).	(Большо́е) спаси́бо.	*(balshóye) spasíba*
You're welcome./ Don't mention it.	Не́ за что.	*nyé za shta*
I don't know.	Я не зна́ю.	*ya ni znáyoo*
I don't understand.	Я не понима́ю.	*ya ni panimáyoo*
I only speak a little bit of Russian.	Я лишь немно́го говорю́ по-ру́сски.	*ya lish nimnóga gavaryóo pa-róoski*
Do you speak English?	Вы говори́те по-англи́йски?	*vy gavarítye pa-anglíski*
Pardon?	Извини́те. Я не понима́ю.	*izviníte. ya nye panimáyoo*
Could you repeat that please?	Повтори́те, пожа́луйста.	*paftarítye, pazhálsta*
More slowly, please.	Поме́дленнее/не так бы́стро, пожа́луйста.	*pamyédliniye/ni tak býstra, pazhálsta*

How do you say it in Russian?	Как по-ру́сски...?	kak pa-róoski...
Excuse me./Sorry.	Прости́те./Извините.	prastítye/izvinítye
I'm sorry.	Мне жаль.	mnye zhal
OK, fine./That's all right.	Хорошо́	kharashó
Cheers! (as toast)	За здоро́вье!	za zdaróvye
What's your name?	Как Вас зову́т?	kak vas zavóot
Pleased to meet you.	О́чень прия́тно.	óchin priyátna
I'd like... (m/f)	Я бы хоте́л/хоте́ла...	ya by khatyél/khatyéla...
Is/are there (any)...?	У Вас есть...?	oo vas yest...
What's this?	Что́ э́то?	shtó éta
How much is it?	Ско́лько (э́то) сто́ит?	skólka (éta) stóit
Can I/we...?	Мо́жно...?	mózhna...
Where is/are...?	Где...?	gdye...
Can you... tell me...? give me...? show me on the map? write it down?	Вы мо́жете... сказа́ть мне...? дать мне... ? показа́ть мне на ка́рте? написа́ть?	vy mózhitye... skazát mnye... dat mnye... pakazát mnye na kártye napisát
Help!	На по́мощь!/Помоги́те!	na pómasch/pamagítye

* numbers

0	ноль	*nol*
1	оди́н	*adín*
2	два	*dva*
3	три	*tri*
4	четы́ре	*chitýri*
5	пять	*pyat*
6	шесть	*shest*
7	семь	*syem*
8	во́семь	*vósim*
9	де́вять	*dyévit*
10	де́сять	*dyésit*
11	оди́ннадцать	*adínatsat*
12	двена́дцать	*dvinátsat*
13	трина́дцать	*trinátsat*
14	четы́рнадцать	*chitýrnatsat*
15	пятна́дцать	*pitnátsat*
16	шестна́дцать	*shisnátsat*
17	семна́дцать	*simnátsat*
18	восемна́дцать	*vasimnátsat*
19	девятна́дцать	*divitnátsat*
20	два́дцать	*dvátsat*
21	два́дцать оди́н	*dvátsat adín*
22...	два́дцать два	*dvátsat dva*
30	три́дцать	*trítsat*
31	три́дцать оди́н	*trítsat adín*
32...	три́дцать два	*trítsat dva*
40	со́рок	*sórak*
50	пятьдеся́т	*piddisyát*
60	шестьдеся́т	*shizdisyát*
70	се́мьдесят	*syémdisyat*
80	во́семьдесят	*vósimdisyat*
90	девяно́сто	*divinósta*

100	сто	*sto*
101	сто один	*sto adín*
102...	сто два	*sto dva*
200	двести	*dvyésti*
250	двести пятьдесят	*dvyésti piddisyát*
300	триста	*trísta*
400	четыреста	*chitýrista*
500	пятьсот	*pitsót*
600	шестьсот	*shissót*
700	семьсот	*simsót*
800	восемьсот	*vasimsót*
900	девятьсот	*divitsót*
1,000	тысяча	*týsicha (coll. týscha)*
2,000	две тысячи	*dvye týsichi*
3,000	три тысячи	*tri týsichi*
4,000	четыре тысячи	*chitýri týsichi*
100,000	сто тысяч	*sto týsich*
one million	один миллион	*adín millión*
one and a half million	полтора миллиона	*paltará millióna*

✳ ordinal numbers

first (m/f/n)	пе́рвый, пе́рвая, пе́рвое	*pyérvy, pyérvaya, pyérvaye*
second (m/f/n)	второ́й, втора́я, второ́е	*ftaroï, ftaráya, ftaróye*
third (m/f/n)	тре́тий, тре́тья, тре́тье	*tréti, trétiya, trétiye*
fourth (m/f/n)	четвёртый, четвёртая, четвёртое	*chitvyórty, chitvyórtaya, chitvyórtaye*

15

fifth (m)	пя́тый	pyáty
sixth (m)	шесто́й	shistóï
seventh (m)	седьмо́й	sidmóï
eighth (m)	восьмо́й	vasmóï
ninth (m)	девя́тый	divyáty
tenth (m)	деся́тый	disyáty

* fractions

a quarter	че́тверть	chyétvirt
a half	полови́на	palavína
three-quarters	три че́тверти	tri chyétvirti
a third	треть	tryet
two-thirds	две тре́ти	dvye tryéti

* days

Monday	понеде́льник	panidyélnik
Tuesday	вто́рник	ftórnik
Wednesday	среда́	sridá
Thursday	четве́рг	chitvyérk
Friday	пя́тница	pyátnitsa
Saturday	суббо́та	soobóta
Sunday	воскресе́нье	vaskrisyénie

* months

January	янва́рь	yinvár
February	февра́ль	fivrál
March	март	mart
April	апре́ль	apryél

May	май	*maï*
June	июнь	*iyóon*
July	июль	*iyóol*
August	а́вгуст	*ávgoost*
September	сентя́брь	*sintyábr*
October	октя́брь	*aktyábr*
November	ноя́брь	*nayábr*
December	дека́брь	*dikábr*

✳ seasons

spring	весна́	*visná*
summer	ле́то	*lyéta*
autumn	о́сень	*ósyen*
winter	зима́	*zimá*

✳ dates

YOU MAY WANT TO SAY...

What day is it today?	Како́й сего́дня день (неде́ли)?	*kakói sivódnya dyen (nidyéli)*
What date is it today?	Како́е сего́дня число́?	*kakóye sivódnya chisló*
When is your birthday?	Когда́ у тебя́/Вас день рожде́ния?	*kogdá oo tibyá/vas dyen razhdyéniya*
(It's) the fifteenth of April.	(Сего́дня) пятна́дцатое апре́ля	*(sivódnya) pitnátsatoye apryélya*
On the fifteenth of April.	Пятна́дцатого апре́ля	*pitnátsatava apryélya*

the basics

17

✳ telling the time

 ● In Russian, 'half past…' is translated literally as half way to the next hour. So, 'half past six' is полседьмого (polsidmóva), literally half way to seven; similarly, 'twenty past three' is двадцать минут четвертого (dvátsat minóot chitvyórtava), twenty minutes off the fourth (hour). 'Ten to five' is five without ten (minutes): без десяти (минут) пять (biz disití [minóot] pyat); 'a quarter to six' is без четверти шесть (bis chyétvirti shest), etc.

● Russia has nine time zones. When travelling in Russia, always check whether the departure and arrival time is Moscow or local.

YOU MAY WANT TO SAY...

● What time is it?	Кото́рый час?/ Ско́лько вре́мени?	katóry chas/ skólka vryémini
● What time does it...	Когда́...	kagdá...
open?	открыва́ется?	atkryváyetsa
close?	закрыва́ется?	zakryváyetsa
start?	начина́ется?	nachináyetsa
finish?	зака́нчивается?	zakánchivayetsa
● It's...	(Сейча́с)...	syeïchás...
10 o'clock	де́сять часо́в	dyésit chisóf
midday	по́лдень	póldin
midnight	по́лночь	pólnach

At...	В...	v...
half past nine	полдесятого	poldisyátava
half past ten	полодиннадца-того	poladínatsatava
quarter past nine	четверь десятого	chyétvirt disyátava
quarter to ten	без четверти десять	bis chyétvirti dyésit
twenty past ten	двадцать минут одиннадцатого	dvátsat minóot adínatsatava
twenty-five to ten	двадцать пять минут одиннадцатого	dvátsat pyat minóot adínatsatava
precisely ten o'clock	ровно десять (часов)	róvna dyésit (chisóf)
In...	Через...	chyéris...
ten minutes	десять минут	dyésit minóot
fifteen minutes	пятнадцать минут	pitnátsat minóot
half an hour	полчаса	polchisá
an hour	час	chas

✳ time phrases

day	день	dyen
week	неделя	nidyélya
fortnight	две недели	dvye nidyéli
month	месяц	myésits
year	год	got

the basics

19

time phrases

today	сегóдня	sivódnya
tomorrow	зáвтра	záftra
the day after tomorrow	послезáвтра	poslizáftra
yesterday	вчерá	fchirá
the day before yesterday	позавчерá	pózafchirá
this morning	сегóдня ýтром	sivódnya óotram
this afternoon	сегóдня пóсле обéда	sivódnya pósli abyéda
this evening/ tonight	сегóдня вéчером	sivódnya vyéchiram
on Friday	в пя́тницу	f pyátnitsoo
on Fridays	по пя́тницам	pa pyátnitsam
every... Monday	кáждый... понедéльник	kázhdy... panidyélnik
every week	кáждую недéлю	kázhdooyoo nidyélyoo
for... a week two weeks two years a month	на... недéлю две недéли два гóда мéсяц	na... nidyélyoo dvye nidyéli dva góda myésits
I'm here for two weeks.	Я пробýду здесь две недéли.	ya prabóodoo zdyes dvye nidyéli
I've been here for a month.	Я здесь ужé мéсяц.	ya zdyes oozhé myésits
I've been learning Russian for two years.	Я учý рýсский язы́к два гóда.	ya oochóo róosski yizýk dva góda

next Tuesday	в следующий вторник	*f slyédooschi ftórnik*
next week	на следующей неделе	*na slyédooscheï nidyéli*
next month	в следующем месяце	*f slyédooschem myésitse*
next year	в следующем году	*f slyédooschem gadóo*
last night	прошлой ночью	*próshlaï nóchyoo*
last week	на прошлой неделе	*na próshlaï nidyéli*
a week ago	неделю назад	*nidyélyoo nazát*
a year ago	год назад	*god nazát*
Since...		
yesterday	со вчерашнего дня	*sa fchiráshniva dnya*
last week	с прошлой недели	*s próshlaï nidyéli*
last month	с прошлого месяца	*s próshlava myésitsa*
last year	с прошлого года	*s próshlava góda*
It's early/late	рано/поздно	*rána/pózna*

MEASUREMENTS

centimetre(s)	сантиметр/ сантиметры	*santimyétr/ santimyétry*
metre(s)	метр/метры	*myetr/myétry*
kilometre(s)	километр/километры	*kilamyétr/kilamyétry*
mile(s)	миля/мили	*mílya/míli*
a litre	литр/литры	*litr/lítry*
25 litres	двадцать пять литров	*dvátsat pyat lítraf*

clothes and shoe sizes

gramme	грамм	*gram*
100 grammes	сто грámм(ов)	*sto grám(af)*
200 grammes	двéсти грámм(ов)	*dvyésti grám(af)*
kilo(s)	килогрámм/ килогрáммы	*kilagrám/kilagrámy*

CONVERSIONS

1km = *0.62 miles*	**1lb** = *450g*
1 mile = *1.61km*	**200g** = *7oz*
1 litre = *1.8 pints*	**¼lb** = *113g*
100g = *3.5oz*	**½lb** = *225g*
1oz = *28g*	**1 kilo** = *2.2lb*

To convert kilometres to miles, divide by 8 and multiply by 5 e.g. 16 kilometres (16/8 = 2, 2 × 5 = 10) = 10 miles.

For miles to kilometres, divide by 5 and multiply by 8 e.g. 50 miles (50/5 = 10, 10 × 8 = 80) = 80 kilometres.

✱ clothes and shoe sizes

WOMEN'S CLOTHES

UK	6	8	10	12	14	16	18	20
Europe	36	38	40	42	44	46	48	50
Russia	40	42	44	46	48	50	52	54

MEN'S CLOTHES							
UK	36	38	40	42	44	46	48
Europe	46	48	50	52	54	56	58

MEN'S SHIRTS							
UK	14	14½	15	15½	16	16½	17
Europe	36	37	38	39/40	41	42	43

SHOES							
UK	2	3	4	5	6	7	8
Europe	36	35.5	37	38	39.5	40.5	42
UK	9	10	11	12			
Europe	43	44.5	45.5	47			

✳ national holidays and festivals

● The New Year is first on the calendar and in popularity. Many celebrate it twice, on January 1 and 14 (which corresponds to January 1 in the Julian calendar, used in Russia before 1918 and which is still used by the Russian Orthodox Church).

● Listed on page 24 are the official national holidays in Russia, on these days banks, offices and most shops are closed.

Listed on page 24

the basics

23

Новый год	*nóvy got*	New Year's Day: 1 January
Новогодние каникулы	*navagódniye kaníkooly*	New Year Holidays
Рождество	*razhdistvó*	**Christmas Day, Russian Orthodox: 7 January**
День защитника Отечества	*dyen zaschítnika atyéchistva*	**Defenders of the Motherland Day: 23 February**
Международный Женский день	*mizhdoonaródny zhénski dyen*	**International Women's Day: 8 March**
Пасха	*páskha*	**Easter**
День Весны и труда	*dyen visný i troodá*	**Spring and Labour Day: 1 May**
День Победы	*dyen pabyédy*	**Victory Day: 9 May**
День России	*dyen rassíi*	**Day of Russia: 12 June**
День Народного единства	*dyen naródnava yidínstva*	**Day of National Unity: 4 November**

general conversation

✳ greetings

● Russian has two words for 'you'. Вы *(vy)* is formal or for more than one person, and ты *(ty)* is informal and is used with children or good friends. In this phrase book, if not stated otherwise, the Вы form is used. If you need to use the ты *(ty)* forms the endings of the verb will change (see **basic grammar**, page 145).

YOU MAY WANT TO SAY...

Hello. (formal) (informal)	Здра́вствуйте! Здра́вствуй!	*zdrástvooïtye* *zdrástvooï*
Hi.	Приве́т!	*privyét*
Good morning.	До́брое у́тро.	*dóbraye óotra*
Good afternoon.	До́брый день.	*dóbry dyen*
Good evening.	До́брый ве́чер.	*dóbry vyéchir*
Good night.	Споко́йной но́чи.	*spakóïnaï nóchi*
Goodbye.	До свида́ния.	*da svidániya*
Bye. (informal)	Пока́.	*paká*
How are you? (lit. how are things)	Как дела́?	*kak dilá*
Fine, thanks.	Спаси́бо, хорошо́.	*spasíba, kharashó*
OK.	Ничего́.	*nichivó*
And you? (formal) (informal)	А у Вас?/А Вы как? А у тебя́?/А ты как?	*a oo vas/a vy kak* *a oo tibya/a ty kak*

general conversation

✳ introductions

● Russians have three names: first name имя *(ímya)*, patronimic отчество *(ótchistva)* and surname фамилия *(famíliya)*. The patronimic is derived from the name of the person's father by adding -ович/-евич *(-ovich/-yevich)* for a man and -овна/-евна *(-ovna/-yevna)* for a woman. For example: father Иван *(Ivan)*; son Иванович *(Ivanovich)*; daughter Ивановна *(Ivanovna)*.

YOU MAY WANT TO SAY...

● **My name is...**	Меня́ зову́т ...	*minyá zavóot*
● **This is...** (referring to a man)	Это ...	*éta ...*
Mr Brown	господи́н Бра́ун	*gaspadín Bráoon*
my husband	мой муж	*moï moosh*
my son	мой сын	*moï syn*
my partner	мой друг	*moï drook*
● **This is...** (referring to a woman)	Это ...	*éta...*
Mrs Brown	госпожа́ Браун	*gaspazhá Bráoon*
my wife	моя́ жена́	*mayá zhiná*
my daughter	моя́ дочь	*mayá doch*
my partner	моя́ подру́га	*mayá padróoga*
● **Pleased to meet you.**	О́чень прия́тно!	*óchin priyátna*
● **Can we use 'ty'?**	Мо́жно на ты?	*mózhna na ty*

* talking about yourself

YOU MAY WANT TO SAY...

● I'm English. (m/f)	Я англича́нин/ англича́нка.	*ya anglichánin/ anglichánka*
● I'm Scottish. (m/f)	Я шотла́ндец/ шотла́ндка.	*ya shatlándits/ shatlánka*
● I'm Irish. (m/f)	Я ирла́ндец/ ирла́ндка.	*ya irlándits/irlánka*
● I'm Welsh. (m/f)	Я валли́ец/ валли́йка.	*ya valíyets/valíĭka*
● I/We come from...	Я/мы из...	*ya/my iz...*
England	А́нглии	*ánglii*
Ireland	Ирла́ндии	*irlándii*
Scotland	Шотла́ндии	*shatlándii*
Wales	Уэ́льса	*ooélsa*
● I/We live in...	Я живу́/мы живём в...	*ya zhivóo/my zhivyóm v...*
London	Ло́ндоне	*lóndanye*
Edinburgh	Эдинбу́рге	*edinbóorgye*
● I'm 25 years old.	Мне два́дцать пять лет.	*mnye dvátsat pyat lyet*
● He's/she's five years old.	Ему́/ей пять лет.	*yimóo/yeĭ pyat lyet*
● I'm a...	Я ...	*ya ...*
web designer	веб-диза́йнер	*veb-dizáĭnyer*
nurse	медсестра́	*mitsistrá*
student (m/f)	студе́нт/ студе́нтка	*stoodyént/ stoodyéntka*

I work in/for…	Я рабо́таю…	ya rabótayoo…
a bank	в ба́нке	v bánkye
a computer firm	в компью́терной фи́рме	v kampyóoternaï fírmi
I'm retired.	Я на пе́нсии.	ya na pyénsii
I'm unemployed.	Я безрабо́тный.	ya byezrabótny
I run my own business.	У меня́ своё де́ло/ своя́ фи́рма.	oo minyá svayó dyéla/ svayá fírma
I'm a freelancer.	Я фрила́нсер.	ya frilánsyer
I'm…	Я…	ya…
married (m/f)	жена́т/за́мужем	zhinát/zámoozhim
divorced (m/f)	разведён/ разведена́	razvidyón/ razvidiná
single (m/f)	не жена́т/ не за́мужем	ni zhinát/ni zámoozhim
widower/widow	вдове́ц/вдова́	vdavyéts/vdavá
I have…	У меня́…	oo minyá…
three children	тро́е дете́й	tróye dityéï
one son/one daughter	оди́н сын/одна́ дочь	adín syn/adná doch
two brothers/ two sisters	два бра́та/две сестры́	dva bráta/dvye sistrý
I don't have…	У меня́…	oo minyá…
any children	нет дете́й	nyet dityéï
any brothers or sisters	нет бра́тьев и́ли сестёр	nyet brátyev íli sistyór
I'm on holiday here.	Я тури́ст.	ya tooríst
I'm here on business.	Я здесь по де́лу/ по рабо́те.	ya zdyes pa dyéloo/ pa rabótye

I'm here with my...	Я здесь с...	ya zdyes s...
wife	моéй женóй	mayéï zhinóï
husband	моúм мýжем	maím móozhim
family	семьёй	simyóï
colleague	коллéгой	kallyégaï
My husband/son is...	Мой муж/сын...	moï moosh/syn...
My wife/daughter is...	Моя женá/дочь...	mayá zhiná/doch...
My husband/wife works in...	Мой муж/моя женá рабóтает в...	moï moosh/mayá zhiná rabótait v...
I speak very little Russian.	Я немнóго говорю по-рýсски.	ya nimnóga gavaryóo pa-róoski

✳ asking about other people

asking about other people

YOU MAY WANT TO SAY...

Where do you come from? (formal/informal)	Откýда Вы/ты?	atkóoda vy/ty
What's your name? (formal/informal)	Как Вас/тебя зовýт?/	kak vas/tibyá zavóot
Are you married? (to m) (to f)	Вы женáты? Вы замýжем?	vy zhináty vy zámoozhim

Do you have...	У Вас есть...	*oo vas yest...*
any children?	дéти?	*dyéti*
any brothers and sisters?	брáтья и́ли сёстры?	*brátya íli syóstry*
a girlfriend/ boyfriend?	подрýга/друг?	*padróoga/drook*
How old are you? (formal/informal)	Скóлько Вам/ тебé лет?	*skólka vam/tibyé lyet*
How old are they?	Скóлько им лет?	*skólka im lyet*
Is this your...	Это...	*éta ...*
husband/wife?	ваш муж/вáша женá?	*vash moosh/vásha zhiná*
boyfriend/ girlfriend?	ваш друг/ вáша подрýга?	*vash drook/vásha padróoga*
What is he/she called?	Как егó/её зовýт?	*kak yivó/yiyó zavóot*
Where are you going? (on foot/ by car)	Кудá Вы идёте/ éдете?	*koodá vy idyótye/ yéditye*
Where are you staying?	Где Вы остановúлись?	*gdye vy astanavílis*
Where do you live?	Где Вы живёте?	*gdye vy zhivyótye*
What do you do?	Чем Вы занимáетесь?	*chem vy zanimáityes*
What are you studying?	Что Вы изучáете?	*shto vy izoocháitye*

general conversation

31

✳ chatting

YOU MAY WANT TO SAY...

- Moscow is very beautiful. | Москва́ о́чень краси́вый го́род. | *maskvá óchin krasívy górat*

- I like Russia (very much). | Мне (о́чень) нра́вится Росси́я. | *mnye (óchin) nrávitsa rassíya*

- It's the first time I've been to Moscow. | Я в пе́рвый раз в Москве́. | *ya f pyérvy raz v maskvyé*

- I come to St. Petersburg often. | Я ча́сто быва́ю в Петербу́рге. | *ya chásta byváyoo v pitirbóorgye*

- Do you live here? | Вы здесь живёте? | *vy zdyes zhivyótye*

- Have you ever been to... | Вы бы́ли в... | *vy býli v...*
    - Liverpool? | Ливерпу́ле? | *livirpóolye*
    - Cambridge? | Ке́мбридже? | *kémbridzhe*

- Did you like it? | Вам понра́вилось? | *vam panrávilas*

YOU MAY HEAR...

- Вам нра́вится Росси́я? | *vam nrávitsya rassíya* | Do you like Russia?

- Вы ра́ньше быва́ли в Росси́и? | *vy ránshe byváli v rassíi* | Have you been to Russia before?

- Вы здесь в пе́рвый раз? | *vy zdyes f pyérvy raz* | Are you here for the first time?

Ско́лько вре́мени Вы здесь бу́дете?	*skólka vryémini vy zdyes bóoditye*	How long will you be here?
Вы хорошо́ говори́те по-ру́сски.	*vy kharashó gavarítye pa-róoski*	Your Russian is very good.
Что Вы ду́маете о...?	*shto vy dóomaitye a…*	What do you think of…?

✳ the weather

YOU MAY WANT TO SAY...

It's a beautiful day!	Чуде́сный день!	*choodyésny dyen*
It's (very)...	(о́чень)...	*(óchin)...*
hot	жа́рко	*zhárka*
cold	хо́лодно	*khóladna*
windy	ве́тренно	*vyétrinna*
damp	сы́ро	*sýra*
slippery	ско́льзко	*skólska*
What's the forecast?	Како́й прогно́з пого́ды?	*kakói pragnós pagódy*
It's...	(Идёт...)	*(idyót...)*
raining	дождь	*dosht*
snowing	снег	*snyek*
hailing	град	*grat*
It's 20 degrees today.	Сего́дня плюс два́дцать.	*sivódnya plyoos dvátsat*
It's minus 10 today.	Сего́дня ми́нус де́сять.	*sivódnya mínoos dyésit*

✳ likes and dislikes

- I like...
  beer/football/
  flowers

  Я люблю
  пи́во/футбо́л/
  цветы́

  *ya lyooblyóo
  píva/footból/tsvitý*

- I don't like...
  vodka/tomatoes

  Я не люблю
  во́дку/помидо́ры

  *ya ni lyooblyóo
  vótkoo/pamidóry*

- I like him/her.

  Он/она́ мне
  нра́вится.

  on/aná mnye nrávitsa

- I don't like him/
  her.

  Он/она́ мне не
  нра́вится.

  *on/aná mnye ni
  nrávitsa*

- I hate...
  swimming

  Я ненави́жу...
  пла́вать.

  *ya ninavízhoo...
  plávat*

- Do you like...
  walking?
  ice cream?

  Вы лю́бите...
  гуля́ть?
  моро́женое?

  *vy lyóobitye...
  goolyát
  marózhinaye*

✳ feelings and opinions

- Are you...
  all right?
  happy?
  sad?

  Всё в поря́дке?
  Вы дово́льны?
  Вы расстро́ены?

  *fsyo f paryátkye
  vy davólny
  vy rastróyeny*

- Are you cold?

  Вам хо́лодно?/Вы
  замёрзли?

  *vam khóladna/vy
  zamyórzli*

- Are you hot?

  Вам жа́рко?

  vam zhárko

I'm (very) tired (m/f)	Я (о́чень) уста́л/ уста́ла.	ya (óchin) oostál/ oostála
I'm bored.	Мне ску́чно.	mnye skóoshna
I'm in good/bad mood.	У меня́ хоро́шее/ плохо́е настрое́ние.	oo minyá kharóshiye/ plakhóye nastrayéniye
What do you think of...?	Что Вы ду́маете о...?	shto vy dóomaitye a...
I/We think it's...	Я ду́маю/мы ду́маем, что э́то...	ya dóomayoo/my dóomaim chto éta...
great	здо́рово/ великоле́пно	zdórava/ velikalyépna
funny	смешно́	smishnó
Did you like it?	Вам понра́вилось?	vam panrávilas
It was...	(Это) бы́ло...	(éta) býla...
beautiful	прекра́сно	prikrásno
fantastic	потряса́юще	patrisáyooschi
awful	ужа́сно	oozhásna
Don't you like it?	Вам не нра́вится?	vam ni nrávitsa
What's your favourite...	Како́й ваш люби́мый...	kakóï vash lyoobímy...
film?	фильм?	film
My favourite... is...	Мой люби́мый...	moï lyoobímy...
How do Russian people feel about...	Что ру́сские ду́мают о...	shto róoskiye dóomayoot a...
the government?	прави́тельстве?	pravítilstvye
the British?	брита́нцах?	britántsakh
drugs?	нарко́тиках?	narkótikakh

✳ making arrangements

What are you doing tonight?	Что Вы де́лаете сего́дня ве́чером?	*shto vy dyélaitye sivódnya vyéchirom*
Would you like…	Вы не хоте́ли бы…	*vy ni khatéli by…*
to come with us?	пойти́ с на́ми?	*païtí s námi*
to go and eat?	пойти́ в рестора́н?	*païtí v ristarán*
to the theatre?	в теа́тр?	*f tiátr*
to the concert?	на конце́рт?	*na kantsért*
Yes, please.	Да.	*da*
No, thank you.	Нет, спаси́бо.	*nyet spasíba*
I'd love to.	С удово́льствием.	*s oodavólstviyem*
What time shall we meet?	Во ско́лько встре́тимся?	*va skólka fstryétimsya*
Where shall we meet?	Где мы встре́тимся?	*gdye my fstryétimsya*
See you later.	До встре́чи.	*da fstryéchi*
Sorry, I/we already have plans.	Извини́те, но у меня́/нас други́е пла́ны.	*izvinítye no oo minyá/ nas droogíye plány*
Please go away.	Уходи́те!	*ookhadítye*
Leave me/us alone!	Оста́вьте меня́/нас в поко́е!	*astáftye minyá/nas f pakóye*
What's your telephone number?	Како́й у Вас/ тебя́ но́мер телефо́на?	*kakóï oo vas/tibyá nómir tilifóna*

| What's your email address? | Какой у Вас/тебя e-mail? | *kakóï oo vas/tibyá i-meïl* |
| My email address is ... at ... dot com. | Мой адрес ... собака ... точка com. | *moï ádris ... sabáka .... tóchka kom* |

* useful expressions

(see **essentials**, page 12)

YOU MAY WANT TO SAY...

Congratulations!	Поздравляю!	*pazdravlyáyoo*
Happy Birthday!	С днём рождения!	*z dnyom razhdyéniya*
Happy Christmas!	С Рождеством!	*s razhdistvóm*
Happy New Year!	С Новым годом!	*s nóvym gódam*
Good luck!	Удачи!	*oodáchi*
That's fantastic!	Великолепно!	*vilikalyépna*
That's terrible!	Ужасно!	*oozhásna*
What a pity!	Как жаль!	*kak zhal*
Bless you! (after sneezing)	Будьте здоровы!	*bóottye zdaróvy*
Have a good journey!	Счастливого пути!	*schaslívava pootí*
Enjoy your meal!	Приятного аппетита!	*priyátnava apitíta*

- **Thank you, same to you.**   Спаси́бо, Вам то́же.   *spasíba, vam tózhe*

- **Cheers!**   За здоро́вье!   *za zdaróvye*

travel&transport

✳ arriving in the country

● Upon arrival you will need to complete an immigration card and a customs declaration. You'll need the immigration card to register your visa and leave the country. Always carry your passport, visa and immigration card with you.

YOU MAY SEE...

Выдача багажа	*výdacha bagazhá*	**baggage reclaim**
Выход	*výkhot*	**exit**
Выхода нет/Нет выхода	*výkhada nyet/nyet výkhada*	**no exit**
Паспортный контроль	*páspartny kantról*	**passport control**
Таможня	*tamózhnya*	**customs**
Таможенная декларация	*tamózhennaya diklarátsiya*	**customs declaration**

YOU MAY WANT TO SAY...

● **I am here on holiday.** (m/f)
Я турист./
Я туристка.
ya tooríst/ya toorístka

● **I am here on business.** (m/f)
Я бизнесмен./
Я бизнесменка.
ya biznismyén/ya biznismyénka

● **It's for my own personal use.**
Это для моего личного пользования.
éta dlya maivó líchnava pólzavaniya

travel and transport

YOU MAY HEAR...

Ваш па́спорт, пожа́луйста.	vash pásport, pazhálsta.	Your passport please.
Ва́ши докуме́нты, пожа́луйста.	váshi dakoomyénty, pazhálsta.	Your documents please.
Где Ва́ша деклара́ция?	gde vásha diklarátsiya?	Where is your customs declaration?
Какова́ цель ва́шего визи́та?	kaková tsel váshiva vizíta	What is the purpose of your visit?
Откро́йте... су́мку/ чемода́н.	atkróïtye... sóomkoo/ chimadán	Please open... this bag/ suitcase.
Пройдёмте со мной/с на́ми.	praïdyómtye sa mnoï/s námi	Come along with me/us please.

✳ directions

YOU MAY SEE...

Больница	balnítsa	hospital
Картинная галерея	kartínnaya galiréya	art gallery
Крепость	kryépast	castle/fortress
Метро	mitró	underground
Музей	moozyéï	museum
Остановка автобуса трамвая	astanófka aftóboosa tramváya	stop bus tram

Площадь	*plóschat*	square
Проспект	*praspyékt*	avenue
Рынок	*rýnak*	market place
Синагога	*sinagóga*	synagogue
Собор	*sabór*	cathedral
Стадион	*stadión*	stadium
Станция	*stántsiya*	station
Стоянки нет	*stayánki nyet*	no parking
Улица	*óolitsa*	street
Церковь	*tsérkaf*	church

YOU MAY WANT TO SAY...

- Excuse me, please. | Извини́те, пожа́луйста. | *izvinítye pazhálsta*

- Where is... the information centre? | Где... спра́вочная? | *gdye... správachnaya*

- Where are... the toilets? | Где туале́т? | *gdye tooalyét*

- How do we get to... (on foot)? | Как дойти́ до ... ? | *kak daïtí da...*

- How do we get to... (by transport)? | Как дое́хать до... ? | *kak dayékhat da...*

- I'm lost. (m/f) | Я заблуди́лся./Я заблуди́лась. | *ya zabloodílsya/ya zabloodílas*

- Is this the right way to... ? | Э́то доро́га в... ? | *éta daróga v...*

Can you show me on the map, please?	Покажите на карте, пожалуйста.	*pakazhítye na kártye, pazhálsta*
Is it far?	Это далеко?	*éta dalikó*
Is there... a bank near here?	Здесь есть... банк?	*zdyes yest bank*
Where is the nearest...	Где здесь...	*gdye zdyes...*

YOU MAY HEAR...

Мы здесь.	*my zdyes*	We are here.
В эту сторону.	*v étoo stóranoo*	This way.
Прямо.	*pryáma*	Straight on.
Поверните... направо.	*pavirnítye... napráva*	Turn... right
Первый/второй поворот... налево.	*pyérvy/ftaróï pavarót... nalyéva*	Take the first/ second on the... left.
Это... напротив... за... рядом с	*éta... naprótif... za... ryádam s*	It's... opposite behind next to
Это очень близко/далеко.	*éta óchin blíska/ dalikó*	It's very near/far away.
Вам нужен автобус номер...	*vam nóozhin aftóboos nómir...*	You have to take bus number...

travel and transport

43

* information and tickets

(see **telling the time**, page 18)

Is there a train/ bus to Novgorod today?	Сегóдня есть пóезд/автóбус в Нóвгород?	*sivódnya yest póist/ aftóboos v nóvgarat*
What time is the... next train	Когда ... слéдующий пóезд	*kagdá... slyédooschi póist*
last train	послéдний пóезд	*paslyédni póist*
first bus ...to Yaroslavl?	пéрвый автóбус ...в Ярослáвль?	*pyérvy aftóboos ... v yaraslávl*
What time does it arrive in Moscow?	Когдá он прибывáет в Москвý?	*kagdá on pribyváit v maskvóo*
Do I have to change?	Нáдо дéлать пересáдку?	*náda dyélat pirisátkoo*
Which platform for... ?	С какóй платфóрмы отправляется пóезд в... ?	*s kakóï platfórmy atpravlyáitsa póist v*
Which bus stop for... ?	Где остановка (автóбуса) в... ?	*gdye astanófka (aftóboosa) v*
Where can I buy... a ticket?	Где мóжно купи́ть... биле́т?	*gdye mózhna koopít... bilyét*
One ticket to..., please.	Оди́н биле́т в...	*adín bilyét v...*

Two tickets to..., please.	Два билета в...	*dva bilyéta v...*
single	в один конец	*v adín kanyéts*
return	туда и обратно	*toodá i abrátna*
For...		
two adults	два взрослых	*dva vzróslykh*
two children	два детских	*dva dyétskikh*
I want to reserve...	Я хочу зарезервировать...	*ya khachóo zarizirvíravat...*
a seat	место	*myésta*
a cabin	каюту	*kayóotoo*
Is there a supplement?	Надо доплатить?	*náda daplatít*
Is there a discount for...	Есть скидки...	*yest skítki...*
students?	студентам?	*stoodyéntam*
senior citizens?	пенсионерам?	*pinsianyéram*

YOU MAY HEAR...

Поезд отходит/ отправляется в 8.20.	*póist atkhódit/ atpravlyáitsa v vósim dvátsat*	The train leaves at 8.20am.
Прибывает в 15.40.	*pribyváit v pitnátsat sórok*	It arrives at 3.40pm.
Время московское.	*vryémya maskófskaye*	Moscow time.
Время местное.	*vryémya myésnaye*	Local time.

Они ходят каждые десять минут.	*ani khódyat kázhdyye dyésit minóot*	They go every ten minutes.
Вам надо сделать пересадку.	*vam náda zdyélat pirisátkoo*	You have to change.
Платформа/пирс номер четыре.	*platfórma/pirs nómir chitýri*	It's platform/pier number four.
Когда Вы хотите ехать?	*kagdá vy khatítye yékhat*	When do you want to travel?
В один конец или туда и обратно?	*v adín kanyéts íli tóoda i abrátna*	Single or return?
Купе или плацкарт?	*koopé íli platskárt*	Four-berth compartment or open car?
Верхняя/нижняя полка?	*vyérkhniya/nízhniya pólka*	Upper or lower berth?
Надо доплатить сто двадцать рублей.	*náda daplatít sto dvátsat rooblyéï*	There's a supplement of 120 roubles.

✳ trains

(see **information and tickets**, page 44)

- You will be asked to show a passport when buying a ticket. Your name and passport number will be on your ticket.

- There are several different types of train in Russia, depending if you are travelling locally or further afield.

YOU MAY SEE...

Автоматические камеры хранения	*aftamatíchiskiye kámiry khranyéniya*	luggage lockers
Билетная касса	*bilyétnaya kássa*	ticket office
Бюро находок	*byooró nakhódak*	lost property
Вагон-ресторан	*vagón ristarán*	restaurant-car
Военная касса	*vayénaya kássa*	ticket office for the military
Входа нет/Нет входа	*fkhóda nyet/nyet fkhóda*	no entry
Зал ожидания	*zal azhidániya*	waiting room
Закрыто	*zakrýta*	closed
Камера хранения	*kámira khranyéniya*	left luggage
Кипяток	*kipitók*	boiled water (for tea)
Купе для отдыха проводников	*koopé dlya óddykha pravadnikóf*	compartment for carriage attendants
Милиция	*milítsiya*	police
Медпункт	*mitpóonkt*	first aid
Место для курения	*myésta dlya kooryéniya*	smoking area
Не курить	*nye koorít*	no smoking
Отменен	*atminyón*	cancelled
Отправление	*atpravlyéniye*	departure
Питьевая вода	*pityiváya vadá*	drinking water
Поезда дальнего следования	*paizdá dálniva slyédavaniya*	long-distance trains
Платформа	*platfórma*	platform
Предварительная продажа билетов	*pridvarítilnaya pradázha bilyétaf*	advance booking
Прибытие	*pribytiýe*	arrivals
Скорый поезд	*skóry póist*	fast train
Служебное купе	*sloozhébnaye koopé*	service compartment
Справочная	*správachnaya*	information

YOU MAY WANT TO SAY...

- I'd like a... ticket to Yekaterinburg please.

  Биле́т... до Екатеринбу́рга, пожа́луйста.

  bilyét... da Yekatyerinbóorga pazhálsta

- Does this train go to Tomsk?

  Э́тот по́езд идёт в Томск?

  etat póist idyót f tomsk

- Excuse me, I've reserved...

  Извини́те, э́то...

  izvinítye éta

  that seat.

  моё ме́сто.

  mayó myésta

  a couchette.

  моя́ по́лка.

  mayá pólka

- Is this seat taken?

  Э́то ме́сто за́нято?

  éta myésta zánita

- May I...

  Мо́жно...

  mózhna

  open the window?

  откры́ть окно́?

  atkrýt aknó

- Where are we?

  Где мы?

  gdye my

- How long does the train stop here?

  Ско́лько стои́т по́езд?

  skólka staít póist

- Can you tell me when we get to Kazan?

  Когда́ мы прибу́дем в Каза́нь?

  kagdá my pribóodim f kazán

- Is the train running late?

  Мы опа́здываем?

  my apázdyvaim

- By how much?

  На ско́лько?

  na skólka

✳ buses and coaches

(see **information and tickets**, page 44)

● Tickets can be bought from a special kiosk киоск *(kiósk)* or from the driver. An alternative to the bus is маршрутка *(marshróotka)*, a minibus-shuttle. They usually have the same numbers as the buses and take the same route. They stop only on request, and you always get a seat. You pay the driver, bus tickets are not valid. You tell the driver where to stop.

YOU MAY SEE...

Автобус	*aftóboos*	coach
Автовокзал	*aftavagzál*	bus station
Вход через переднюю дверь	*vkhot chyéris piryédniyoo dvyer*	enter by the front door
Выход через заднюю дверь	*výkhat chyéris zádniyoo dvyer*	exit by the back door
За безбилетный проезд штраф 100 рублей	*za bizbilyétny prayést shtraf sto rooblyéï*	100 rouble penalty for travel without a valid ticket
Междугородний автобус	*mizhdoogaródni aftóboos*	long-distance coach
Места для пассажиров с детьми и инвалидов	*mistá dlya passazhíraf z ditmí i invalídaf*	seats for disabled persons and passengers with children

YOU MAY WANT TO SAY...

Where does the bus to the town centre leave from?	Откуда идёт автобус в центр?	atkóoda idyót aftóboos v tsentr
Does the bus to the airport leave from here?	Автобус в аэропорт (идёт) отсюда?	aftóboos v aerapórt (idyót) atsyóoda
What number is it?	Какой номер?	kakóï nómir
Does this bus go to...	Автобус идёт...	aftóboos idyót...
the train station?	до вокзала?	da vagzála
Which stop is it for the... museum?	В музей какая остановка?	v moozyéï kakáya astanófka
Can you tell me/us where to get off, please?	Можете сказать мне/нам, где выходить?	mózhitye skazát mnye/nam gdye vykhadít
The next stop, please.	На следующей остановите.	na slyédooscheï astanavítye
Stop (here) please.	(Здесь) остановите, пожалуйста.	(zdyes) astanavítye pazhálsta

YOU MAY HEAR...

Пятьдесят седьмой идёт до метро.	piddisyát sidmóï idyót da mitró	The number 57 goes to the underground station.
Извините, я выхожу.	izvinítye ya vykhazhóo	Excuse me, I'm getting off here.

| Вам на́до вы́йти на сле́дующей (остано́вке). | vam náda výiti na slyédooscheï (astanófkye) | You have to get off at the next stop. |
| Вы прое́хали остано́вку. | vy prayékhali astanófkoo | You've missed the stop. |

✳ underground

(see **information and tickets**, page 44)

● Metro entrances are marked with a large red letter 'M'. Underground maps can be purchased at newspaper kiosks (not at the Metro ticket offices).

YOU MAY SEE...

Ка́сса	kássa	ticket office
Метро́	mitró	underground
Перехо́д на ста́нцию...	pirikhód na stántsiyoo	transfer (to another line)
Перехо́д прекраща́ется в 1 час но́чи	pirikhót prikraschaïtsa v adín chas nóchi	transfer is closed at 1 am
Поса́дки нет	pasátki nyet	no boarding
Спра́вочная	správachnaya	information
Ста́нция	stántsiya	station

YOU MAY WANT TO SAY...

● I'd like a monthly ticket please. | Проездно́й на ме́сяц, пожа́луйста. | praiznóï na myésits pazhálsta

travel and transport

51

For a single journey	На одну́ пое́здку	*na adnóo payéstkoo*
For two journeys	На две пое́здки	*na dvye payéstki*
For 5/10/20 journeys	На пять/де́сять/ два́дцать пое́здок	*na pyat/dyésit/ dvátsat payézdak*
One token	Оди́н жето́н	*adín zhitón*
Two/three/four tokens	Два/три/четы́ре жето́на	*dva/tri/chitýri zhitóna*
Do you have a map of the underground?	У вас есть схе́ма метро́?	*oo vas yest skhyéma mitró*
Is this the right stop for Gorky Park?	Парк Го́рького на э́той ста́нции?	*park górkava na étaï stántsii*
Does this train go to the university?	Э́тот по́езд идёт до университе́та?	*état póist idyót da oonivirsityéta*
Where is there a metro station near here?	Где (здесь) (ста́нция) метро́?	*gdye (zdyes) (stántsiya) mitró*

YOU MAY HEAR...

Вам на́до перейти́.	*vam náda piriïtí*	You have to change.
Сле́дующая оста́новка.	*slyédooschaya astanófka*	It's the next stop.
Сле́дующая ста́нция...	*slyédooschaya stántsiya...*	The next station is...

✳ boats and ferries

(see **information and tickets**, page 44)

(see **information and tickets**, page 44)

YOU MAY SEE...

Каюта	*kayóota*	cabin
Круиз	*krooís*	cruise
Паром	*paróm*	ferry
Пирс	*pirs*	pier
Порт	*port*	port
Причал	*prichál*	quay
Речной вокзал	*richnóï vagzál*	river station
Спасательная лодка	*spasátilnaya lótka*	lifeboat
Спасательный жилет	*spasátilny zhilyet*	life jacket

YOU MAY WANT TO SAY...

- I'd like a return ticket to Novgorod please.

  Билет в Нижний Новгород и обратно, пожалуйста.

  bilyét v nízhni nóvgarad i abrátna pazhálsta

- Is there a ferry to Kaliningrad today?

  Сегодня есть паром в Калининград?

  sivódnya yest paróm f kaliningrád

- Are there any boat trips?

  Есть водные прогулки?

  yest vódnyye pragóolki

- How long is the cruise/boat trip?

  Сколько длится круиз/прогулка?

  skólka dlítsa krooís/ pragóolka

- Is it possible to go out on deck?

  Можно выйти на палубу?

  mózhna výїti na pálooboo

travel and transport

53

✻ air travel

(see **information and tickets**, page 44)

YOU MAY WANT TO SAY...

- **Is there a flight to Chelyabinsk?**
  today
  tomorrow

  Есть рейс в Челябинск?
  сегодня
  завтра

  yest ryéïs f chilyábinsk
  sivódnya
  záftra

- **I want to change/ cancel my ticket.**

  Я хочу поменять/ сдать билет.

  ya khachóo paminyát/ zdat bilyét

● **Is there a delay?**	Самолёт задéрживается?	*samalyót zadyérzhivaitsa*
● **Which gate is it?**	Какóй вы́ход на посáдку?	*kakóï vы́khat na pasátkoo*
● **My luggage hasn't arrived.**	Я не получи́л багáж.	*ya ni paloochíl bagásh*
● **Is there a bus to the centre of the town from here?**	Отсю́да хóдит автóбус в центр?	*atsyóoda khódit aftóboos v tsentr*

WORDS TO LISTEN OUT FOR... ?

Вы́ход на посáдку	*vы́khat na pasátkoo*	**gate**
Задéрживается	*zadyérzhivaitsya*	**delay**
Закáнчивается регистрáция	*zakánchivaitsa rigistrátsiya*	**last call**
Отменя́ется	*atminyáitsa*	**cancelled**
Рейс	*ryéïs*	**flight**

✳ taxis

(see **directions**, page 41)

YOU MAY WANT TO SAY... 💬

● **I need a taxi...**	Мне нýжно такси́	*mnye nóozhna taksí*
immediately.	немéдленно	*nimyédlina*
for tomorrow at 9am.	зáвтра в дéвять утрá	*záftra v dyévit ootrá*

taxis

Is there a taxi rank round here?	Где стоянка такси?	*gdye stayánka taksí*
To this address, please.	Вот адрес.	*vot ádris*
How much will it cost?	Сколько будет стоить?	*skólka bóodit stóit*
I'm in a hurry.	Я спешу.	*ya spishóo*
Stop here, please.	Остановите здесь, пожалуйста.	*astanavítye zdyes pazhálsta*
Can you wait for me, please?	Вы можете подождать?	*vy mózhitye padazhdát*
Keep the change.	Сдачи не надо.	*zdáchi ni náda*

YOU MAY HEAR...

Это десять километров.	*etá dyésit kilamyétraf*	It's ten kilometres away.
(Это будет стоить) восемьсот рублей.	*(etá bóodit stóit) vasimsót rooblyéï*	It'll cost 800 roubles.

✳ hiring cars and bicycles

YOU MAY WANT TO SAY...

- I'd like to hire... | Я хочу́ взять напрока́т | ya khachóo vzyat naprakát

    two bicycles | два велосипе́да | dva vilasipyéda
    a small car | ма́ленькую маши́ну | málinkooyoo mashínoo

- For... | На... | na...
    one day. | оди́н день. | adín dyen
    a week. | неде́лю. | nidyélyoo

- Until... | До... | da...
    Friday. | пя́тницы. | pyátnitsy

- How much is it... | Ско́лько сто́ит... | skólka stóit...
    per day? | оди́н день? | adín dyen
    per week? | одна́ неде́ля? | adná nidyélya

- Is kilometrage/ mileage included? | Э́то включа́ет пробе́г? | éta fklyoocháit prabyék

- My husband/ colleague wants to drive too. | Мой муж/колле́га то́же бу́дет води́ть. | moï moosh/kallyéga tózhe bóodit vadít

- Can I leave the car... | Я могу́ оста́вить маши́ну... | ya magóo astávit mashínoo...
    at the airport? | в аэропорту́? | v aerapartóo
    in the town centre? | в це́нтре го́рода? | v tséntri górada

YOU MAY HEAR...

Како́й велосипе́д/ каку́ю маши́ну Вы хоти́те? | kakóï vilasipyéd/ kakóoyoo mashínoo vy khatítye | What kind of car/bicycle do you want?

На ско́лько?	*na skólka*	**For how long?**
Ва́ши права́, пожа́луйста.	*váshi pravá pazhálsta*	**Your driving licence, please.**
Пробе́г не ограни́чен.	*prabyék ni agraníchin*	**There's unlimited kilometrage.**
Вам нужна́ дополни́тельная страхо́вка?	*vam noozhná dapalnítilnaya strakhóvka*	**Do you want extra insurance?**
Верни́те маши́ну с по́лным ба́ком.	*virnítye mashínoo s pólnym bákom*	**Please return the car with a full tank.**
Верни́те маши́ну/ велосипе́д до ше́сти часо́в.	*virnítye mashínoo/ vilasipyéd da shistí chisóf*	**Please return the car/bicycle before six o'clock.**

✳ driving

● Driving is on the right. Seat belts are compulsory for drivers and passengers in the front seat.

● At petrol stations, you typically find 86, 92, 95 and sometimes 98 octane fuel. 92 octane and greater is unleaded. The Diesel pump is marked with the Russian Cyrillic D sign (Д), or as соля́рка *(salyárka)*. You have to pay before you fill up with petrol. Most outlets will not accept cards.

driving

YOU MAY SEE...

Автозаправка (АЗС)	*aftazapráfka (a ze es)*	petrol station
Автосервис	*aftasyérvis*	car service
Дорога закрыта	*daróga zakrýta*	road closed
ДПС	*de pe es*	road police
Нет обгона/Обгон запрещен	*nyet abgóna/abgón zaprischón*	no overtaking
Объезд	*ob-yést*	diversion
Одностороннее движение	*adnastarónniye dvizhénie*	one-way traffic
Опасно	*apásna*	danger
Стоп	*stop*	stop
Стоянка	*stayánka*	car park
Стоянки нет	*stayánki nyet*	no parking
Съезд	*s-yest*	exit

YOU MAY WANT TO SAY...

- **Where is the nearest petrol station?** Где (здесь) заправка? *gdye (zdyes) zapráfka*

- **300 roubles worth of 95 octane petrol, please.** На триста рублей девяносто пятого, пожалуйста. *na trísta rooblyéï divinósta pyátava pazhálsta*

- **20 litres of 92 octane petrol.** Двадцать литров девяносто второго. *dvátsat litraf divinósta ftaróva*

- **A full tank, please** Полный бак, пожалуйста. *pólny bak pazhálsta*

- **A half-litre of oil.** Поллитра масла. *pollítra másla*

- **Where is the water/air, please?** Где вода/воздух? *gdye vadá/vózdookh*

travel and transport

mechanical problems

Что Вы хотите?	chto vy khatítye	What would you like?
Ско́лько?	skólka	How much do you want?
Ключи́, пожа́луйста	klyoochí pashálsta	The key, please.

* mechanical problems

YOU MAY WANT TO SAY...

My car has broken down.	Слома́лась маши́на.	slamálas mashína
I have a puncture.	У меня́ проко́л.	oo minyá prakól
I don't know what's wrong.	(Я) не зна́ю, в чём пробле́ма.	(ya) ni znáyoo f chom prablyéma
I think it's the... clutch	Ду́маю, что... сцепле́ние	dóomayoo chto... stsiplyéniye
The ... doesn't work.	...не рабо́тает.	ni rabótait
Is it serious?	Это серьёзно?	éta sir-yózna
Can you repair it today?	Вы мо́жете сде́лать сего́дня?	vy mózhitye zdyélat sivódnya
When will it be ready?	Когда́ бу́дет гото́во?	kagdá bóodit gatóva
How much will it cost?	Ско́лько бу́дет сто́ить?	skólka bóodit stóit

travel and transport

60

YOU MAY HEAR...

Что случилось?/ В чём проблéма?	shto sloochílas/ f chom prablyéma	What's wrong with it?
У меня нет запчастéй.	oo minyá nyet zapchistyéï	I don't have the necessary parts.
Приходите во вторник.	prikhadítye va ftórnik	Come back next Tuesday.
Будет готово... чéрез час. в понедéльник.	bóodit gatóva... chyéris chas f panidyélnik	It'll be ready... in an hour. on Monday.

✳ car parts

YOU MAY WANT TO SAY...

accelerator	акселерáтор	aksilirátar
back tyre	зáднее колесó	zádniye kalisó
battery	аккумулятор	akoomoolyátar
bonnet	капóт	kapót
boot	багáжник	bagázhnik
brakes	тормозá	tarmazá
carburettor	карбюрáтор	karbyoorátar
distributor	распределитель зажигáния	raspridilítel zazhigániya
engine	мотóр	matór
exhaust pipe	выхлопнáя трубá	vykhlapnáya troobá
fanbelt	ремéнь вентилятора	rimyén vintilyátara
front tyre	перéднее колесó	piryédniye kalisó
fuel gauge	бензиномéр	binzinamýer
gear box	корóбка передáч	karópka piridách

headlights	фáры	*fary*
ignition	зажигáние	*zazhigániye*
indicator	указáтель поворóта	*ookazátil pavaróta*
radiator	радиáтор	*radiátar*
reversing light	фонáрь зáднего хóда	*fanár zádniva khóda*
spark plugs	свéчи	*svyéchi*
starter motor	стáртер	*stárter*
steering wheel	руль	*rool*
window	окнó	*aknó*
windscreen	лобовóе стеклó	*labavóye stikló*
windscreen wiper(s)	двóрник(и)	*dvórnik(i)*

✳ bicycle parts

YOU MAY WANT TO SAY... 💬

back light	зáдний свет	*zádni svyet*
chain	цепь	*tsep*
frame	рáма	*ráma*
front light	передний свет	*piryédni svyet*
gear(s)	передáча/передáчи	*piridácha/piridáchi*
handlebars	руль	*rool*
inner tube	кáмера шины	*kámira shíny*
pump	насóс	*nasós*
saddle	седлó	*sidló*
spoke	спица	*spítsa*
tyre	шина	*shína*
wheel	колесó	*kalisó*

accommodation

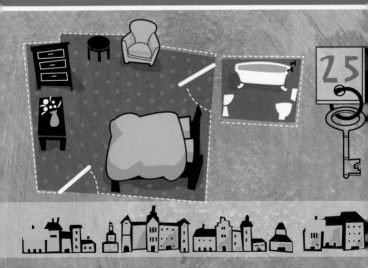

✳ accommodation

● Ground floor in English corresponds to Russian first floor: первый этаж *(pyérvy etásh)*, English first floor is Russian second floor: второй этаж *(ftaróï etásh)* etc.

YOU MAY SEE...

Буфет	*boofyét*	bar
Вестибюль/фойе/ холл	*vistibyóol/faïyé/khol*	lounge
Гараж	*garásh*	garage
Гостиница	*gastínitsa*	hotel
Душ	*doosh*	showers
Лифт	*lift*	lift
Молодежное общежитие	*maladyózhnaye apschizhítiye*	youth hostel
Обслуживание номеров	*apslóozhivaniye namiróf*	room service
Питьевая вода	*pityiváya vadá*	drinking water
Прачечная	*práchishnaya*	laundry
Регистрация	*rigistrátsiya*	reception
Ресторан	*ristarán*	restaurant
Стоянка/парковка	*stayánka/parkófka*	parking
Тариф	*taríf*	charge, tariff
Турбаза	*toorbáza*	tourist camp

✱ booking in advance

(see **telephones**, page 124; **the internet**, page 127)

YOU MAY WANT TO SAY... 💬

● Do you have...	У Вас есть...	oo vas yest...
a single room?	одноме́стный но́мер?	adnamyésny nómir
a double room?	двухме́стный но́мер?	dvookhmyésny nómir
a family room?	семе́йный но́мер?	simyéiny nómir
a twin-bedded room?	но́мер с разде́льными крова́тями?	nómir s razdyélnymi kravátyami
space for a tent?	ме́сто для пала́тки?	myésta dlya palátki
● I'd like to rent...	Я хочу́ снять...	ya khachóo snyat...
an apartment	кварти́ру	kvartíroo
● For...	на...	na...
one night	одну́ ночь/ одни́ су́тки	adnóo noch/ adní sóotki
two nights	дво́е су́ток	dvóye sóotak
a week	неде́лю	nidyélyoo
● from... to...	с... по ...	s... pa...
● for tonight	на сего́дня	na sivódnya
● with bath/shower	с ва́нной/ду́шем	s vánnaï/dóoshim
● We have a two-person tent.	У нас двухме́стная пала́тка.	oo nas dvóokhmyésnaya palátka
● How much is it...	Ско́лько сто́ит...	skólka stóit...
per night?	в су́тки?	f sóotki?
per week?	в неде́лю?	v nidyélyoo

accommodation

65

booking in advance

- Is breakfast included? | С за́втраком? | *z záftrakom*

- Is there a reduction for children? | У Вас есть ски́дки для дете́й? | *oo vas yest skítki dlya dityéï*

- Is there wheelchair access? | Мо́жно прое́хать на инвали́дной коля́ске? | *mózhna prayékhat na invalídnaï kalyáskye*

- Do you have anything cheaper? | Есть что́-нибудь подеше́вле? | *yest chtó-nobóod padishévli*

- Do you have a website? | У Вас есть (интерне́т) сайт? | *oo vas yest (internét) sáït*

- What's your email address? | Како́й у Вас e-mail? | *kakóï oo vas i-méïl*

YOU MAY HEAR...

- Я Вас слу́шаю. | *ya vas slóoshayoo* | Can I help you?

- Когда́ Вы прибу́дете? | *kagdá vy pribóodítye* | When do you want to come?

- На ско́лько су́ток? | *na skólka sóotak* | For how many nights?

- Ско́лько челове́к? | *skólka chilavyék* | For how many people?

- Кака́я/како́го разме́ра у Вас па́латка? | *kakáya/kakóva razmyera oo vas palátka* | What size is your tent?

- Как Ва́ша фами́лия? | *kak vásha famíliya* | What's your name, please?

accommodation

66

... рублéй в сутки, с зáвтракам.	... rooblyéï f sóotki, z záftrakam	It's ... roubles per night, including breakfast.
Извинúте, (свобóдных) мест нет.	izvinítye (svabódnykh) myest nyet	I'm sorry, we're full.

* checking in

YOU MAY WANT TO SAY...

I (m/f) have a reservation for... tonight	Я закáзывал/-а нóмер на... сегóдня	ya zakázyval/-a nómir na... sivódnya
It's in the name of...	На úмя...	na ímya...
Do you accept credit cards?	Вы принимáете кредúтные кáрты?	vy primáitye kridítnyye kárty

REGISTRATION CARD INFORMATION

Имя	first name
Фамилия	surname
Домашний адрес	home address
Город/Улица/Номер дома	city/street/number
Индекс	postcode
Национальность	nationality
Дата рождения	date of birth
Номер паспорта	passport number
Дата	date
Подпись	signature

accommodation

67

✳ hotels, B&Bs and hostels

YOU MAY WANT TO SAY...

- Where can I park?
  Где мóжно постáвить машúну?
  gdye mózhna pastávit mashínoo

- Do you have...
  a room with a view?
  a bigger room?
  У Вас есть...
  нóмер с вúдом из окнá?
  нóмер побóльше?
  oo vas yest...
  nómir s vídam iz akná
  nómir pabólshe

- What time...
  is breakfast?
  Во скóлько...
  зáвтрак?
  va skólka...
  záftrak

- Where is...
  the bar?
  the restaurant?
  Где...
  буфéт?
  ресторáн?
  gdye...
  boofyét
  ristarán

- Is there...
  an internet connection here?
  Здесь есть...
  интернéт?
  zdyes yest...
  internét

YOU MAY HEAR...

- Извинúте, но свобóдных номерóв нет.
  izvinítye, no svabódnykh namiróf nyet
  I'm afraid we don't have any rooms available tonight.

- Мы смóжем переселúть Вас зáвтра.
  my smózhim pirisilít vas záftra
  We might be able to change your room tomorrow.

- Входнáя дверь закрывáется в...
  fkhadnáya dvyer zakryváitsa v...
  We lock the front door at...

- Обслýживание номерóв с... до...
  apslóozhivaniye namiróf s... da...
  There's room service from... to...

✳ camping

(see **directions**, page 41)

YOU MAY WANT TO SAY...

- **Can we camp here?**
  Мы мóжем постáвить здесь палáтку?
  my mózhim pastávit zdyes palátkoo

- **It's a two-person tent.**
  Э́то двухмéстна палáтка.
  éta dvóokhmyésnaya palátka

- **Where are...**
  the toilets?
  Где...
  туалéты?
  gdye...
  tooalyéty

- **Do we pay extra for the showers?**
  За душ платúть отдéльно?
  za doosh platít adyélna

- **Is this drinking water?**
  Э́то питьевáя водá?
  éta pityiváya vadá

YOU MAY HEAR...

- Кéмпинг...
  в пятú киломéтрах
  kyémpink...
  f pití kilamyétrakh atsyóoda
  The campsite is...
  five kilometres away

- Здесь нельзя́ стáвить палáтку.
  zdyes nilzyá stávit palátkoo
  You can't camp here.

- Розéтка там.
  razyétka tam
  The electric point is over there.

∗ requests and queries

YOU MAY WANT TO SAY...

- I'm expecting...
  a phone call

  Мне должны́...
  позвони́ть

  *mnye dalzhný...
  pazvanít*

- Can I...
  leave this in
  the safe?

  put it on my
  room bill?

  Я могу́...
  положи́ть это в
  сейф?

  Запиши́те это
  на мой счёт?

  *ya magóo...
  palazhít éta f syéif*

  *zapishítye éta na
  moï schyot*

- Can you...
  order me a taxi?

  Вы мо́жете...
  заказа́ть мне
  такси́?

  *vy mózhitye...
  zakazát mnye taksí*

- Do you have...
  another
  pillow?
  an adaptor?

  У Вас есть...
  ещё одна́
  поду́шка?
  ада́птер?

  *oo vas yest...
  yeschó adná
  padóoshka
  adápter*

- I've lost my key.
  (m/f)

  Я потеря́л/
  потеря́ла ключ.

  *ya patiryál/patiryála
  klyooch*

YOU MAY HEAR...

- Вам сообще́ние/
  факс.

  *vam saapschyéniye/
  faks*

  There's a message/
  fax for you.

- Вас разбуди́ть?

  vas razboodít

  Do you want a
  wake up call?

- В како́е вре́мя?

  f kakóye vryémya

  (For) what time?

✳ problems and complaints

● Excuse me.	Извините.	*izvinítye*
● The room is too...	В номере слишком...	*v nómirye slíshkam...*
hot	жарко	*zhárka*
cold	холодно	*khóladna*
noisy	шумно	*shóomna*
● The room is too small.	Номер слишком маленький.	*nómir slíshkam mályenki*
● There isn't any...	Нет...	*nyet...*
hot water	горячей воды	*garyácheï vadý*
power	электричества	*eliktríchistva*
● There aren't any...	Нет...	*nyet...*
towels	полотенец	*palatyénits*
● The bed is uncomfortable.	Кровать неудобная.	*kravát nioodóbnaya*
● The bathroom/ toilet is dirty.	В ванной/туалете грязно.	*v vánnaï/tooalyétye gryázna*
● The toilet doesn't flush.	В туалете не работает смыв.	*v toalyétye ni rabótait smyf*
● The key doesn't work.	Ключ не подходит.	*klyooch ni patkhódit*
● The shower/ remote control is not working.	Душ/пульт не работает.	*doosh/poolt ni rabótait*
● There's a smell of gas.	Пахнет газом.	*pákhnit gázam*
● I want to see the manager!	Позовите менеджера!	*pazavítye myénedzhera*

checking out

Одну минуту, пожалуйста.	*adnóo minóotoo pazhálsta*	Just a moment, please.
Завтра починим/ исправим.	*záftra pachínim/ isprávim*	We'll fix it for you tomorrow.
Извините, ничем не могу помочь.	*izvinítye nichém ni magóo pamóch*	I'm sorry, there's nothing I can do.

✱ checking out

YOU MAY WANT TO SAY...

The bill, please.	Счёт, пожалуйста.	*schot pazhálsta*
What time is check out?	Во сколько надо освободить номер?	*va skólka náda asvabadít nómir*
Can I leave my luggage here?	Я могу оставить здесь свой багаж?	*ya magóo astávit zdyes svoí bagásh*
There's a mistake in the bill.	В счёте ошибка.	*f schótye ashípka*
I/We've had a (very) good time here.	Мне/нам здесь (очень) понравилось.	*mnye/nam zdyes (óchin) panrávilas*

YOU MAY HEAR...

Сколько у Вас вещей/мест?	*skólka oo vas vischéi/ myest*	How many bags?
Оставьте здесь.	*astávtye zdyes*	Leave them here.
Давайте проверю.	*daváitye pravyéryoo*	Let me check it.
Приезжайте ещё.	*priyizzháitye yischó*	Come again!

* self-catering/second homes

(see **problems and complaints**, page 71)

YOU MAY WANT TO SAY...

My surname is...	Моя фамилия...	mayá famíliya...
Can you give me the key, please?	Дайте, пожалуйста, ключ.	dáïtye pazhálsta klyooch
Where is... the fusebox?	Где... пробки?	gdye... própki
How does the cooker work?	Как работает плита?	kak rabótait plitá
How does the hot water work?	Как включать горячую воду?	kak fklyoochát garyáchooyoo vódoo
Is there... another gas bottle?	Здесь есть... другой газовый баллон?	zdyes yest... droogóï gázavy balón
Are there any shops round here?	Где здесь магазин?	gdye zdyes magazín
Where do I/we put the rubbish?	Куда выбрасывать мусор?	koodá vybrásyvat móosar
When do they come to clean?	Когда приходит уборщица?	kagdá prikhódit oobórschitsa
I need... a plumber an electrician	Мне нужен... сантехник электрик	mnye nóozhin... santyékhnik elyéktrik
How can I contact you?	Как с Вами связаться?	kak s vami svizátsa
What shall we do with the key when we leave?	Куда деть ключ, когда будем уезжать?	koodá det klyooch kagdá bóodim ooizhát

YOU MAY HEAR...

Нажми́те кно́пку/ поверни́те выключа́тель.	*nazhmítye knópkoo/pavirnítye vyklyoochátil*	Press this button/ turn on the switch.
На себя́/от себя́	*na sibyá/at sibyá*	Pull/push.
Запасны́е одея́ла/поду́шки в шкафу́.	*zapasnýye adiyála/ padóoshki f shkafóo*	There are spare blankets/pillows in the cupboard.
Му́сор выбра́сывать...	*móosar vybrásyvat...*	Put the rubbish...
в му́сорный бак на у́лице	*v móosarny bak na óolitse*	in the rubbish-container outside
Убо́рщица придёт в...	*oobórschitsa pridyót v...*	The cleaner comes on...
Но́мер моего́ моби́льника/ Мой моби́льный но́мер...	*nómir maivó mabílnika/ móï mabílny nómir...*	My mobile number is...

food&drink

✳ food and drink

● Traditional Russian breakfast завтрак *(záftrak)* is substantial: porridge, eggs, sausage etc. Russian lunch is usually a warm meal, as is dinner ужин *(óozhin)*.

YOU MAY SEE...

Бар	*bar*	bar
Блинная	*blínnaya*	pancake house
Буфет	*boofyét*	buffet
Гардероб	*gardirób*	cloakroom
Закусочная	*zakóosachnaya*	snack bar
Кафе	*kafé*	café
Кафе-мороженое	*kafé-marózhinaye*	ice-cream parlour
Кондитерская	*kandítirskaya*	snack bar serving cakes
Кофейня	*kafyéïnya*	coffee bar
Куры-гриль	*kóory-gril*	roast chicken takeaway
Кухня	*kóokhnya*	kitchen
Меню	*minyóo*	menu
На вынос	*na výnas*	takeaway
Пельменная	*pilmyénnaya*	dumpling house
Пиццерия	*pitsiríya*	pizzeria
Ресторан	*ristarán*	restaurant
Столовая	*stalóvaya*	canteen
Туалеты	*tooalyéty*	toilets

✲ making bookings

(see **time phrases**, page 19)

YOU MAY WANT TO SAY...

I'd like to reserve a table for...	Я бы хотéл/хотéла заказáть стóлик на...	ya by khatyél/ khatyéla zakazát stólik na...
two people	двоúх	dvaíkh
tomorrow evening at half past eight	зáвтра в половúне девя́того	záftra f palavínye divyátava
this evening at nine o'clock	сегóдня в дéвять вéчера	sivódnya v dyévit vyéchira
My name is...	На úмя...	na ímya...
Could you get us a table...	Нельзя́ ли...	nilzyá li...
earlier?	порáньше?	paránshe
later?	попóзже?	papózhzhe

YOU MAY HEAR...

На какóе врéмя?	na kakóye vryémya	What time would you like the table for?
На скóлько человéк?	na skólka chilavyék	For how many people?
Извинúте, но свобóдных мест нет.	izvinítye no svabódnykh myest nyet	I'm sorry we're fully booked.

food and drink

77

✳ at the restaurant

I/We've booked a table.	У меня/нас заказан столик.	*oo minyá/nas zakázan stólik*
We haven't booked.	Мы не заказывали.	*my ni zakázyvali*
Have you got a table for four, please?	У Вас есть столик на четверых?	*oo vas yest stólik na chitvirýkh*
Have you got a high chair?	У Вас есть детский стульчик?	*oo vas yest dyétski stóolchik*
How long's the wait?	Долго надо будет ждать?	*dólga náda bóodit zhdat*
Do you take credit cards?	Вы принимаете кредитные карты?	*vy primáitye kridítnye kárty*

Вы заказывали (столик)?	*vy zakazyváli (stólik)*	Have you got a reservation?
Где желаете сидеть?	*gdye zhiláitye sidyét*	Where would you like to sit?
Столик для курящих или некурящих?	*stólik dlya kooryáshchikh íli nikooryáshchikh*	Smoking or non-smoking?
Будете ждать?	*booditye zhdat*	Would you like to wait?

✳ ordering your food

ordering your food

YOU MAY WANT TO SAY...

- addressing your
  waiter
  - (to f)   Де́вушка!   *dyévooshka*
  - (to m)   Молодо́й челове́к!   *maladói chilavyék*

- Do you have the   У Вас есть   *oo vas yest minyóo*
  menu in English?   меню́ на   *na anglískom*
      англи́йском (языке)?   *(yizykyé)*

- Do you have...   У Вас есть...   *oo vas yest...*
  - a children's   де́тское меню́?   *dyétskaye minyóo*
    menu?
  - vegetarian   вегетариа́нские   *vigitariánskie*
    food?   блю́да?   *blyóoda*

- We're ready to   Мы хоти́м   *my khatím zakazát*
  order.   заказа́ть.

- I'd like...   Я бу́ду...   *ya bóodoo...*

- What does this   Что на гарни́р   *chto na garnír zdyes*
  dish come with?   здесь?

- What's this   Что э́то (тако́е)?   *shtó eta (takóye)*
  please?

- Excuse me, I've   Извини́те, я   *izvinítye ya*
  changed my   переду́мал/-а.   *piridóomal/*
  mind. (m/f)   *piridóomala*

YOU MAY HEAR...

- Что бу́дете пить?   *shto bóoditye pit*   **What would you like to drink?**

food and drink

Вы гото́вы заказа́ть?/ Вы уже́ вы́брали?	*vy gatóvy zakazat/vy oozhé výbrali*	Are you ready to order?
К сожале́нию, э́то зако́нчилось.	*k sazhalyéniyoo éta zakónchilas*	I'm sorry, that's finished.
Что-нибудь ещё?	*shtó-nibood yischó*	Anything else?
Бу́дете... кóфе? десе́рт?	*bóoditye... kófe disyért*	Would you like... coffee? dessert?

✳ ordering your drinks

Can we see the wine list, please?	Ви́нную ка́рту, пожа́луйста.	*vínnooyoo kártoo pazhálsta*
A bottle of this wine please.	Буты́лку э́того вина́, пожа́луйста.	*bootýlkoo étava viná pazhálsta*
Half a litre of this please.	Поллитра э́того (вина́).	*pollítra étava (viná)*
A glass of the... please. red wine white wine	Бока́л... кра́сного (вина́) бе́лого (вина́)	*bakál... krásnava (viná) byélava (viná)*
What beers do you have?	Како́е у вас пи́во?	*kakóye oo vas píva*
Is that a bottle or draught?	В буты́лках и́ли разливно́е?	*v bootýlkakh íli razlivnóye*
For me please... a gin and tonic	Мне, пожа́луйста... джин с то́ником	*mnye pazhálsta... dzhin s tónikam*

food and drink

- **Do you have any liqueurs?** | У Вас есть ликёры? | *oo vas yest likyóry*
- **A bottle of mineral water, please.** | Буты́лку минера́льной воды́, пожа́луйста. | *bootýlkoo minirálnaï vadý pazhálsta*
- **What juices do you have?** | Како́й у вас сок? | *kakóï oo vas sok*

YOU MAY HEAR...

Лёд, лимо́н?	*lyot, limon*	**Ice and lemon?**
Во́ду жела́ете?	*vódoo zhiláitye*	**Would you like water as well?**
С га́зом или без?	*z gázam ili byes*	**Sparkling or still water?**
Большу́ю/ма́ленькую буты́лку?	*balshóoyoo/málinkoyoo bootýlkoo*	**A large or small bottle?**

* bars and cafés

YOU MAY WANT TO SAY...

- **I'll have...** | (Мне), пожа́луйста... | *(mnye) pazhálsta...*
  - **a coffee** | ко́фе | *kófye*
  - **a white coffee** | ко́фе с молоко́м | *kófye s malakóm*
  - **a black coffee** | чёрный ко́фе | *chyórny kófye*
  - **a cup of tea** | чай | *chaï*
  - **a fruit tea** | фрукто́вый чай | *frooktóvy chaï*
    - **...please**

food and drink

• with milk/lemon	с молоко́м/ с лимо́ном	*s malakóm/s limónam*

• A glass of...
   water
   apple juice
   wine
	Стака́н ...
	   воды́
	   я́блочного со́ка
	   Бока́л вина́
		stakán...
		   vadý
		   yáblachnava sóka
		   bakál viná

• A shot of vodka	Рю́мку во́дки.	*ryóomko vótki*
• No ice, thanks.	Лёд не на́до.	*lyot ni náda*
• Same again please.	Мо́жно ещё, пожа́луйста.	*mózha yischó* *pazhálsta*
• How much is that?	Ско́лько э́то сто́ит?	*skólka éta stóit*

YOU MAY HEAR... ?

• Что жела́ете?	*shto zhiláitye*	**What would you like?**
• Мале́нький, большо́й?	*mályenki/balshói*	**Small or large?**
• Вам счита́ть вме́сте и́ли отде́льно?	*vam schitát vmyésti* *íli addyélna*	**Are you paying together or separately?**

✳ special requirements

YOU MAY WANT TO SAY... 💬

• I'm diabetic.	У меня́ диабе́т.	*oo minyá diabyét*

• I'm allergic to...
   nuts
   seafood
	У меня́ аллерги́я на...
	   оре́хи
	   морепроду́кты
		oo minyá allirgíya na...
		   aryékhi
		   moripradóokty

• I'm vegetarian.	Я вегетариа́нец/Я не ем мя́са.	*ya vigitariánits/ya ni yem myása*
• I don't eat meat or fish.	Я не ем ни мя́со, ни ры́бу.	*ya ni yem ni myása ni rýby*
• I can't eat...	Я не ем	*ya ni yem...*
dairy products	моло́чные проду́кты	*malóchnyye pradóokty*
wheat products	проду́кты, содержа́щие пшени́цу	*pradóokty sadirzháschiye pshinítsoo*
• Do you have anything without...	У Вас есть что́-нибудь без...	*oo vas yest shtó-nibood byez...*
meat?	мя́са?	*myása*
• Is that cooked with...	Это...	*éta...*
nuts?	с оре́хами?	*s aryékhami*

YOU MAY HEAR...

• Всё в порядке́?	*fsyó f paryátkye*	**Is everything all right?**
• Я спрошу́ у по́вара.	*ya sprashóo oo póvara*	**I'll check with the kitchen.**

✳ problems and complaints

YOU MAY WANT TO SAY...

- This is...
  cold
  burnt

  Это...
  холо́дное
  подгоре́ло

  éta...
  khalódnaye
  padgaryéla

- I didn't order this. (m/f)

  Я э́то не зака́зывал/-а.

  ya éta ni zakázyval/-a

- Is our food coming soon?

  Когда́ принесу́т наш зака́з?

  kagdá prinisóot nash zakás?

- Can I/we have more... , please?
  water

  Ещё... пожа́луйста.

  во́ды

  yischó... pazhálsta

  vadý

✳ paying the bill

YOU MAY WANT TO SAY...

- The bill, please.

  Счёт, пожа́луйста.

  schót pazhálsta

- There's a mistake here.

  Здесь оши́бка.

  zdyes ashípka

- That was fantastic, thank you.

  Всё бы́ло о́чень вку́сно, спаси́бо.

  fsyo býla óchin fkóosna, spasíba

YOU MAY HEAR...

- Как Вас обслужи́ли?

  kak vas apsloozhíli

  How was everything?

- Извини́те, опла́та то́лько нали́чными.

  izvinítye, apláta tólka nalíchnymi

  Sorry, we only accept cash.

food and drink

* buying food

 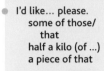

- I'd like... please.
  some of those/
  that
  half a kilo (of ...)
  a piece of that

  (Мне)... пожáлуйста,
  немнóго вот
  этого/тогó
  полкилó...
  кусóк этого/тогó

  (mnye)... pazhálsta
  nimnóga vot
  étava/tavó
  polkiló...
  koosók étava/tavó

- How much is that? Скóлько это стóит? skólka éta stóit

- What's that, please? Что это такóе? shtó eta takóye

- A bit more/less,
  please.

  Чуть бóльше/
  мéньше.

  choot bólshe/
  myénshe

- That's enough,
  thank you.

  Достáточно,
  спасíбо.

  dastátachna, spasíba

- Where's the...
  fruit and
  vegetable
  section?

  Где у Вас...
  фрýкты и óвощи?

  gdye oo vas ...
  fróokty i óvaschi

- Can I have a bag,
  please?

  Мóжно пакéт? mózhna pakyét

YOU MAY HEAR...

- Что желáете?/
  Что Вам?

  shto zhiláitye/shto
  vam

  What would you
  like?

- Скóлько? skólka How much/many
  would you like?

- Чтó(-нибудь) ещё? shtó(-nibood) yischó Anything else?

food and drink

85

menu reader

GENERAL

Завтрак	*záftrak*	breakfast
Обед	*abyét*	lunch
Ужин	*óozhin*	dinner
Закуски	*zakóoski*	starters
Шведский стол	*shvyétski stol*	buffet
Первые блюда	*pyérvyye blyóoda*	first course
Вторые блюда	*ftarýye blyóoda*	second (main) course
Гарнир	*garnír*	side dishes
Блюдо дня	*blyóoda dnya*	dish of the day
Комплексный обед	*kómplyeksny abyét*	set menu
Традиционные блюда	*traditsiónnyye blyóoda*	typical dishes
Мясные блюда	*misnýye blyóoda*	meat dishes
Рыбные блюда	*rýbnyye blyóoda*	fish dishes
Десерт	*disyért*	dessert
Безалкагольные напитки	*bizalkagólnyye napítki*	soft drinks
Горячие напитки	*garyáchie napítki*	hot drinks
Все цены с учетом НДС	*vse tsény s oochyótam en de es*	tax included
Мы (не) принимаем кредитные карты	*my (ni) prinimáim kridítnyye kárty*	we (don't) accept credit cards

DRINKS

бренди	*bréndi*	brandy
бутылка	*bootýlka*	bottle
вино	*vinó*	wine
сухое	*sookhóye*	dry
домашнее	*damáshniye*	house wine
красное	*krásnaye*	red
сладкое	*slátkaye*	sweet
белое	*byélaye*	white
виски	*víski*	whisky
водка	*vótka*	vodka
горячий шоколад/ какао	*garyáchi shikalát/ kakáo*	hot chocolate
графин	*grafín*	jug, pitcher
коктейль	*kaktéïl*	cocktail
кофе	*kófye*	coffee
черный	*chórny*	black
без кофеина	*byes kafiína*	decaffeinated
со льдом	*sa ldom*	iced
лед, со льдом	*lyot, sa ldom*	ice, with ice
лимонад	*limanát*	lemonade
марочное вино	*márachnaye vinó*	vintage
минеральная вода (с газом/ без газа)	*minirálnaya vadá (z gázam/byez gáza)*	mineral water (fizzy/still)
молоко (горячее/ холодное)	*malakó (garyáchiye/ khalódnaye)*	milk (hot/cold)
молочный коктейль	*malóchny kaktéïl*	milkshake
пиво	*píva*	beer
безалкагольное	*bizalkagólnaye*	alcohol-free
бутылочное	*bootýlachnaye*	bottled
светлое	*svyétlaye*	light
темное	*tyómnaye*	dark
разливное	*razlivnóye*	draught

ром	*rom*	rum
сидр	*sidr*	cider
сок	*sok*	juice
ананасовый	*ananásavy*	pineapple
апельсиновый	*apilsínavy*	orange
грейпфрутовый	*greïpfróotavy*	grapefruit
томатный	*tamátny*	tomato
яблочный	*yáblachny*	apple
тоник	*tónik*	tonic
херес	*khyéris*	sherry
чай	*chaï*	tea
зеленый	*zilyóny*	green
черный	*chórny*	black
с молоком/	*s malakóm/*	with milk/
лимоном	*limónam*	lemon
мятный	*myátny*	mint
ромашковый	*ramáshkavy*	camomile
фруктовый	*frooktóvy*	fruit
шампанское	*shampánskaye*	champagne

STYLES OF COOKING

вареный/отварной	*varyóny/otvarnóï*	boiled
жаренный	*zháriny*	roasted, grilled
запеченный	*zapichóny*	baked
копченый	*kapchóny*	smoked
маринованные	*marinóvanny*	marinated
мороженый	*marózhiny*	frozen
паровой	*paravóï*	steamed
свежий	*svyézhi*	fresh
соленый	*salyóny*	pickled
тушеный	*tooshóny*	stewed
фаршированный	*farshiróvany*	stuffed

FOOD

абрикос	*abrikós*	apricot
авокадо	*avakáda*	avocado
азу	*azóo*	azu (diced meat, usually beef, with pickles)
антрекот	*antrikót*	entrecôte
апельсин	*apilsín*	orange
баклажан	*baklazhán*	aubergine
банан	*banán*	banana
баранина	*baránina*	lamb
беляш	*bilyásh*	belyash (fried meat pastry)
бефстроганов	*bifstróganaf*	beef stroganoff
бифштекс	*bifshtéks*	steak
блины	*bliný*	pancakes
бобы	*babý*	beans
борщ	*borsch*	borsch
брокколи	*brókali*	broccoli
буженина	*boozhinína*	cold boiled pork
булочка	*bóolachka*	roll
бульон	*boolyón*	broth
с клецками	*s klyótskami*	with dumplings
с фрикадельками	*s frikadélkami*	with meatballs
бутерброд	*bootirbrót*	sandwich
вареники	*varyéniki*	dumplings
варенье	*varyénye*	(runny) jam
ватрушка	*vatróoshka*	cottage cheese pastry
ветчина	*vitchiná*	ham
взбитые сливки	*vzbítyye slífki*	whipped cream
виноград	*vinagrát*	grapes

гамбургер	*gámboorgir*	hamburger
говядина	*gavyádina*	beef
голубцы	*galooptsý*	stuffed cabbage
горчица	*garchítsa*	mustard
грибы	*gribý*	mushrooms
грудинка	*groodínka*	bacon
груша	*gróosha*	pear
гуляш	*goolyásh*	goulash
гусь	*goos*	goose
дыня	*dýnya*	melon
желе	*zhilyé*	jelly
жульен	*zhoolyén*	mushrooms with sour cream
запеканка	*zapikánka*	baked pudding
зеленый горошек	*zilyóny garóshik*	peas
земляника	*zimliníka*	wild strawberries
изюм	*izyóom*	raisin
икра	*ikrá*	caviar
кабачковая	*kabachkóvaya*	marrow puree
зернистая	*zirnístaya*	unpressed caviar
красная	*krásnaya*	red
лососевая	*lasasyóvaya*	salmon
черная	*chórnaya*	black
индейка	*indyéika*	turkey
йогурт	*yógoort*	yoghurt
кабачки	*kabachkí*	marrows/courgettes
камбала	*kambalá*	plaice
капуста	*kapóosta*	cabbage
картофель/ картошка	*kartófil/kartóshka*	potato
каша	*kásha*	porridge
квашенная капуста	*kváshinaya kapóosta*	sauerkraut
кекс	*kyeks*	fruit cake

кисель	kisyél	kissel (kind of blancmange)
клубника	kloobníka	strawberry
клюква	klyóokva	cranberry
колбаса	kalbasá	sausage
конфеты	kanfyéty	sweets
корица	karítsa	cinnamon
котлеты	katlyéty	cutlets
краб	krap	crab
креветки	krivyétki	prawns
крыжовник	kryzhóvnik	gooseberry
кукуруза	kookooróoza	sweet corn
кулебяка	koolibyáka	kulebyaka (pie)
курица	kóoritsa	chicken
лапша	lapshá	noodles
лимон	limón	lemon
лосось	lasós	salmon
лук	look	onion
майонез	mayinés	mayonnaise
малина	malína	raspberry
масло растительное	másla rastítilnaye	oil
масло сливочное	másla slívachnaye	butter
мед	myot	honey
миндаль	mindál	almonds
морепродукты	moripradóokty	seafood
морковь	markóf	carrot
мороженое	marózhinaye	ice-cream
мясо	myása	meat
огурец	agooryéts	cucumber
окрошка	akróshka	cold soup
окунь	ókoon	perch

оладьи	aládyi	sweet pancakes
оливки	alífki	olives
оливье	aliv-yé	Russian potato salad
омар	amár	lobster
омлет	amlyét	omelette
орех	aryékh	nuts
орехи грецкие	aryékhi gryétskiye	walnuts
орехи земляные	aryékhi zimlinýe	peanuts
отбивная	atbivnáya	chop
паштет	pashtyét	pâté
пельмени	pilmyéni	dumplings
перец	pyérits	pepper
петрушка	pitróoshka	parsley
печенка/печень	pichyónka/pyéchin	liver
пирог	pirók	large pie
пирожки	pirashkí	small pies
с капустой	s kapóostaï	with cabbage
с картошкой	s kartóshkaï	with potato
с мясом	s myásam	with meat
с рисом и яйцом	s rísam i yiïtsóm	with rice and eggs
помидор	pamidór	tomato
почки	póchki	kidneys
пряники	pryániki	honey cake
рак	rak	crab
рис	ris	rice
рулет мясной	roolyét misnóï	meat loaf
рыба	rýba	fish
салат	salát	salad
сардельки	sardélki	frankfurter sausage
сахар	sákhar	sugar
свекла	svyókla	beetroot
свекольник	svikólnik	cold beetroot soup

свинина	*svinína*	pork
севрюга	*sivryóoga*	sturgeon
селедка	*silyótka*	herring
селедка под шубой	*silyótka pat shóobaï*	herring salad with beetroot and mayonnaise
сельдерей	*sildiréï*	celery
скумбрия	*skóombriya*	mackerel
слива	*slíva*	plum
сливки	*slífki*	cream
сметана	*smitána*	sour cream
солянка	*salyánka*	solyanka (soup with cucumbers)
сосиски	*sasíski*	sausages
соус	*sóoos*	sauce
спагетти	*spagyétti*	spaghetti
спаржа	*spárzha*	asparagus
суп	*soop*	soup
сыр	*syr*	cheese
сырники	*sýrniki*	syrniki (small fried cakes filled with cottage cheese)
творог	*tvórak*	cottage cheese
телятина	*tilyátina*	veal
тефтели	*tiftyéli*	meatballs
торт	*tort*	cake
треска	*triská*	cod
тыква	*týkva*	pumpkin
уксус	*óoksoos*	vinegar
утка	*óotka*	duck
уха	*ookhá*	fish soup
фасоль	*fasól*	beans

форель	farél	trout
харчо	kharchó	mutton soup
хлопья	khlópya	cornflakes
хлеб	khlyep	bread
белый/черный	byély/chórny	white/brown
холодец	khaladyéts	aspic
хрен	khryen	horseradish
цветная капуста	tsvitnáya kapóosta	cauliflower
черешня	chiryéshnya	cherries
черника	chirníka	blackberries
чернослив	chirnaslíf	prunes
чеснок	chisnók	garlic
шампиньоны	shampinióny	(field) mushrooms
шоколад	shikalát	chocolate
шпинат	shpinát	spinach
шпроты	shpróty	sprats
щавель	schavyél	sorrel
щи	schi	cabbage soup
щука	schóoka	pike
яблоко	yáblaka	apple
язык	yizýk	tongue
яичница	yiíshnitsa	fried eggs
яйца	yáïtsa	eggs
вкрутую	fkrootóoyoo	hard-boiled
всмятку	fsmyátkoo	soft-boiled
под майонезом	pad mayinézam	with mayonnaise

sightseeing
&activities

* at the tourist office

● If you cannot find the tourist office ask at reception of your hotel for information. Usually hotels will have plenty of leaflets and free maps.

YOU MAY SEE...

Билеты	*bilyéty*	tickets
Гостиницы	*gastínitsy*	hotels
Закрыто	*zakrýta*	closed
Открыто	*atkrýta*	open
Экскурсии	*ekskóorsii*	(day) trips

YOU MAY WANT TO SAY...

● **Do you speak English?** — Вы говорите по-английски? — *vy gavarítye pa-anglíski*

● **Do you have...** — У Вас есть... — *oo vas yest...*
    a map of the town? — карта города? — *kárta górada*
    a list of hotels? — список гостиниц? — *spísak gastínits*

● **Do you have information in English?** — У Вас есть информация на английском? — *oo vas yest infarmátsiya na anglískam*

● **Can you book for me/us ...** — Вы можете заказать мне/нам... — *vy mózhitye zakazát mnye/nam...*
    a hotel room? — гостиницу? — *gastínitsoo*
    this day trip? — эту экскурсию? — *étoo ekskóorsiyoo*

sightseeing and activities

- **Where is...** Где... *gdye...*
    the art gallery? карти́нная *kartínnaya*
      галере́я? *galiryéya*
    the museum? музе́й? *moozyéï*
    the bank? банк? *bank*

- **Is there a post office near here?** Где здесь по́чта? *gde zdyes póchta*

✳ opening times
(see **telling the time**, page 18)

YOU MAY WANT TO SAY...

- **What time does the... close?** Во ско́лько закрыва́ется... *va skólka zakryváitsa...*
    museum музе́й? *moozyéï*

- **When does the... open?** Когда́ открыва́ется... *kagdá atkryváitsya...*
    exhibition вы́ставка? *výstafka*

- **Is it open... at the weekend?** Он/она́ рабо́тает... по выходны́м? *on/aná rabótait... pa vykhadným*

- **Is it open to the public?** Он/она́ откры́т/а для посети́телей? *on/aná atkrýt/atkrýta dlya pasitítilyeï*

YOU MAY HEAR...

- ...рабо́тает ка́ждый день кро́ме... *rabótait kázhdy dyen krómye* It's open every day except...

- ...рабо́тает с... до ... *rabótait s... da...* It's open from... to...

sightseeing and activities

97

| ...закры́т(-a/o) на реставра́цию | zakrýt(-a/o) na ristavrátsiyoo | It's closed for repairs. |

* visiting places

YOU MAY SEE...

Биле́ты	bilyéty	ticket office
Вход	fkhot	entrance
Вхо́да нет	fkhóda nyet	no entry
Гардеро́б/Ка́мера хране́ния	gardiróp/kámira khranyéniya	cloakroom
Рука́ми не тро́гать	rookámi ni trógat	do not touch
Служе́бное помеще́ние	sloozhébnaye pamischéniye	private
Фо́то и видеосъёмка запрещены́	fóto i videos-yómka zaprischiný	use of photographic and recording equipment prohibited
Экску́рсии	ekskóorsii	guided tours

YOU MAY WANT TO SAY...

- **How much does it cost?** Ско́лько э́то сто́ит? *skólka éta stóit*

- **Two adults, please.** Два́ взро́слых *dva vzróslykh*

- **One adult and two children, please.** Оди́н взро́слый и два де́тских, пожа́луйста. *adín vzrósly i dva dyétskikh, pazhálsta*

Is there a discount for... | Есть скидки... | yest skítki...
students? | студéнтам? | stoodyéntam
children? | дéтям? | dyétyam

Do you have ... | У Вас есть ... | oo vas yest...
an audio tour? | аудиотýр? | aoodiatóor

Are there guided tours (in English)? | Есть экскýрсии (на англúйском)? | yest ekskóorsii (na anglískam)

Can I take photos? | Мóжно фотографúровать? | mózhna fatagafíravat

Can you take a photo of us? | Вы мóжете меня/нас сфотографúровать? | vy mózhitye minya/ nas sfatagrafíravat

When was this built? | Когдá это бýло пострóено? | kagdá éta býla pastróina

Who painted this picture? | Чья это картúна? | ch-yá éta kartína

YOU MAY HEAR...

Билéт стóит ... рублéй. | bilyét stóit ... rooblyéi | It costs ... roubles per person.

Вход свобóдный. | fkhot svabódny | Admission is free.

Скúдки... | skítki... | There's a discount for...

пенсионéрам | pinsianyéram | senior citizens

Дéти до... лет беспла́тно. | dyéti da... lyet bisplátna | Children under... go free.

99

going on tours and trips

У Вас есть студе́нческий (биле́т)?	*oo vas yest stoodyénchiski (bilyét)*	Do you have a student card?
Су́мку/рюкза́к на́до сдать (в ка́меру хране́ния).	*sóomkoo/ryookzák náda zdat (f kámiroo khranyéniya)*	You must leave your bag/rucksack in the cloak-room.
К сожале́нию, на инвали́дной коля́ске не прое́хать.	*k sazhalyéniyoo na invalídnaï kalyáskye ni prayékhat*	I'm sorry, it's not suitable for wheelchairs.
Аудиоту́р сто́ит... рубле́й.	*aoodiatóor stóit... rooblyéï*	The audio tour costs ... Roubles.
Э́то рабо́та худо́жника/ архите́ктора ...	*éta rabóta khoodózhnika/ arkhityéktara...*	The painter/ architect was...

✳ going on tours and trips

YOU MAY WANT TO SAY...

I'd like to join the tour to...	Я хочу́ пое́хать на экску́рсию в ...	*ya khachóo payékhat na ekskóorsiyoo v...*
What time does it...	Когда́ ...	*kagdá*
leave?	нача́ло?	*nachála*
get back?	мы вернёмся?	*my virnyómsya*
Where does it leave from?	Отку́да она́ отправля́ется?	*atkóoda aná atpravlyáitsa*
Does the guide speak English?	Экскурсово́д/гид говори́т по-англи́йски?	*ekskóorsavod/git gavarít pa-anglíski*

How much is it?	Ско́лько сто́ит?	skólka stóit
Is... included?	С...	s...
lunch	обе́дом?	abyédam
accommodation	прожива́нием?	prazhivániyem
When's the next...	Когда́ сле́дующая...	kagdá slyédooschaya...
boat trip?	прогу́лка на теполохо́де?	pragóolka na tiplakhódye
day trip?	экску́рсия?	ekskóorsiya
Can we hire...	Мы мо́жем наня́ть...	my mózhim nanyát...
an English-speaking guide?	англогово-ря́щего ги́да?	anglagava-ryáschiva gída
I've lost my group. (m/f)	Я отста́л/отста́ла от гру́ппы.	ya atstál/atstála at gróopy

---

YOU MAY HEAR... ❓

Нача́ло экску́рсии в...	nachála ekskóorsii v...	It leaves at...
Оконча́ние экску́рсии в...	akanchániye ekskóorsii v...	It gets back at...
Она́ отправля́ется от...	aná atpravlyáitsa at...	It leaves from...
Он/она́ берёт... рубле́й в день.	on/aná biryót... rooblyéi v dyen	He/She charges... Roubles per day.

sightseeing and activities

101

* tourist glossary

Башня	*báshnya*	tower
Выставка	*výstafka*	exhibition
Горячий источник	*garyáchi istóchnik*	hot spring
Дворец	*dvaryéts*	palace
Зоопарк	*zaapárk*	zoo
Картинная галерея	*kartínnya galiryéya*	art gallery
Кладбище	*kládbische*	cemetery
Крепость	*kryépast*	fortress
Памятник	*pámitnik*	monument
Парк	*park*	park
Площадь	*plóschat*	square
Сады	*sadý*	gardens
Собор	*sabór*	cathedral
Стадион	*stadión*	stadium
Царица	*tsarítsa*	tsarina
Царь	*tsar*	tsar

* entertainment

Балет	*balyét*	ballet
Балкон	*balkón*	upper circle
Без антракта	*byez antrákta*	there is no interval
Билетов нет	*bilyétaf nyet*	sold out
Гардероб	*gardiróp*	cloakroom
Кино	*kinó*	cinema
Концертный зал	*kantsyértny zal*	concert hall

Кукольный театр	*kóokalny tiátr*	**puppet theatre**
Ложа	*lózha*	**box**
Матч	*mach*	**match**
Ночной клуб	*nachnóï kloop*	**nightclub**
Опера	*ópira*	**opera**
Оркестр	*arkyéstr*	**orchestra**
Партер	*partér*	**stalls**
Ряд	*ryat*	**row**
Театр	*tiátr*	**theatre**
Цирк	*tsirk*	**circus**

YOU MAY WANT TO SAY...

- **What is there to do in the evenings here?** | Куда можно пойти вечером? | *koodá mózhna paití vyéchiram*

- **Is there... round here?**
  a cinema? | Где здесь... кинотеатр? | *gdye zdyes... kinatiátr*

- **What's on...**
  tomorrow?
  at the theatre? | Что идёт завтра? в театре? | *shto idyót záftra? f tiátrye*

- **Is there a football match on this weekend?** | В выходные будет футбольный матч? | *v vykhadnýye bóodit footbólny mach*

- **What time does the... start?**
  game | Во сколько начало... игры? | *va skólka nachála... igrý*

- **How long is the performance?** | Сколько длится представление? | *skólka dlítsa pritstavlyéniye*

entertainment

- **Where can I get tickets?** — Где мо́жно купи́ть биле́ты? — *gdye mózhna koopít bilyéty*

- **Is it suitable for children?** — Это подойдёт де́тям? — *éta padaïdyót dyétyam*

- **Has the film got subtitles?** — Фильм с субти́трами? — *film s sooptítrami*

- **Is it dubbed?** — Фильм дубли́рован? — *film dooblíravan*

- **Who's...** — Кто... — *kto...*
  - **singing?** — поёт? — *payót*
  - **playing?** — игра́ет? — *igráit*

✳ booking tickets

YOU MAY WANT TO SAY...

- **Can you get me tickets for...
  the ballet?**
  Вы мо́жете зака-за́ть биле́ты...
  на бале́т?
  *vy mózhitye zakazát bilyéty...
  na balyét*

- **Are there any seats left for Saturday?**
  Есть биле́ты на суббо́ту?
  yest bilyéty na soobótoo

- **I'd like to book...
  two seats**
  Пожа́луйста...
  два биле́та
  *pazhálsta...
  dva bilyéta*

- **In the stalls.**
  В парте́ре.
  f partére

- **In the upper circle.**
  На балко́не.
  na balkónye

- **Do you have anything cheaper?**
  Есть что́-нибудь подеше́вле?
  yest shtó-nibood padishévli

- **Is there wheelchair access?**
  Мо́жно прое́хать на инвали́дной коля́ске?
  mózhna prayékhat na invalídnaï kalyáskye

YOU MAY HEAR...

- Ско́лько?
  skólka
  How many?

- На како́е число́?
  na kakóye chisló
  When for?

- Извини́те, но на э́то число́ биле́тов нет.
  izvinítye no na éta chisló bilyétaf nyet
  I'm sorry we're sold out.

sightseeing and activities

105

✳ at the show

YOU MAY WANT TO SAY...

What is on tonight?	Что сегодня показывают?	*shto sivódnya pakázyvayoot*
Two for tonight's performance, please.	Два билета на сегодня, пожалуйста.	*dva bilyéta na sivódnya pazhálsta*
We'd like to sit...	Я хочу сидеть...	*ya khachóo sidyét...*
at the front	впереди	*fpiridí*
at the back	подальше/в заднем ряду	*padálshye/v zádnim ridóo*
in the middle	в середине	*f siridínye*
We've reserved seats.	Мы заказывали билеты.	*my zakázyvali bilyéty*
It's in the name of...	На имя...	*na ímya...*
Is there an interval?	Будет антракт?	*bóodit antrákt*
Where are the toilets?	Где туалеты?	*gdye tooalyéty*
Can you stop talking, please?!	Можно потише, пожалуйста?!	*mózhna patíshi pazhálsta*

YOU MAY HEAR...

Извините, на сегодня билетов нет.	*izvinítye na sivódnya bilyétaf nyet*	Sorry, we're full tonight.
Вам какие места?	*vam kakíye mistá*	Where do you want to sit?
Вам нужна программка?	*vam noozhná pragrámka*	Would you like a programme?

✳ sports and activities

YOU MAY SEE...

Бассейн	*basséïn*	swimming pool
Верховая езда	*virkhaváya yizdá*	horse riding
Купаться запрещено	*koopátsa zaprischinó*	no swimming
Медпункт	*mitpóonkt*	first aid
Опасно	*apásna*	danger
Площадка/поле для игры в гольф	*plaschátka/pólye dlya igrý v golf*	golf course
Пляж	*plyash*	beach
Подъемник	*pad-yómnik*	ski lift
Прокат лыж	*prakát lysh*	ski hire
Сауна	*sáoona*	sauna
Спортивный центр	*spartívny tsentr*	sports centre
Теннисный корт	*ténnisny kort*	tennis court
Футбольное поле	*footbólnaye pólye*	football pitch

YOU MAY WANT TO SAY...

- Where can I/we...   Где мóжно   gdye mózhna
                         поигрáть...   paigrát...
    play tennis?   в тéннис?   f ténis
    play golf?   в гольф?   v golf

- Can I/we...   Здесь мóжно ...   zdyes mózhna...
    go fishing   рыбáчить?   rybáchit
    here?
    go swimming   купáться?   koopátsa
    here?

- I'm...   Я...   ya ...
    a beginner   новичóк   navichók
    quite   óпытный   ópytny
    experienced   спортсмéн/   spartsmyén/
    (m/f)   óпытная   ópytnaya
                           спортсмéнка   spartsmyénka

- How much does   Скóлько стóит...   skólka stóit...
  it cost...
    per hour?   в час?   f chas
    per day?   в день?   v dyen
    per round?   пáртия?   pártiya
    per game?   йгра?   igrá

- Can I/we hire...   Мóжно взять   mózhna vzyat
                         напрокáт ...   naprakát...
    raquets?   ракéтки?   rakyétki
    skis?   лы́жи?   lýzhi

- Do you give   Вы даёте урóки?   vy dayótye ooróki
  lessons?

- Do I/we have to   Нýжно быть   nóozhna byt
  be a member?   члéном клýба?   chlyénam klóoba

| Is there a discount for children? | Есть скидки для детей? | *yest skítki dlya dityéï* |

YOU MAY HEAR...

Это стóит... рублéй в час.	*éta stóit... rooblyéï f chas*	It costs... roubles per hour.
Нýжно заплатúть/ остáвить залóг... рублéй.	*nóozhna zaplatít/ astávit zalók... rooblyéï*	There's a deposit of... roubles.
Всё зáнято.	*vsyo zánita*	We're fully booked.
Зайдúте пóзже.	*zaïdítye pózhzhe*	Come back later.
Есть местá на зáвтра.	*yest mistá na záftra*	We've got places tomorrow.
Какóй у Вас размéр?	*kakóï oo vas razmyér*	What size are you?
Какóй у Вас рост?	*kakóï oo vas rost*	How tall are you?
Вам нужнá... фотогрáфия страхóвка	*vam noozhná... fatagráfiya strakhófka*	You need... a photo insurance

✳ at the beach, river or pool

YOU MAY WANT TO SAY...

● **Can we swim here?**	Здесь мо́жно купа́ться?	*zdyes mózhna koopátsa*
● **When is high/low tide?**	Когда́ (быва́ет) прили́в/отли́в?	*kagdá (byváit) prilíf/ atlíf*
● **Is the water clean?**	Вода́ чи́стая?	*vadá chístaya*
● **Where is the... lifeguard?**	Где... спаса́тель?	*gdye... spasátil*

YOU MAY HEAR...

● Осторо́жно, опа́сно!	*astarózhna, apásna*	Be careful, it's dangerous.
● Тече́ние о́чень си́льное.	*tichyéniye óchin sílnaye*	The current is very strong.
● О́чень си́льный ве́тер.	*óchin sílny vyétir*	It's very windy.

YOU MAY SEE...

Лови́ть рыбу запрещено́/ Рыба́лка запрещена́	*lavít rýboo zaprischinó/ rybálka zaprischiná*	**no fishing**
Ныря́ть запрещено́.	*nyryát zaprischinó*	**no diving**

shops&services

* shopping

● Generally you pay for all goods at the till before leaving the shop. You may come across the system where you pay for goods at a cash desk first and then collect them. Don't forget the receipt or you won't get your items.

YOU MAY SEE...

(Аварийный) выход	avaríiny výkhat	(emergency) exit
Антиквариат	antikvariát	antiques
Аптека	aptyéka	chemist's/pharmacy
Булочная	bóolashnaya	bakery
Вход	fkhot	entry
Газеты-журналы	gazyéty-zhoornály	newsagent's
Диета	diyéta	health foods
Закрыто	zakrýta	closed
Игрушки	igróoshki	toys
Канцелярские товары	kantsilyárskiye taváry	stationer's
Касса	kássa	cashier
Книги/Книжный магазин	kníги/knízhny magazín	bookshop
Кожа	kózha	leather goods
Компьютеры	kampyóotery	computers
Кондитерская	kandítirskaya	cake shop/confectioner's
Мебель	myébil	furniture shop
Меха	mikhá	furs
Молоко	malakó	milk
Мороженое	marózhinaye	ice-cream
Мясо	myása	butcher's

Обувь	óboof	footwear/shoe shop
Овощи-фрукты	óvaschi-fróokty	greengrocer
Одежда	adyézhda	clothing/fashion
Оптика	óptika	optician's
Открыто	atkrýta	open
Парикмахерская	parikmákhirskaya	hairdresser's
Парфюмерия	parfyoomyériya	perfumery
Подарки	padárki	gifts
Почта	póchta	post office
Примерочные	primyérachnyye	fitting rooms
Продукты	pradóokty	groceries
Распродажа	raspradázha	sales
Розничная цена	róznichnaya tsiná	retail price
Руками не трогать	rookámi ni trógat	do not touch
Рыба	rýba	fishmonger's
Самообслуживание	sámaapslóozhivaniye	self-service
Специальное предложение	spitsiálnaye pridlazhéniye	special offer
Спорттовары	spórttaváry	sports goods
Сувениры	sooviníry	souvenirs
Супермаркет	sóopirmárkit	supermarket
Табак	tabák	tobacconist's
Торговый центр	targóvy tsentr	shopping centre
Универмаг	oonivirmák	department store
Фотография	fatagráfiya	photographer's
Химчистка	khimchístka	dry-cleaners
Хлеб	khlyep	bakery
Цветы	tsietý	florist's
Электроника	eliktrónika	electronics
Электротовары	elyéktrataváry	electrical goods
Ювелирный магазин	yoovilírny magazín	jeweller's

Where is... the shopping centre?	Где... торго́вый центр?	gdye... targóvy tsentr
Where can I buy... a city map?	Где мо́жно купи́ть... ка́рту го́рода?	gdye mózhna koopít... kártoo górada
I'd like ..., please. that one there this one here two of those	Пожа́луйста..., вот то вот э́то два таки́х	pazhálsta... vot to vot éta dva takíkh
Have you got... ?	У Вас есть... ?	oo vas yest...
How much does it/do they cost?	Ско́лько э́то сто́ит?	skólka éta stóit
Can you write it down please?	Мо́жете написа́ть?	mózhitye napisát
I'm just looking.	Я (про́сто) смотрю́.	ya (prósta) smatryóo
There's one in the window.	Как на витри́не.	kak na vitrínye
I'll take it.	Я возьму́ э́то.	ya vazmóo éta
Is there a guarantee?	Есть гара́нтия?	yest garántiya
Can you... keep it for me? order it for me?	Вы мо́жете... э́то отложи́ть? э́то заказа́ть?	vy mózhitye... éta atlazhít éta zakazát
I need to think about it.	Я поду́маю.	ya padóomayoo

YOU MAY HEAR...

Я Вас слу́шаю.	ya vas slóoshayoo	Can I help you?
(Это сто́ит)... рубле́й.	(éta stóit) ... rooblyéï	It costs ... roubles.
Извини́те, но э́то зако́нчилось.	izvinítye no éta zakónchilas	I'm sorry, we've sold out.
Я могу́ для Вас заказа́ть.	ya magóo dlya vas zakazát	I can order it for you.

✳ paying

● The official Russian currency is the rouble (рубль *roobl*) (RUR). One rouble equals 100 kopecks (копейка *kapyéïka*). Currently there are banknotes of 10, 50, 100, 500 and 1,000 roubles, and coins of 1, 5, 10, 50 kopecks and of 1, 2 and 5 roubles.

● There are many cash machines in all major Russian cities, and a lot of shops and restaurants accept cards. However, as soon as you go to smaller towns, you will find it hard to use your credit card.

YOU MAY WANT TO SAY...

Where do I pay?	Где ка́сса?	gdye kássa
Do you take credit cards?	Вы принима́ете креди́тные ка́рты?	vy prinimáitye kridítnyye kárty
Can you wrap it, please?	Вы мо́жете заверну́ть?	vy mózhitye zavirnóot

shops and services

115

buying clothes and shoes

- **Can I have...**   Дáйте,   *dáïtye, pazhálsta...*
  please?   пожáлуйста,...
  - **a receipt**   чек   *chyek*
  - **a bag**   пакéт   *pakyét*

- **Sorry, I haven't**   Извинúте, у менá   *izvinítye oo minyá*
  got any change.   нет мéлочи.   *nyet myélachi*

YOU MAY HEAR...

Это подáрок?	*éta padárak*	**Is it a gift?**
Пакéт нýжен?	*pakyét nóozhin*	**Do you want a bag?**
Пожáлуйста...,	*pazhálsta...*	**Can I see... please?**
какóй-нибýдь	*kakóï-nibóod*	**some ID**
докумéнт	*dakoomyént*	
пáспорт	*páspart*	**your passport**
У Вас есть/	*oo vas yest/bóodit*	**Have you got any**
бýдет помéльче?	*pamyélchi*	**smaller notes?**
У менá нет сдáчи.	*oo minyá nyet zdáchi*	**I have no change.**
Идúте менáйте.	*idítye minyáïtye*	**You will need to get some change.**

✱ buying clothes and shoes
(see **clothes and shoe sizes** page 22)

YOU MAY WANT TO SAY...

- **Have you got...**   У Вас есть...   *oo vas yest...*
  - **a smaller size?**   на размéр   *na razmyér*
                           мéньше?   *myénshe*
  - **a larger size?**   на размéр бóльше?   *na razmyér bólshe*
  - **other colours?**   другóго цвéта?   *droogóva tsvyéta*

- I'm a size... У меня... разме́р. *oo minyá... razmyér*
- I'm looking for... Я ищу́... *ya ischóo...*
    - a shirt руба́шку *roobáshkoo*
    - a jumper джéмпер *dzhémpir*
    - a jacket пи́джак *pidzhák*
    - a hat ша́пку *shápkoo*
- A pair of...
    - trousers брю́ки *bryóoki*
    - boots боти́нки *batínki*
- Where are the changing rooms? Где приме́рочная? *gdye primyérachnaya*

✳ changing rooms

YOU MAY WANT TO SAY...

- Can I try this on, please? Я могу́ приме́рить? *ya magóo primyérit*
- It doesn't fit. Не подхо́дит. *ni patkhódit*
- It's too... (Сли́шком...) *(slíshkam...)*
    - big. велико́ *vilikó*
    - small. мало́ *maló*
- It doesn't suit me. Мне не идёт. *mnye ni idyót*

YOU MAY HEAR...

Хоти́те/жела́ете приме́рить?	*khatítye/zhiláitye primyérit*	Would you like to try it/them on?
Како́й разме́р?	*kakóï razmyér*	What size are you?
Вам идёт.	*vam idyót*	It suits/they suit you.

✱ exchanges and refunds

YOU MAY WANT TO SAY...

- I'd like...
  to return this.
  to change this.

  Я хочу́...
  э́то верну́ть.
  э́то поменя́ть.

  ya khachóo...
  éta virnóot
  éta paminyát

- This is faulty.

  Здесь брак.

  zdyes brak

- This doesn't fit.

  Не подошло́.

  ni padashló

- I'd like a refund.

  Я хочу́ получи́ть
  де́ньги обра́тно.

  ya khachóo paloochít
  dyéngi abrátna

YOU MAY HEAR...

- У Вас есть...
  чек?
  гаранти́йный
  та́лон?

  oo vas yest...
  chyek
  garantíiny talón

  Have you got...
  the receipt?
  the guarantee?

- Извини́те, мы не
  возвраща́ем
  де́ньги.

  izvinítye my ni
  vazvrascháim dyéngi

  Sorry, we don't
  give refunds.

- Вы мо́жете
  обменя́ть.

  vy mózhitye
  abminyát

  You can exchange
  it.

shops and services

118

* photography

YOU MAY WANT TO SAY...

- **Can you print photos from a memory card?** — Вы печáтаете фотогрáфии с кáрты пáмяти? — *vy pichátayetye fatagráfii s kárty pámiti*

- **I'd like to develop this film.** — Я хочý проявить плёнку. — *ya khachóo prayivít plyónkoo*

- **When will it/they be ready?** — Когдá бýдет готóво? — *kagdá bóodit gatóva*

- **Do you have an express service?** — Вы дéлаете срóчные закáзы? — *vy dyélaitye sróchnyye zakázy*

- **How much does it cost...** — Скóлько стóит... — *skólka stóit...*
  per print? — один снимок? — *adín snímak*

- **I'd like,... please.** — Пожáлуйста,... — *pazhálsta...*
  an 8MB memory card — кáрту пáмяти на вóсемь мегабáйтов — *kártoo pámiti na vósim migabáitov*

YOU MAY HEAR...

- Матóвые или глянцевые? — *mátavyye íli glyántsivyye* — Do you want them matt or gloss?

- Приходите... — *prikhadítye...* — Come back...
  зáвтра — *záftra* — tomorrow
  чéрез час — *chyéris chas* — in an hour

- На скóлько мегабáйтов (кáрту пáмяти)? — *na skólka migabáïtaf (kártoo pámiti)* — What size memory card do you want?

at the tobacconist, off-licence

✱ at the tobacconist

- Can I have a packet of... , please?

  Пáчку... , пожáлуйста.

  páchkoo... pazhálsta

- Do you sell...

  У Вас есть...

  oo vas yest...

  - matches? спи́чки? *spíchki*
  - lighters? зажигáлки? *zazhigálki*
  - loose tobacco? табáк? *tabák*
  - cigars? сигáры? *sigáry*

✱ at the off-licence

- Have you got any...

  У Вас есть...

  oo vas yest...

  - local wine? мéстное винó? *myésnaye vinó*
  - imported beer? и́мпортное пи́во? *ímpartnaye píva*

- Is this sweet or dry?

  Это слáдкое или сухóе?

  éta slátkaye íli sookhóye

- I'll take... please.

  Я возьмý...

  ya vazmóo...

  - a bottle/two bottles буты́лку/две буты́лки *bootýlkoo/dvye bootýlki*
  - a pack упакóвку *oopakófkoo*

✳ at the post office

YOU MAY WANT TO SAY...

- A stamp for... please.
  Europe
  America

  Ма́рку для письма́ в... пожа́луйста.
  Евро́пу
  Аме́рику

  márkoo dlya písma v... pazhálsta
  yevrópoo
  amyérikoo

- Five stamps please.

  Пять ма́рок, пожа́луйста.

  pyat márak pázhalsta

- For...
  postcards
  letters

  Для...
  откры́ток
  пи́сем

  dlya...
  atkrýtak
  písim

- Can I send this...
  registered?
  by airmail?

  Мо́жно посла́ть...
  заказны́м?
  а́виа?

  mózhna paslát...
  zakazným
  ávia

- It contains a present.

  Э́то – пода́рок.

  éta padárok

- Can I have a receipt, please?

  Квита́нцию да́йте, пожа́луйста.

  kvitántsiyoo dáïtye, pazhálsta

- Do you change money here?

  Я могу́ здесь обменя́ть де́ньги?

  ya magóo zdyes abminyát dyéngi

YOU MAY HEAR...

Положи́те на весы́.

palazhítye na visý

Put it on the scales, please.

Что внутри́?

shto vnootrí

What's in it?

Запо́лните тамо́женную деклара́цию, пожа́луйста.

zapólnitye tamózhinooyoo diklarátsiyoo pazhálsta

Please fill in this customs declaration form.

at the bank, changing money

✳ at the bank

- Excuse me, where's the foreign exchange counter?

  Извините, где окно обмена валюты?

  izvinítye gdye aknó abmyéna valyóoty

- Is there a cash machine here?

  Здесь есть банкомат?

  zdyes yest bankamát

- The cash machine has eaten my card.

  Банкомат сьел мою карту.

  bankamát s-yel mayóo kártoo

- I've forgotten my pin number. (m/f)

  Я забыл/-а свой пин-код.

  ya zabýl/zabýla svoï pin-kot

- My name is...

  Моя фамилия...

  mayá famíliya...

- Has my money arrived yet?

  Деньги пришли?

  dyéngi prishlí

✳ changing money

- You can change money at banks or licensed bureau de change. Look for Обмен валюты (*abmyén valyóoty*) or Обменный пункт (*abmyénny poonkt*) signs. The smaller bureaus may accept US dollars and Euros only. Never change money on the street, even if you are offered a better rate.

YOU MAY WANT TO SAY...

- I'd like to change ...
  - these travellers' cheques
  - one hundred pounds

Я хочу́...
обнали́чить доро́жные че́ки
обменя́ть сто фу́нтов

ya khachóo...
abnalíchit darózhnye chyéki
abminyát sto fóontaf

- Can you give me...
  - small notes?

Вы мо́жете разменя́ть...
поме́льче?

vy mózhitye razminyát...
pamyélchi

- What's the rate today...
  - for the pound?
  - for the dollar?
  - for the euro?

Како́й сего́дня курс...
фу́нта?
до́ллара?
е́вро?

kakóï sivódnya koors...
fóonta
dóllara
yévra

YOU MAY HEAR...

Ско́лько?	skólka	How much?
Па́спорт, пожа́луйста.	páspart pazhálsta	Passport, please.
Распиши́тесь здесь, пожа́луйста.	raspishítis zdyes pazhálsta	Sign here, please.
Курс пятьдеся́т два рубля́ за оди́н фунт.	koors piddisyát dva rooblyá za adín foont	It's 52 roubles to the pound.

shops and services

123

✳ telephones

● To make a phone call from a public telephone you'll need a telephone card телефонная карточка (*tilifónnaya kártachka*) or a token жетон (*zhitón*). They can be purchased from a newspaper kiosk, a post office or an underground ticket office.

YOU MAY WANT TO SAY...

● **Where's the (nearest) phone?** — Где здесь телефóн? — *gdye zdyes tilifón*

● **Is there a public phone?** — Здесь есть телефóн-автомáт? — *zdyes yest tilifón-aftamát*

● **I'd like to...** — Я хочý... — *ya khachóo...*
　buy a phone card. — купúть телефóнную кáрточку. — *koopít tilifónnooyoo kártachkoo*
　call England. — позвонúть в Áнглию. — *pazvanít v ángliyoo*
　make a reverse charge call. — позвонúть за счёт вызывáемого абонéнта. — *pazvanít za schyot vyzyváimava abanyénta*

● **How much does it cost per minute?** — Скóлько стóит минýта? — *skólka stóit minóota*

● **What's the code for... ?** — Какóй код у... ? — *kakóï kot oo...*

● **Hello.** — Аллó. — *alló*

● **It's... speaking.** — Говорúт.../Это... — *gavarít.../éta...*

- **Can I speak to... ?** — Могу я поговорить с... — *magóo ya pagavarít s...*
- **When will he/she be back?** — Когда он/она будет? — *kagdá on/aná bóodit*
- **I'll ring back.** — Я перезвоню. — *ya pirizvanyóo*
- **Can I leave a message?** — Могу я оставить сообщение? — *magóo ya astávit saapschyéniye*
- **My number is...** — Мой телефон... — *móї tilifón...*
- **It's a bad line.** — Плохо слышно/плохая связь. — *plókha slýshna/plakháya svyas*
- **I've been cut off.** — Связь прервалась. — *svyas prirvalás*

YOU MAY HEAR...

- Кто говорит?/Это кто? — *kto gavarít/éta kto* — Who's calling?
- Извините, его/её нет. — *izvinítye yivó/yiyó nyet* — Sorry, he/she's not here.
- Минуточку/одну минуту. — *minóotachkoo/adnóo minóotoo* — Just a moment.
- Какой Ваш телефон? — *kakóї vash tilifón* — What's your number?
- Занято. — *zánita* — It's engaged.
- Не отвечает. — *ni atvicháit* — There's no answer.
- Будете ждать? — *bóoditye zhdat* — Do you want to hold?

mobiles

• Вы ошиблись (номером)/Вы не туда попали.	vy ashíblis (nómirom)/vy ni toodá papáli	Sorry, wrong number.
• Неправильно набран номер.	niprávilna nábran nómir	The number you have dialled is incorrect.

✳ mobiles

• I need a charger for this phone.	Мне нужна зарядка устройство для этого телефона.	mnye nóozhná zarýatka oostróïstva dlya étava tilifóna
• I need a SIM card for the local network.	Мне нужна SIM-карта для местной сети.	mnye noozhná sim-kárta dlya myésnaï syetí
• I'd like to top-up my mobile phone.	Я хочу положить деньги на телефон.	ya khachóo palazhít dyéngi na tilifón

shops and services

126

✳ the internet

- Is there an internet café near here?

  Где здесь интернет-кафе?

  gdýe zdyés internét-kafé

- I'd like to check my emails.

  Я хочу проверить почту.

  ya khachóo pravyérit póchtoo

- How much is it per minute?

  Сколько стоит минута?

  skólka stóit minóota

- I can't log on.

  Я не могу войти.

  ya ni magóo vaïtí

- It's not connecting.

  Не соединяется.

  ni saidinyáitsa

- It's very slow.

  Очень медленно.

  óchin myédlinno

- Can I...
    print this?
    scan this?

  Я могу...
    распечатать?
    отсканировать?

  ya magóo...
    raspichátat
    atskaníravat

- Can I...
    use my memory stick?

  Я могу...
    использовать свою (карту памяти) USB?

  ya magóo...
    ispólzavat svayóo (kártoo pámiti) yoo es bee?

- Do you have...
    a CD-ROM?

  У Вас есть...
    сидиром?

  oo vas yest...
    sidiróm?

- How do I switch to an English keyboard?

  Как переключить на английскую клавиатуру?

  kak piriklyoochít na anglískooyoo klaviatóoroo?

the internet

Имя пользователя	*ímya pólzavatilya*	username
Пароль	*paról*	password
Нажать/кликнуть	*nazhát/klíknoot*	click here
Ссылка	*ssýlka*	link

✳ faxes

YOU MAY WANT TO SAY...

- **What's your fax number?** — Какой у Вас номер факса? — *kakóï oo vas nómir fáksa*

- **Can you send this fax for me, please?** — Вы можете отправить факс? — *vy mózhitye atprávit faks*

- **How much is it?** — Сколько это стоит? — *skólka éta stóit*

health&safety

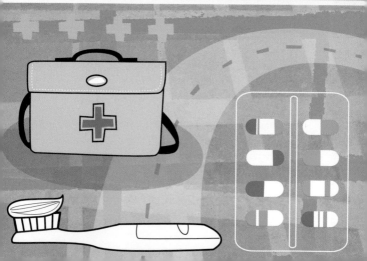

* at the pharmacy

● Pharmacy booths аптечный киоск (*aptyéchny kiósk*) can be found near metro stations and in supermarkets. They sell basic over the counter medication.

YOU MAY WANT TO SAY...

● Have you got something for... | У вас есть что-нибудь от... | *oo vas yest shtó-nibood at...*
  headaches? | головной бóли? | *galavnói bóli*
  | бóли в гóрле? | *bóli v górlye*

  a cold? | простýды | *prastóody*
  diarrhoea? | понóса/диарéи? | *panósa/diaryéi*

● I need some... please. | У Вас есть... | *oo vas yest...*

  condoms | презервативы | *prizirvatívy*
  insect repellent | срéдство от насекóмых | *sryédstva at nasikómykh*
  painkillers | обезбóливаю-щее | *abizbólivayoo-schiye*

  plasters | плáстырь | *plástyr*
  tampons | тампóны | *tampóny*
  toothpaste | зубнáя пáста | *zoobnáya pásta*

● Can you make up this prescription, please? | Вы мóжете приготóвить лекáрство по этому рецéпту? | *vy mózhitye prigatóvit likárstva pa étamoo ritséptoo*

YOU MAY HEAR...

Вы э́то ра́ньше принима́ли?	vy éta ránshe prinimáli	Have you taken this before?
У Вас есть реце́пт?	oo vas yest ritsépt	Have you got a prescription?
Óтпуск то́лько по реце́пту.	ótpoosk tólka pa ritséptoo	Available only with a prescription.

✳ at the doctor's

(see **medical complaints and conditions**, page 133)

YOU MAY WANT TO SAY...

I need a doctor (who speaks English).	Мне ну́жен врач, (кото́рый говори́т по-англи́йски).	mnye nóozhin vrach (katóry gavarít pa-anglíski)
Can I make an appointment for...	Мо́жно попа́сть (на прие́м) к врачу́...	mózhna papásĺ (na priyóm) k vrachóo...
today?	сего́дня?	sivódnya
I've run out of my medication.	У меня́ зако́нчилось лека́рство.	oo minyá zakónchilas likárstva
He/She has had a ... vaccination.	У него́/неё есть приви́вка от	oo nivó/niyó yest privífka at
polio	полиомиэли́та	poliomielíta
measles	ко́ри	kóri
Can I have a receipt for my health insurance, please?	Мне нужна́ квита́нция для страхо́вки.	mnye noozhná kvitántsiya dlya strakhófki

✱ describing your symptoms

(for **parts of the body**, see page 136)

I don't feel well.	Я себя плохо чувствую.	ya sibyá plókho chóostvooyoo
It hurts here.	Вот здесь больно/болит.	vot zdyes bólna/balít
My ... hurts. head	У меня болит... голова	oo minyá balít... galavá
My ... hurt. feet	У меня болят... ноги	oo minyá balyát... nógi
I've got... a sore throat swollen glands a rash diarrhoea	У меня... болит горло увеличены гланды сыпь понос/диарея	oo minyá... balít górla oovilíchiny glándy syp panós/diaryéya
I'm dizzy.	У меня кружится голова.	oo minyá króozhitsa galavá
I feel sick.	Меня тошнит.	minyá tashnít
I can't... breathe sleep	Я не могу... дышать спать	ya ni magóo... dyshát spat
I've burnt myself. (m/f)	Я порезался/порезалась	ya paryézalsya/paryézalas
I've cut myself. (m/f)	Я обжёгся/обожглась.	ya abzhóksya/abazhglás
I've been sick.	Меня вырвало./Меня рвало.	minyá výrvala/minyá rvaló

medical complaints and conditions

✳ medical complaints and conditions

YOU MAY WANT TO SAY...

- I'm... У меня ... *oo minyá...*
  - arthritic артрит *artrít*
  - asthmatic áстма *ástma*
  - diabetic диабéт *diabyét*
  - epileptic эпилéпсия *epilyépsiya*

- I'm... Я ... *ya...*
  - blind (m/f) слепóй/слепáя *slipói/slipáya*
  - deaf (m/f) глухóй/глухáя *glookhói/ glookháya*
  - pregnant берéменная *biryéminaya*

- I've got... У меня ... *oo minyá...*
  - high/low blood высóкое/нúзкое *vysókaye/nískaye*
    pressure давлéние *davlyéniye*
  - a heart больнóе сéрдце *balnóye syértse*
    condition

- I use a Я инвалúд на *ya invalít na*
  wheelchair. коляске. *kalyáskye*

- I have difficulty Я с трудóм хóжу. *ya s troodóm*
  walking. *khazhóo*

- I'm HIV positive. У меня СПИД. *oo minyá spit*

- I'm allergic to... У меня аллергúя на ... *oo minyá alirgíya na...*
  - antibiotics антибиóтики *antibióliki*
  - cortisone кортизóн *kartizón*
  - nuts орéхи *aryékhi*
  - penicillin пеницилúн *pinitsilín*

- I suffer from... У меня ... *oo minyá*
  - hayfever сеннáя *sinnáya likharátka*
    лихорáдка
  - angina стенокардúя *stinakardíya*

health and safety

133

medical complaints and conditions

YOU MAY HEAR...

Где болит/ бóльно?	gdye balít/bólna	Where does it hurt?
Здесь болит/ бóльно?	zdyes balít/bólna	Does it hurt here?
Как давнó э́то у Вас?	kak dávno éta oo vas	How long have you been feeling like this?
Вы принимáете какúе-нибудь лекáрства?	vy prinimáitye kakíye-nibood likárstva	Are you on medication?
У Вас есть аллергúя?	oo vas yest alirgíya	Are you allergic to anything?
Надо измéрить температýру.	náda izmyérit timpiratóoroo	I need to take your temperature.
Раздéньтесь, пожáлуйста.	razdyéntis pazhálsta	Get undressed, please.
Ложúтесь, пожáлуйста.	lazhítis pazhálsta	Lie down here, please.
Ничегó серьёзного.	nichivó siryóznava	It's nothing serious.
У Вас инфéкция.	oo vas infyéktsiya	You've got an infection.
(Вам) нáдо сдéлать... анáлиз крóви мочú кáла	(vam) náda zdyélat análiz... króvi machí kála	I need a ... sample. blood urine stool
(Вам) нáдо сдéлать рентгéн.	(vam) náda zdyélat rintgyén	You need an X-ray.

medical complaints and conditions

Я сде́лаю Вам уко́л.	ya zdyélayoo vam ookól	I'm going to give you an injection.
Принима́йте три ра́за в день.	prinimáïtye tri ráza v dyen	Take this three times a day.
во вре́мя еды́ по́сле еды́ до еды́	va vryémya yedý pósli yedý da yedý	with food after meals before meals
Вам на́до отдохну́ть.	vam náda oddakhnóot	You must rest.
Никако́го спиртно́го/алкого́ля.	nikakóva spirtnóva/alkagólya	You mustn't drink alcohol.
Когда́ прие́дете домо́й, обяза́тельно сходи́те к врачу́.	kagdá priyédityе damóï abizátilna skhadítye k vrachóo	You should see a doctor when you go home.
Вам на́до в больни́цу.	vam náda v balnítsoo	You need to go to hospital.
У Вас растяже́ние... лоды́жки	oo vas rastizhéniye... ladýshki	You've sprained your... ankle
У Вас перело́м... рёбер	oo vas pirilóm... ryóbir	You've broken your... ribs
У Вас... грипп аппендици́т отравле́ние	oo vas... grip apinditsít atravlyéniye	You've got... flu appendicitis food poisoning
У Вас серде́чный при́ступ.	oo vas sirdyéchny prístoop	It's a heart attack.

✳ parts of the body

YOU MAY WANT TO SAY...		
ankle	лоды́жка	ladýshka
appendix	аппе́ндикс	appyéndiks
arm	рука́	rooká
artery	арте́рия	artériya
back	спина́	spiná
bladder	мочево́й пузы́рь	machivóï poozýr
blood	кровь	krof
body	те́ло	tyéla
bone	кость	kost
bowels	кише́чник	kishéchnik
breast	грудь	groot
chest	грудь/грудна́я кле́тка	groot/groodnáya klyétka
collar bone	ключи́ца	klyoochítsa
ear	у́хо	óokha
elbow	ло́коть	lókot
eye	глаз	glas
face	лицо́	litsó
finger	па́лец	pálits
foot	ступня́	stoopnyá
genitals	генита́лии	ginitálii
glands	гла́нды	glándy
hair	во́лос	vólos
hand	рука́, кисть	rooká, kist
head	голова́	galavá
heart	се́рдце	syértse
heel	пя́тка	pyátka
hip	бедро́	bidró
jaw	че́люсть	chyélyoost

joint	суста́в	*soostáf*
kidney	по́чка	*póchka*
knee	коле́но	*kalýena*
leg	нога́	*nagá*
ligament	свя́зка	*svyáska*
liver	пе́чень	*pyéchin*
lung	лёгкие	*lyókhkiye*
mouth	рот	*rot*
muscle	мы́шца	*mýshtsa*
nail	но́готь	*nógat*
neck	ше́я	*shéya*
nerve	нерв	*nyerf*
nose	нос	*nos*
penis	пе́нис	*pyénis*
rib	ребро́	*ribró*
shoulder	плечо́	*plichó*
skin	ко́жа	*kózha*
spine	позвоно́чник	*pazvanóchnik*
stomach	желу́док	*zhilóodak*
tendon	сухожи́лие	*sookhazhíliye*
testicle	яи́чко	*yiíchka*
thigh	бедро́	*bidró*
throat	го́рло	*górla*
thumb	большо́й па́лец	*balshóï pálits*
toe	па́лец ноги́	*pálits nagí*
tongue	язы́к	*yizýk*
tonsils	минда́лины	*mindáliny*
tooth	зуб	*zoop*
vagina	ваги́на/влага́лище	*vagína/vlagálische*
vein	ве́на	*vyéna*
wrist	запя́стье	*zapyástye*

✳ at the dentist's

YOU MAY WANT TO SAY...

I need a dentist (who speaks English).	Мне нýжен зубнóй врач (котóрый говорúт по-англúйски).	*mnye nóozhin zoobnóï vrach (katóry gavarít pa-anglíski)*
I've got toothache.	У меня болúт зуб.	*oo minyá balít zoop*
It's my wisdom tooth.	Это зуб мýдрости.	*éta zoop móodrasti*
I've lost a filling.	У меня вы́пала плóмба.	*oo minyá výpala plómba*
I've lost a crown/cap.	У меня слетéла корóнка.	*oo minyá slityéla karónka*
I've broken a tooth.	У меня сломáлся зуб.	*oo minyá slamálsya zoop*
Can you fix it temporarily?	Вы мóжете залечúть врéменно?	*vy mózhitye zalichít vryéminno*
How much will it cost?	Скóлько это бýдет стóить?	*skólka éta bóodit stóit*

YOU MAY HEAR...

Откройте рот.	*atkróïtye rot*	**Open wide.**
Прикусите.	*prikoosítye*	**Close your jaws together.**
Вы (не)беременны?	*vy (ni)biryéminny*	**Are you pregnant?**
Надо поставить пломбу.	*náda pastávit plómboo*	**You need a filling.**
Зуб надо удалить.	*zoop náda oodalít*	**I'll have to take it out.**
Я сделаю Вам укол.	*ya zdyélayoo vam ookól*	**I'm going to give you an injection.**
Я поставлю Вам временную... пломбу коронку	*ya pastávlyoo vam vryéminnooyoo... plómboo karónkoo*	**I'm going to give you a temporary...** filling crown

✳ emergencies

EMERGENCY TELEPHONE NUMBERS:

Fire 01
Пожарная служба (*pazhárnaya slóozhba*)

Police 02
Милиция (*milítsiya*)

Ambulance 03
Скорая медицинская помощь (*skóraya miditsínskaya pómasch*)

YOU MAY SEE...

Больница	*balnítsa*	hospital
Медпункт	*mitpóonkt*	first aid
Поликлиника	*paliklínika*	health centre
Приемное отделение	*priyómnaye addilyénie*	admissions
Скорая помощь	*skóraya pómasch*	ambulance
Травмпункт	*travmpóonkt*	accident and emergency
Врач	*vrach*	doctor
Медсестра	*mitsistrá*	nurse
Инструкция по применению	*instróoktsiya pa priminyéniyoo*	instructions for use
Наружное/для наружнего пользования	*naróozhnaye/dlya naróozhniva pólzavaniya*	for external use only
Перед употреблением взбалтывать	*pyérid oopatriblyéniem vzbáltyvat*	shake before use
Яд	*yat*	poison

YOU MAY WANT TO SAY...

- I need...
  - a doctor
  - an ambulance

  - the fire brigade
  - the police

Вы́зовите...
врача́
ско́рую
(по́мощь)
пожа́рных
мили́цию

výzavitye...
vrachá
skórooyoo
(pómasch)
pazhárnykh
milítsiyoo

- **Immediately!** | Неме́дленно! | *nimyédlino*
- **Help!** | Помоги́те! | *pamagítye*
- **There's a fire!** | Пожа́р! | *pazhár*
- **There's been an accident.** | Ава́рия. | *avária*
- **I have to use the phone.** | Мне на́до позвони́ть. | *mnye náda pazvanít*
- **I'm lost. (m/f)** | Я заблуди́лся/ заблуди́лась. | *ya zabloodílsya/ zabloodílas*
- **I've lost my son.** | Мой сын потеря́лся. | *moï syn patiryálsya*
- **I've lost my daughter.** | Моя́ дочь потеря́лась. | *mayá doch patiryálas*
- **Stop!** | Стоп! | *stop*

YOU MAY HEAR...

- Где Вы (нахо́дитесь)? | *gdye vy (nakhódityes)* | **Where are you?**
- Ваш а́дрес? | *vash ádris* | **What's your address?**

✳ police

YOU MAY WANT TO SAY...

- **Sorry, I didn't realise it was against the law.** | Извини́те, я не знал, что э́то притивозако́нно. | *izvinítye, ya ni znal shto éta prativazakónna*

141

● Here are my documents.	Вот мой докуме́нты.	*vot maí dakoomyénty*
● I haven't got my passport on me.	У меня́ нет с собо́й па́спорта.	*oo minyá nyet s saboï pásparta*
● I don't understand.	Я не понима́ю.	*ya ni panimáyoo*
● I'm innocent.	Я не вино́вен.	*ya ni vinóvin*
● I need a lawyer (who speaks English).	Мне ну́жен адвока́т (кото́рый говори́т по-англи́йски).	*mnye nóozhin advakát (katóry gavarít pa-anglíski)*
● I want to contact my...	Я хочу́ связа́ться с...	*ya khachóo svizátsa s...*
embassy	посо́льством	*pasólstvam*
consulate	ко́нсульством	*kónsoolstvam*

● Ва́ши докуме́нты, пожа́луйста.	*váshi dakoomyénty pazhálsta*	**Your documents please.**
● У Вас есть докуме́нты, удостоверя́ющие ли́чность?	*oo vas yest dakoomyénty oodastaviryáyooschiye líchnast*	**Have you got any proof of identity?**
● Придётся запла- ти́ть штраф.	*pridyótsa zaplatít shtraf*	**You'll have to pay a fine.**
● Пройдёмте со мно́й.	*praïdyómtye sa mnoï*	**Come with me.**
● Вы аресто́ваны.	*vy aristóvany*	**You're under arrest.**

✳ reporting crime

YOU MAY WANT TO SAY... 💬

I want to report a theft.	Я хочу заявить о краже.	*ya khachóo zayivít a krázhe*
My ... has been stolen.	У меня украли...	*oo minyá ookráli...*
purse/wallet	кошелёк	*kashilyók*
passport	паспорт	*páspart*
My car has been broken into.	У меня обокрали машину.	*oo minyá abakráli mashínoo*
My car has been stolen.	У меня угнали машину.	*oo minyá oognáli mashínoo*
I've lost my...	Я потерял...	*ya patiryál...*
credit cards	кредитные карты	*kridítnyye kárty*
luggage	свой багаж	*svoï bagásh*
I've been mugged/ attacked.	На меня напали.	*na minyá napáli*

YOU MAY HEAR... ❓

Когда/где это случилось?	*kagdá/gdye éta sloochílas*	When/where did it happen?
Что случилось?	*shto sloochílas*	What happened?
Как он/а выглядел/а?	*kak on/aná výglidil/a*	What did he/she look like?
Как они выглядели?	*kak aní výglidili*	What did they look like?
Заполните этот бланк, пожалуйста.	*zapólnitye étot blank pazhálsta*	Fill in this form please.

YOU MAY WANT TO SAY...

- It happened...   Это случи́лось...   *éta sloochílas...*
  - five minutes ago   пять мину́т наза́д   *pyat minóot nazát*
  - last night   вчера́ ве́чером   *fchirá vyéchiram*
  - on the beach   на пля́же   *na plyázhe*

- He/She had...   У него́/неё...   *oo nivó/niyó...*
  - blonde hair   бы́ли све́тлые во́лосы   *býli svyétlyye vólasy*
  - a knife   был нож   *byl nosh*

- He/She was...   Он/а был/а́...   *on/ana byl/bylá...*
  - tall   высо́кий/высо́кая   *vysóky/vysókaya*
  - young   молодо́й/молода́я   *maladóï/maladáya*
  - short   небольшо́го ро́ста   *nibalshóva rósta*

- He/She was wearing...   На нём/ней бы́ли...   *na nyom/nyéï býli...*
  - jeans   джи́нсы   *dzhínsy*
  - a dark jacket with a hood   тёмная ку́ртка с капюшо́ном   *tyómnaya kóortka s kapishónom*

basic grammar

✶ articles (a, an, the)

There are no definite articles or indefinite articles in Russian.

✶ nouns

Nouns have three genders: masculine, feminine, or neuter. The gender of inanimate nouns is determined by their ending. Masculine nouns usually end in a consonant or -й: стол (table), чай (tea). Feminine nouns usually end in -а or -я: виза (visa), фамилия (surname). Nouns ending in a soft sign -ь can be either masculine or feminine. Neuter nouns usually end in -о, -е/ё e.g. окно (window), солнце (sun). There are a few nouns ending in -мя, e.g. время (time).

plurals

The endings of nouns change in the plural. For masculine and feminine nouns the most common plural ending is -ы or -и, e.g:

гостиница - гостиницы   (hotel, hotels)
ключ - ключи   (key, keys)

Some masculine nouns have -а in the plural, e.g:

поезд - поезда   (train, trains)
дом - дома   (house, houses)

The typical neuter plural ending is -а, e.g:

место - места   (place, places)

Neuter nouns in -мя have their plural in -ена, e.g:

имя - имена   (name, names)

Some commonly used nouns have irregular plurals:

человéк - лю́ди (a man/person, people)
ребёнок - де́ти (a child, children)

There are a few words that exist only in the plural, e.g. де́ньги (money).

case

Russian has six cases: nominative, accusative, genitive, dative, instrumental, and prepositional. Nouns appear in different forms, i.e. with different endings, depending on their role in the sentence.

The form listed in the dictionary is the nominative. It is used for the subject of the sentence. The accusative is used for the direct object of the sentence, and after prepositions в and на indicating the motion 'to' and 'into'. The genitive corresponds to English 'of' or 's. It is used after certain prepositions, e.g. по́сле (after), без (without), от (from), из (from, out of), для (for), о́коло (around), до (till), у (at). The genitive is also used after мно́го (a lot of, much), ма́ло (little, few) and after нет (there is no).

The dative is used for indirect objects and after the preposition к (towards). The instrumental points to the means by which an action is performed. It is also used after certain prepositions, e.g. с (together with), пе́ред (in front of), под (under), над (over). The prepositional case is used after the prepositions о (about), в (in) and на (at, when indicating location).

Some nouns, usually loan words from other languages, never change their endings. They stay the same in all cases and also in the plural, e.g. такси́ (taxi), кафе́ (café).

animate nouns

CASE	MASCULINE SING	PL	FEMININE SING	PL
nom	ма́льчик	ма́льчики	де́вочка	де́вочки
acc	ма́льчика	ма́льчиков	де́вочку	де́вочек
gen	ма́льчика	ма́льчиков	де́вочки	де́вочек
dat	ма́льчику	ма́льчикам	де́вочке	де́вочкам
instr	ма́льчиком	ма́льчиками	де́вочкой	де́вочками
prep	ма́льчике	ма́льчиках	де́вочке	де́вочках

мальчик (boy), девочка (girl)

masculine inanimate nouns

CASE	SING	PL	SING	PL
nom	стол	столы́	рубль	рубли́
acc	стол	столы́	рубль	рубли́
gen	стола́	столо́в	рубля́	рубле́й
dat	столу́	стола́м	рублю́	рубля́м
instr	столо́м	стола́ми	рублём	рубля́ми
prep	столе́	стола́х	рубле́	рубля́х

стол (table), рубль (rouble)

feminine inanimate nouns

CASE	SING	PL	SING	PL
nom	неде́ля	неде́ли	пло́щадь	пло́щади
acc	неде́ли	неде́ли	пло́щадь	пло́щади
gen	неде́ли	неде́ль	пло́щади	площаде́й
dat	неде́ле	неде́лям	пло́щади	площадя́м
instr	неде́лей	неде́лями	пло́щадью	площадя́ми
prep	неде́ле	неде́лях	пло́щади	площадя́х

неделя (week), площадь (square)

neuter nouns

CASE	SING	PL	SING	PL
nom	ме́сто	места́	вре́мя	времена́
acc	ме́сто	места́	вре́мя	времена́
gen	ме́ста	мест	вре́мени	времён
dat	ме́сту	места́м	вре́мени	времена́м
instr	ме́стом	места́ми	вре́менем	времена́ми
prep	ме́сте	места́х	вре́мени	времена́х

ме́сто (place), вре́мя (time)

✳ adjectives

Adjectives agree with nouns they describe in gender, number and case. In dictionaries you usually find the nominative singular masculine form.

Typical adjective endings are: for masculine -ый/-ий, -ой; for feminine -ая/-яя; for neuter -ое/-ее; for plural -ые/-ие.

Below are tables for adjectives referring to inanimate nouns.

CASE	MASC./NEUT. SING	FEM. SING	PLURAL
nom	кра́сный (m) кра́сное (n)	кра́сная	кра́сные
acc	кра́сный (m) кра́сное (n)	кра́сную	кра́сные
gen	кра́сного	кра́сной	кра́сных
dat	кра́сному	кра́сной	кра́сным
instr	кра́сным	кра́сной	кра́сными
prep	кра́сном	кра́сной	кра́сных

кра́сный (red)

CASE	MASC./NEUT. SING	FEM. SING	PLURAL
nom	после́дний (m)	после́дняя	после́дние
	после́днее (n)		
acc	после́дний (m)	после́днюю	после́дние
	после́днее (n)		
gen	после́днего	после́дней	после́дних
dat	после́днему	после́дней	после́дним
instr	после́дним	после́дней	после́дними
prep	после́днем	после́дней	после́дних

после́дний (last)

✱ personal pronouns (I, you, he, she etc.)

CASE	SINGULAR				PLURAL		
	I	you	he/it	she	we	you	they
nom	я	ты	он/оно́	она́	мы	вы/Вы	они́
acc	меня́	тебя́	его́	её	нас	вас	их
gen	меня́	тебя́	(н)его́	(н)её	нас	вас	(н)их
dat	мне	тебе́	(н)ему́	(н)ей	нам	вам	(н)им
instr	мной	тобо́й	(н)им	(н)ей	на́ми	ва́ми	(н)и́ми
prep	мне	тебе́	нём	ней	нас	вас	них

The (н)-forms are used after prepositions.

✱ possessive pronouns (my, your, his, her etc.)

Possessives have different endings in different cases. They follow the adjective pattern.

мой (my)

CASE	MASC./NEUT. SING	FEM. SING	PLURAL
nom	мой (m), моё (n)	моя́	мои́
acc	as nom* or gen**	мою́	as nom* or gen**
gen	моего́	мое́й	мои́х
dat	моему́	мое́й	мои́м
instr	мои́м	мое́й	мои́ми
prep	моём	мое́й	мои́х

наш (our)

CASE	MASC./NEUT. SING	FEM. SING	PLURAL
nom	наш (m), на́ше (n)	на́ша	на́ши
acc	as nom* or gen**	на́шу	as nom* or gen**
gen	на́шего	на́шей	на́ших
dat	на́шему	на́шей	на́ших
instr	на́шим	на́шей	на́шими
prep	на́шем	на́шей	на́ших

Твой (your sing) has the same endings as мой, and ваш (your pl) has the same endings as наш. Его́ (his, its), её (her) and их (their) never change.

* for inanimate nouns, ** for animate nouns

✳ adverbs

Adverbs are usually formed by taking off the adjective ending and adding -о.

краси́в-ый → краси́в-о   (beautiful)
ме́дленн-ый → ме́дленн-о   (slow)

✳ comparatives

Comparatives are formed by placing the word бо́лее (more) or ме́нее (less) in front of the relevant adjective. These words stay the same whatever the gender, number or case of the adjective.

The short form of the comparative can be formed by taking off the adjective ending and adding -ee, e.g: краси́в-ый → краси́вее, бы́стр-ый → быстре́е. The comparative forms are followed by a noun in the genitive, or чем (than).

The superlatives can be built by placing са́мый (most) – with the correct case ending – in front of the adjective, e.g: прия́тный → са́мый прия́тный/са́мая прия́тная/са́мые прия́тные etc. (pleasant)

✳ verbs

The infinitive is usually given in dictionaries. Russian infinitives usually end in -ть, with some ending in -ти and -чь. Russian verbs have two aspects, imperfective and perfective. Usually these are obvious pairs, formed by prefixes, or internal modification or by changing the stress pattern. In a dictionary, both aspect forms are given with a slash, with the imperfective form first.
чита́ть/прочита́ть (to read)
зака́зывать/заказа́ть (to order)

Some frequently used verbs have aspect forms derived from entirely different roots, e.g.
говори́ть/сказа́ть (to say)
брать/взять (to take)

The imperfective aspect is used when we do not know if the action was completed. It also denotes frequently repeated actions, and focuses on an action in progress. It describes a single completed action and emphasises the result.

✳ verb tenses

Verbs have different endings depending on the subject of the sentence. The verbs follow two main patterns, called conjugations. The verbs of the first conjugation commonly end in -ать or -ять, the verbs of the second conjugation end in -ить.

Only the imperfective aspect is used for the present tense.

the verb 'to work': рабо́тать

PRESENT TENSE: FIRST CONJUGATION		
я	рабо́та-ю	I work
ты	рабо́та-ешь	you work
он/а́	рабо́та-ет	he/she works
мы	рабо́та-ем	we work
вы	рабо́та-ете	you work
они́	рабо́та-ют	they work

the verb 'to say': говори́ть

PRESENT TENSE: SECOND CONJUGATION		
я	говор-ю́	I say
ты	говор-и́шь	you say
он/а́	говор-и́т	he/she says
мы	говор-и́м	we say
вы	говор-и́те	you say
они́	говор-я́т	they say

Some frequently used verbs have irregular forms, e.g.

the verb 'to eat': есть

PRESENT TENSE		
я	ем	I eat
ты	ешь	you eat
он/а́	ест	he/she eats
мы	еди́м	we eat
вы	еди́те	you eat
они́	едя́т	they eat

the verb 'to be': быть

This does not occur in the present tense, there are no words for 'am', 'is' and 'are' in Russian.

Я бизнесме́н.	I (am a) businessman.
Мы из А́нглии.	We (are) from England.
Где Ва́ша ви́за?	Where (is) your visa?

To translate 'to have' use the preposition у followed by the genitive case of the possessor, followed by:

есть (or omit) in the present
был/-а/-л/-и in the past
бу́дет/бу́дут in the future

The object of possession is put into the nominative case:

У неё большо́й дом.   She has a big house.

To put verbs into the past tense, take off the -ть ending of the infinitive and add:

-л	for masculine singular subject
-ла	for feminine singular subject
-ло	for neuter singular subject
-ли	for plural subject

To form the future tense for single actions use the perfective aspect with present tense endings. For actions that will repeatedly happen in the future, or that will spread over time, use the future of the verb 'to be' followed by the imperfective infinitive of the corresponding verb, e.g. вспоминáть 'remember':

я бу́ду вспоминáть	I'll remember
ты бу́дешь вспоминáть	you'll remember
он/á бу́дет вспоминáть	he/she'll remember
мы бу́дем вспоминáть	we'll remember
вы бу́дете вспоминáть	you'll remember
они́ бу́дут вспоминáть	they'll remember

✳ negation

To form negatives, use не or нет in front of the verb. Note that after нет the genitive is used.

Я (не) тури́ст.	I am (not) a tourist.
Я (не) понимáю.	I (don't) understand.

✳ word order

Word order is rather flexible, though the neutral and most common order is Subject-Verb-Object.

✳ questions

You can ask a question by changing the intonation. In questions with question words, there is no need to rearrange the sentence as in English, the word order stays the same as in the statement.

(see **pronunciation guide**, page 6)

English – Russian Dictionary

Russian nouns are given with their gender in brackets: (m) for masculine, (f) for feminine, (n) for neuter, (s) for singular, (pl) for plural. Other abbreviations: *(adj.)* adjective, and *(coll.)* for colloquialisms. See **basic grammar**, page 145, for further explanations.

There's a list of **car parts** on page 61 and **parts of the body** on page 136. See also the **menu reader** on page 87, and **numbers** on page 14.

A

about *(approximately)* о́коло, приблизи́тельно *ókala, priblizítilna*
» *(relating to)* о,об *a, ab*
abroad за грани́цей/за рубежо́м *za granítsei, za roobizhóm*
to accept *(to receive)* принима́ть/ приня́ть *prinimát/prinyát*
accident ава́рия (f), несча́стный слу́чай (m) *aváriya, nischásny slóochaï*
accommodation жильё (n) *zhil-yó*
account *(bank)* счёт (m) *schot*
accountant бухга́лтер (m) *boogáltir*
to accuse обвиня́ть/обвини́ть *abvinyát/abvinít*
ache боль (f) *bol*
across: across the road че́рез доро́гу *chéris darógoo*
actor актёр (m) *aktyór*
actress актри́са (f) *aktrísa*
adaptor ада́птер (m) *adápter*
address а́дрес (m) *ádris*
adult взро́слый (m) *vzrósly*
advance: in advance зара́нее *zarániye*

advertisement, advertising рекла́ма (f), объявле́ние (n) *rikl[á]ma, ab-yivlyéniye*
aeroplane самолёт (m) *samalyót*
after по́сле *pósli*
afterwards пото́м, по́зже *patóm, pózhe*
aftershave лосьо́н (m) по́сле бритья́ *lasyón pósli brit-yá*
again сно́ва, опя́ть *snóva, apyát*
ago наза́д *nazát*
AIDS СПИД (m) *spit*
air во́здух (m) *vózdookh*
» **by air** самолётом *samalyótam*
» **air mail** авиапо́чта (f) *aviapóchta*
air conditioning: with air conditioning с кондиционе́ром *s kanditsianyéram*
airport аэропо́рт (m) *aerapórt*
aisle прохо́д (m) *prakhót*
» **aisle seat** ме́сто у прохо́да *mésta oo prakhóda*
alarm трево́га (f) *trivóga*
» **alarm clock** буди́льник (m) *boodílnik*
alcohol алкого́ль (m), спиртно́е (n) *alkagól, spirtnóye*

alcoholic *(person)* алкоголик (m) *alkagólik*

all весь (m), вся (f), всё (n), все (pl) *vyes, fsya, fsyo, fsye*

allergic аллергический *alirgíchiski*

» **I am allergic to** у меня аллергия на ... *oo minyá alirgíya na*

to **allow** позволять/позволить *pazvalyát/pazvólit*

all right *(OK)* всё в порядке *fsyo f paryátkye*

along вдоль *vdol*

already уже *oozhé*

also тоже, также *tózhe, tákzhe*

always всегда *fsigdá*

ambulance скорая помощь (f) *skóraya pómasch*

American *(adj.)* американский *amirikánski*

» *(people)* американец/американка (m/f) *amirikánits, amirikánka*

amount количество (n) *kalíchistva*

anaesthetic *(local)/(general)* местный/общий наркоз (m) *myésny/ópschi narkós*

and и *i*

angry злой *zloí*

animal животное (n) *zhivótnaye*

antibiotics антибиотик (m) *antibiótik*

antique античный *antíchny*

any любой *lyoobóí*

» **have you got any bread?** у вас есть хлеб? *oo vas yést khlep?*

anyone кто-нибудь *któ-nibood*

anything что-нибудь *shtó-nibood*

» **anything else** что-нибудь ещё *shtó-nibood yischó*

anywhere где-нибудь *gdyé-nibood*

apartment квартира (f) *kvartíra*

appendicitis аппендицит (m) *apinditsít*

appetite аппетит (m) *apitít*

apple яблоко (n) *jáblaka*

appointment приём (m) *priyóm*

» **I** *(m/f)* **have an appointment** я записан/а на приём *ya zapísan/a na priyóm*

approximately приблизительно *priblizítilna*

architect архитектор (m) *arkhityéktar*

area *(measurement)* площадь (f) *plóschat*

» *(region, zone)* район (m), зона (f) *rayón, zóna*

arm рука (f) *rooká*

armbands *(swimming)* (надувные) крылышки (pl) *(nadoovnýye) krýlyshki*

army армия (f) *ármiya*

to **arrange** устраивать/устроить *oostráivat/oostróit*

arrest арест (m) *aryest*

» **under arrest** под арестом *pad aryéstam*

arrival прибытие (n) *pribýtiye*

to **arrive** прибывать/прибыть *pribyvát/pribýt*

art искусство (n) *iskóostva*

» **art gallery** картинная галерея *kartínnaya galiryéya*

arthritis артрит (m) *artrít*

artificial искусственный *iskóostviny*

artist артист (m) *artíst*

as *(like)* как *kak*

ashtray пепельница (f) *pyépilnitsa*

to **ask** спрашивать/спросить *spráshivat/sprasít*

aspirin аспирин (m) *aspirín*

asthma астма (f) *ástma*

at once сразу *srázoo zhe*

attractive привлекательный *privlikátilny*

aunt тётя (f) *tyótya*

Australian *(adj.)* австралийский *afstralíski*

» *(people)* австралиец/австралийка (m/f) *afstralíyits/afstralíka*

author автор (m) *áftar*

automatic автомати́ческий *aftamatíchiski*

to avoid избега́ть/избежа́ть *izbigát/ izbizhát*

awful ужа́сный *oozhásny*

B

baby младе́нец (m), малы́ш (m) *mladyénits, malýsh*

» **baby food** де́тское пита́ние (n) *dyétskaye pitániye*

» **baby wipes** вла́жные салфе́тки (pl) *vlázhnyye salfyétki*

babysitter ня́ня (f), бебиси́ттер (m) *nyánya, byébisítter*

back (reverse side) обра́тная сторона́ (f) *abrátnaya staraná*

backwards наза́д *nazát*

bad плохо́й *plakhóy*

bag су́мка (f) *sóomka*

bakery бу́лочная (f) *bóolachnaya*

balcony (theatre etc.) балко́н (m) *balkón*

bald лы́сый *lýsy*

ball мяч (m) *myach*

ballet бале́т (m) *balyét*

balloon возду́шный шар (m) *vazdóoshny shar*

banana бана́н (m) *banán*

bank банк (m) *bank*

banknote банкно́т (m) *banknót*

bar бар (m) *bar*

bar (chocolate) шокола́дка (f) *shikalátka*

barber's парикма́херская (f) *parikmákhirskaya*

basin (bowl) ра́ковина (f) *rákavina*

bath ва́нна (f) *vána*

» **to have a bath** принима́ть/ приня́ть ва́нну *prinimát/prinyát vánoo*

bathhouse ба́ня (f) *bánya*

bathroom ва́нная (ко́мната) (f) *vánnaya (kómnata)*

bathtub ва́нна (f) *vána*

battery (car) аккумуля́тор (m) *akoomoolyátar*

» (radio) батаре́йка (f) *bataryéïka*

beach пляж (m) *plyásh*

beard борода́ (f) *baradá*

beautiful краси́вый *krasívy*

because потому́ что *patamóo shta*

bed крова́ть (f) *kravát*

bedroom спа́льня (f) *spálnya*

bee пчела́ (f) *pchilá*

to begin начина́ть/нача́ть *nachinát/ nachát*

» **it begins at 8pm** нача́ло в 8 часо́в *nachála v vósim chisóf*

beginner начина́ющий (m) *nachináyooschi*

behind за *za*

to believe ве́рить/пове́рить *vyérit/ pavyérit*

bell звоно́к (m) *zvanók*

below под *pod*

belt реме́нь (m), по́яс (m) *rimyén, póyis*

best лу́чший *lóochshi*

better лу́чше *lóochshe*

between ме́жду *myézhdoo*

bicycle велосипе́д (m) *vilasipyét*

bidet биде́ (n) *bidé*

big большо́й *balshóy*

bill счёт (m) *schot*

bird пти́ца (f) *ptítsa*

birthday день (m) рожде́ния *dyen razhdyéniya*

biscuit пече́нье (n) *pichén-ye*

to bite куса́ть/укуси́ть *koosát/ookoosít*

bitter го́рький *górki*

black чёрный *chórny*

» **black and white** (film) чёрно-бе́лый *chórna-byély*

» **black coffee** чёрный ко́фе (m) *chórny kófye*

blanket одея́ло (n) *adiyála*

bleach хло́рка (f) *khlórka*

to bleed кровото́чить *kravatóchit*

blind слепо́й *slipóy*

blister волды́рь (m), мозо́ль (f) *valdýr, mazól*

blonde блонди́нка (m/f) *blandín/ka*

blood кровь (f) *krof*

blouse блу́зка (f) *blóoska*

blue си́ний *síni*

» **light blue** голубо́й *galoobói*

to board сади́ться /сесть в самолёт *sadítsa/syest f samalyót*

boarding card поса́дочный тало́н (m) *pasádachny talón*

boat кора́бль *karábl*

» **boat trip** во́дная прогу́лка (f) *vódnaya pragóolka*

body те́ло (n) *tyéla*

to boil кипяти́ть/вскипяти́ть *kipitít/ vskipitít*

» **boiled egg** варёное яйцо́ (n) *varyónaye yitsó*

boiler бо́йлер (m), парово́й котёл (m) *bóilyer, paravói katyól*

bone кость (f) *kost*

book кни́га (f) *kníga*

to book зака́зывать/заказа́ть *zakázyvat/zakazát*

» **booking office** биле́тная ка́сса (f) *bilyétnaya kássa*

booklet букле́т (m) *booklyét*

bookshop кни́жный магази́н (m) *knízhny magazín*

border *(frontier)* грани́ца (f) *granítsa*

boring ску́чный *skóoshny*

both о́ба (m/n)/о́бе (f) *óba/óbye*

bottle буты́лка (f) *bootýlka*

bottle opener открыва́лка (f) *atkryválka*

bowl ми́ска (f) *míska*

box коро́бка (f) *karópka*

» *(theatre)* ло́жа (f) *lózha*

box office театра́льная ка́сса (f) *tiatrálnaya kássa*

boy ма́льчик (m) *málchik*

boyfriend друг (m), бойфре́нд (m) *drook, boifrént*

bra бюстга́льтер (m) ли́фчик (m, *coll.*) *byoosgáltir, lífchik*

bracelet брасле́т (m) *braslyét*

bread хлеб (m) *khlyep*

» **bread roll** бу́лочка (f) *bóolachka*

» **wholemeal bread** цельнозерново́й хлеб *tselnazirnavói khlyeb*

to break лома́ть/слома́ть *lamát/slamát*

to break down лома́ться/слома́ться *lamátsa/slamátsa*

breakfast за́втрак (m) *záftrak*

to breathe дыша́ть *dyshát*

bribe взя́тка (f) *vzyátka*

bride неве́ста (f) *nivyésta*

bridegroom жени́х (m) *zhiníkh*

bridge мост (m) *most*

briefcase портфе́ль (m) *partfyél*

bright я́ркий *yárki*

to bring приноси́ть/принести́ *prinasít/ prinistí*

British *(adj.)* брита́нский *británski*

» *(people)* брита́нец/брита́нка (m/f) *británits/británka*

broadband широкополо́сный интерне́т *shirakapalósny internét*

broken сло́манный *slómanny*

bronchitis бронхи́т (m) *brankhít*

brother брат (m) *brat*

bruise синя́к (m) *sinyák*

brush щётка (f) *schótka*

buffet буфе́т (m) *boofyét*

to build стро́ить/постро́ить *stróit/ pastróit*

building зда́ние (n) *zdániye*

to burn горе́ть/сгоре́ть *garyét/zgaryét*

bus авто́бус (m) *aftóboos*

» **by bus** авто́бусом *aftóboosam*

business би́знес (m) *bíznis*

» **business trip** командиро́вка (f) *kamandirófka*

» **on business** по де́лу *pa dyéloo*

businessman/woman бизнесме́н/ка (m/f) *biznismyén/ka*

bus station автовокзал (m), автобусная станция (f) *aftavagzál, aftóboosnaya stántsiya*

bus stop остановка (f) автобуса *astanófka aftóboosa*

busy *(restaurant etc)* оживлённый *azhivlyónny*

but но *no*

butter масло (n) *másla*

button пуговица (f) *póogavitsa*

to **buy** покупать/купить *pakoopát/ koopít*

by: by train/by plane на поезде/на самолёте *na póizdye/na samalyóye*

C

cable car фуникулёр (m) *foonikoolyór*

café кафе (n) *kafé*

cake торт (m) *tort*

to **call** *(to pay a visit)* заходить/зайти *zakhadít/zaití*

» *(to name)* называть/назвать *nazyvát/nazvát*

calm спокойный *spakóiny*

camera фотоаппарат (m), камера (f) *fataparát, kámira*

campsite палаточный городок (m); кемпинг (m) *palátachny garadók; kyémpink*

can *(to be able)* мочь/смочь *moch/ smoch*

can *(tin)* банка (f) *bánka*

can opener консервный нож (m) *kansyérvny nosh*

to **cancel** отменять/отменить *atminyát/atminít*

cancer рак (m) *rak*

candle свеча (f) *svichá*

capital *(city)* столица (f) *stalítsa*

car машина (f), автомобиль (m) *mashína, aftamabíl*

» **by car** на машине *na mashínye*

careful осторожный *astarózhny*

car park автостоянка (f) *aftastayánka*

carriage *(train)* вагон (m) *vagón*

carrier bag пакет (m), сумка (f) *pakyét, sóomka*

to **carry** носить/нести *nasít/nistí*

cash наличные (pl) *nalíchnyye*

» **to pay cash** платить/ заплатить наличными *platít/ zaplatít nalíchnymi*

cash desk касса (f) *kása*

cashpoint банкомат (m) *bankamát*

castle замок (m) *zámak*

cat кот/кошка (m/f) *kot/kóshka*

cathedral собор (m) *sabór*

Catholic *(adj.)* католический *katalíchiski*

» *(people)* католик/католичка (m/f) *katólik/katalíchka*

CD компакт-диск (m), сиди (m) *kampákt-disk, sidí*

» **CD-Rom** сидиром (m) *sidiróm*

centimetre сантиметр (m) *santimyétr*

central центральный *tsintrálny*

central heating центральное отопление (n) *tsintrálnaye ataplyéniye*

centre центр (m) *tsentr*

century век (m) *vyek*

CEO *(chief executive officer)* Главный исполнительный директор (m) *glávny ispalnítilny diryéktar*

certificate сертификат (m), свидетельство (n) *sirtifikát, svidyétilstva*

chair стул (m), стулья (pl) *stool, stóol-ya*

» **chair lift** (подвесной) подъёмник (m) *(padvisnói) pad-yómnik*

champagne шампанское (n) *shampánskaye*

championship чемпионат (m) *chimpianát*

change *(coins)* мéлочь (f) *myélach*

to change *(clothes)* переодевáться/переодéться *piriadivátsa/piriadyétsa*

» *(money)* обмéнивать/обменя́ть *abmyénivat/abminyát*

» *(trains)* пересáживаться/пересéсть *pirisázhivatsa/pirisyést*

changing room *(sport)* раздевáлка (f) *razdiválka*

» *(shop)* примéрочная (f) *primyérachnaya*

chapel часóвня (f) *chisóvnya*

cheap дешёвый *dishóvy*

» **cheaper** дешéвле *dishévli*

checked *(pattern)* в клéтку *f klyétkoo*

check-in *(desk)* регистрациóнная стóйка (f) *rigistratsiónnaya stóïka*

to check-in регистри́роваться/зарегистри́роваться *rigistríravatsa/zarigistríravatsa*

Cheers! За (Вáше) здорóвье! *za (váshe) zdaróvye*

chewing gum жевáтельная рези́нка (f) жвáчка (f *coll.*), *zhivátilnaya rizínka, zhváchka*

child ребёнок (m) *ribyónak*

children дéти (pl) *dyéti*

chocolate шоколáд (m) *shikalát*

to choose выбирáть/вы́брать *vybirát/výbrat*

Christian *(adj.)* христиáнский *khristiánski*

» *(people)* христиани́н/христиáнка (m/f) *khristianín/khristiánka*

» **Christian name** и́мя (n) *ímya*

Christmas Рождествó (n) *razhdistvó*

» **Christmas tree** рождéственская ёлка (f) *razhdyéstvinskaya yólka*

» **Christmas Eve** сочéльник (m) *sachyélnik*

church цéрковь (f) *tsérkaf*

cigar сигáра (f) *sigára*

cigarette сигарéта (f) *sigaryéta*

cinema кинó (n) *kinó*

circle круг (m) *krook*

» **dress-circle** *(in theatre)* бельэтáж (m) *byeletásh*

circus цирк (m) *tsirk*

city гóрод (m) *górat*

class класс (m) *klass*

classical класси́ческий *klassíchiski*

» **classical music** класси́ческая мýзыка (f) *klassíchiskaya móozyka*

claustrophobia клаустрофóбия (f) *klaoostrafóbiya*

clean чи́стый *chísty*

clear я́сный *yásny*

clever ýмный *óomny*

climate кли́мат (m) *klímat*

to climb лáзить, лезть *lázit, lyest*

clinic кли́ника (f) *klínika*

cloakroom гардерóб (m) *gardiróp*

clock часы́ (pl) *chisý*

close *(by)* ря́дом с *ryádam s*

closed закры́то *zakrýta*

clothes одéжда (f) *adyézhda*

cloudy óблачный *óblachny*

club клуб (m) *kloop*

coach *(instructor)* трéнер (m), репети́тор (m), *tryénir, ripítítor*

» *(bus)* междугорóдный автóбус (m) *mezhdoogaródny aftóboos*

coast бéрег (m) *byérik*

coat пальтó (n) *paltó*

coat-hanger вéшалка (f) *vyéshalka*

coin монéта (f) *manyéta*

cold холóдный *khalódny*

(noun) простýда (f) *prastóoda*

» **I'm cold** мне хóлодно *mne khóladna*

» **I have a cold** у меня́ простýда *oo minyá prastóoda*

collar воротни́к (m) *varatník*

colleague коллéга (m/f) *kallyéga*

college коллéдж (m) *kalyédsh*

colour цвéт (m), цветá (pl) *tsvyet, tsvitá*

» *(adj.)* цветнóй *tsvitnói*

colour-blind дальтóник (m) *daltónik*

comb расчёска (m) *raschóska*

to come приходи́ть/прийти́ *prikhadít/ priití*

» **come in!** Входи́те! *fkadíte*

comedy коме́дия (m) *kamyédiya*

comfortable (m) удо́бный *oodóbny*

comic (magazine) ко́микс (m) *kómiks*

commercial комме́рческий *kamyérchiski*

common (usual) обы́чный, обыкнове́нный *abýchny, abyknavyény*

» (shared) о́бщий *ópschi*

commission коми́ссия (f) *kamíssiya*

company компа́ния (f) *kampániya*

compared with по сравне́нию с *pa sravnyéniyoo*

compartment купе́ (n) *koopé*

to complain жа́ловаться/ пожа́ловаться *zhálavatsa/ pazhálavatsa*

complaint жа́лоба (f) *zhálaba*

complete по́лный *pólny*

complicated сло́жный *slózhny*

composer компози́тор (m) *kampazítar*

compulsory обяза́тельный *abizátilny*

computer компью́тер (m) *kamp-yóoter*

concert конце́рт (m) *kantsért*

concession усту́пка (f) *oostóopka*

to conclude заключа́ть/заключи́ть *zaklyoochát/zaklyoochít*

conclusion заключе́ние (n), вы́вод (m) *zaklyoochéniye, vývat*

concussion сотрясе́ние (n) мо́зга *satrisyéniye mózga*

condition усло́вие (n) *ooslóviye*

condom презервати́в (m) *prizirvatíf*

conference конфере́нция (f), совеща́ние (n) *kanfiryéntsiya, savischániye*

to confirm подтвержда́ть/ подтверди́ть *patvirzhdát/patvirdít*

conjunctivitis конъюнктиви́т (m) *kan-yoonktivít*

connection связь (f) *svyas*

conservation сохране́ние (n), охра́на (f) *sakhranyéniye, akhrána*

conservative консервати́вный *kansirvatívny*

constipation запо́р (m) *zapór*

consulate ко́нсульство (n) *kónsoolstva*

contact lens конта́ктные ли́нзы (pl) *kantáktnyye línzy*

» **contact lens cleaner/solution** раство́р для конта́ктных линз *rastvór dlya kantáktnykh lins*

contagious зара́зный *zarázny*

continent контине́нт (m), матери́к (m) *kantinyént, matirík*

to continue продолжа́ть/продо́лжить *pradalzhát/pradólzhit*

contraceptive контрацепти́в (m) *kantratsiptíf*

control (passport) контро́ль (m) *kantról*

convenient удо́бный *oodóbny*

to cook гото́вить/пригото́вить *gatóvit/ prigatóvit*

cool прохла́дный *prakhládny*

corkscrew што́пор (m) *shtópar*

corner у́гол (m) *óogal*

correct пра́вильный *právilny*

corridor коррид́ор (m) *karidór*

cosmetics косме́тика (f) *kasmyétika*

to cost сто́ить *stóit*

cot де́тская крова́тка (f) *dyétskaya kraváтka*

cotton (material) хло́пок (m) *khlópak*

» (thread) ни́тки (pl) *nítki*

cotton wool ва́та (f) *váta*

to cough ка́шлять/кашляну́ть *káshlit/ kashlinóot*

to count счита́ть/сосчита́ть *schitát/ saschitát*

counter (post office) окно́ (n) *aknó*

country страна́ (f) *straná*

» **in the country** за́ городом, на да́че *zá garadam, na dáche*
couple *(pair)* па́ра (f) *pára*
course *(lessons)* курс (m) *koors*
» *(of meal)* блю́до (n) *blóoda*
court *(law)* суд (m) *soot*
» *(tennis)* корт (m) *kort*
cover *(lid)* кры́шка (f) *krýshka*
cramp су́дорога (f) *sóodaraga*
cream *(lotion)* крем (m) *kryem*
» *(colour)* кре́мовый *kryémavy*
credit card креди́тная ка́рта (f) *kridítnaya kárta*
to **cross** пересека́ть/пересе́чь *pirisikát/pirisyéch*
crossroad перекрёсток (m) *pirikryóstak*
crowded перепо́лненный *piripólniny*
cruise круи́з (m) *krooís*
crutch косты́ль (m) *kastýl*
to **cry** пла́кать/запла́кать *plakát/zaplakát*
crystal криста́лл (m) *kristál*
cup ча́шка (f) *cháshka*
curler *(hair)* пло́йка (f), щипцы́ (pl) для зави́вки *plóïka, shiptsý dlya zavífki*
current *(electrical)* ток (m) *tok*
curtain занаве́ска (f), што́ра (f) *zanavyéska, shtóra*
to **cut** ре́зать *ryézat*
to **cut oneself** поре́заться *paryézatsa*
cutlery столо́вые прибо́ры (pl) *stalóyye pribóry*
cycling велоспо́рт (m) *vilaspórt*
cystitis цисти́т (m) *tsistít*

D

daily ежедне́вный *yezhidnyévny*
dairy products моло́чные проду́кты (pl) *malóchnyye pradóokty*
damage вред (m), уще́рб (m) *vryet, ooschérb*
damp вла́жный, сыро́й *vlázhny, syróï*

to **dance** танцева́ть/станцева́ть *tantsivát/stantsivát*
danger опа́сность (f) *apásnast*
dangerous опа́сный *apásny*
dark тёмный *tyómny*
darling дорого́й, ми́лый *daragóï, míly*
date *(day)* да́та (f), число́ (n) *dáta, chisló*
» *(fruit)* фи́ник (m) *finik*
daughter дочь (f), до́чери (pl) *doch, dóchiri*
day день (m), дни (pl) *dyen, dni*
» **day after tomorrow** послеза́втра *poslizáftra*
» **day before yesterday** позавчера́ *pazafchirá*
dead end тупи́к (m) *toopík*
deaf глухо́й *glookhóï*
dear *(loved)* ми́лый, дорого́й *míly, daragóï*
» *(expensive)* дорого́й *daragóï*
death смерть (f) *smyert*
debt долг (m) *dolk*
decaffeinated coffee ко́фе (m) без кофеи́на *kófye byes kafiína*
deck па́луба (f) *pálooba*
to **decide** реша́ть/реши́ть *rishát/rishít*
deep глубо́кий *gloobóki*
deer оле́нь (m) *alyén*
definitely определённо, то́чно *apridilyónna, tóchna*
degree *(temperature)* гра́дус (m) *grádoos*
» *(university)* дипло́м (m) *diplóm*
delay заде́ржка (f) *zadyérshka*
delicate делика́тный *dilikátny*
delicious вку́сный *fkóosny*
delighted: I am delighted to... я с удово́льствием... *ya s oodavólstviyem*
to **deliver** доставля́ть/доста́вить *dastavlyát/dastávit*
delivery доста́вка (f) *dastáfka*

demonstration демонстра́ция (f), пока́з (m) *dimanstrátsiya, pakás*

denim джи́нсовый *dzhínsavy*

dentist зубно́й врач (m), стомато́лог (m) *zoobnói vrach, stamatólok*

denture зубно́й проте́з (m) *zoobnói pratés*

deodorant дезодора́нт (m) *dezadaránt*

to depart отправля́ться/отпра́виться *atpravlyátsa/atprávitsa*

department *(in shop)* отде́л (m) *addyél*

department store универма́г (m) *oonivirmák*

departure отправле́ние (n) *atpravlyéniye*

departure lounge зал (m) ожида́ния *zal azhidániya*

depth глубина́ (f) *gloobiná*

to describe опи́сывать/описа́ть *apísyvat/apisát*

dessert десе́рт (m) *disyért*

destination пункт (m) назначе́ния *poonkt naznachéniya*

detergent мо́ющее сре́дство (n) *móyooschiye sryétstva*

to develop *(cause to unfold)* развива́ть/разви́ть *razvivát/razvít*

» *(photo)* проявля́ть/прояви́ть *prayivlyát/prayivít*

diabetic диабе́тик (m) *diabyétik*

to dial набира́ть/набра́ть но́мер *nabirát/nabrát nómir*

dialling code код (m) *kot*

dialling tone гудо́к (m) *goodók*

diamond алма́з (m) *almás*

diarrhoea диаре́я (f), поно́с (m) *diaryéya, panós*

dice игра́льные ко́сти (pl) *igrálnyye kósti*

dictionary слова́рь (m) *slavár*

to die умира́ть/умере́ть *oomirát/oomiryét*

diesel ди́зель (m), соля́рка (f) *dízyel, salyárka*

diet дие́та (f) *diyéta*

different ра́зный, разли́чный *rázny, razlíchny*

difficult тру́дный *tróodny*

digital цифрово́й *tsifravói*

» **digital camera** цифрово́й фотоаппара́т (m) *tsifravói fataparát*

dinghy надувна́я ло́дка (f) *nadoovnáya lótka*

dining room столо́вая (f) *stalóvaya*

dinner *(midday meal)* обе́д (m) *abyét*

» *(evening meal)* у́жин (m) *óozhin*

dinner jacket смо́кинг (m) *smókink*

diplomat диплома́т (m) *diplamát*

direct *(train)* прямо́й, без переса́дки *primói, byes pirisátki*

direction направле́ние (n) *napravlyéniye*

dirty гря́зный *gryázny*

disabled инвали́д (m) *invalít*

disco дискоте́ка (f) *diskatyéka*

discount ски́дка (f) *skítka*

dish блю́до (n) *blyóoda*

dishwasher посудомо́ечная маши́на (f) *pasoodamóyichnaya mashína*

disinfectant дезинфици́рующее сре́дство (n) *dezinfitsírooyooschiye sryétstva*

dislocated вы́вихнутый *vývikhnooty*

disposable однора́зовый *adnarázovy*

» **disposable camera** однора́зовый фотоаппара́т (m) *adnarázovy fataparát*

» **disposable nappies** однора́зовые подгу́зники (pl), па́мперсы (pl coll.) *adnarázavyye padgóozniki, pámpirsy*

distance расстоя́ние (n) *rastayániye*

district райо́н (m) *rayón*

to disturb беспоко́ить *bispakóit*

to dive ныря́ть/нырну́ть *nyryát/nyrnóot*

diversion объе́зд (m) *ab-yést*

divorced разведённый *razvidyónny*

dizzy: I feel dizzy у меня́ кру́жится голова́ *oo minyá króozhitsa galavá*

to do де́лать/сде́лать *dyélat/zdyélat*

doctor до́ктор (m), врач (m) *dóktar, vrach*

document докуме́нт (m) *dakoomyént*

dog соба́ка (f) *sabáka*

doll ку́кла (f) *kóokla*

» **Russian doll** матрёшка (f) *matryóshka*

dollar до́ллар (m) *dólar*

dome ку́пол (m) *kóopal*

donkey осёл (m), иша́к (m) *asyól, ishák*

door дверь (f) *dvyer*

double двойно́й *dvaïnói*

double bed двуспа́льная крова́ть (f) *dvoospálnaya kravát*

down вниз *vnis*

download загружа́ть/загрузи́ть *zagroozhát/zagroozít*

downstairs внизу́ *vnizóo*

draught beer разливно́е пи́во (n) *razlivnóye píva*

to draw (picture) рисова́ть/нарисова́ть *risavát/narisavát*

drawer я́щик (m) *yáschik*

drawing рису́нок (m) *risóonak*

dress пла́тье (n) *plát-ye*

to dress, get dressed одева́ться/ оде́ться *adivátsa/adyétsa*

dressing (medical) перевя́зочный материа́л (m), бинт (m) *pirivyázachny matirial, bint*

» (salad) припра́ва (f) *pripráva*

drink напи́ток (m) *napítak*

to drink пить/вы́пить *pit/výpit*

drinking water питьева́я вода́ (f) *pityiváya vadá*

to drive води́ть/вести́ *vadít/vistí*

driving licence води́тельские права́ (pl) *vaditilskiye pravá*

drowsiness сонли́вость (f) *sanlívast*

drug нарко́тик (m) *narkótik*

» **drug addict** наркома́н (m) *narkamán*

dry-cleaner's химчи́стка (f) *khimchístka*

dubbed (film) дубли́рованный *dubliravany*

dummy (baby's) со́ска (f) *sóska*

during во вре́мя *va vryémya*

dust пыль (f) *pyl*

dusty пы́льный *pýlny*

duty (tax) нало́г (m) *nalók*

duty-free беспо́шлинный *bispóshlinny*

duvet одея́ло (n) *adiyálo*

DVD дивиди́ (m) *dividí*

» **DVD-player** дивиди́-пле́ер (m) *dividí-pléyer*

dyslexic: he is dyslexic он дисле́к-сик *on dislyéksik*

E

each ка́ждый *kázhdy*

ear у́хо (n), (pl) у́ши *óokha, óoshi*

ear infection ушна́я инфе́кция *ooshnáya infyéktsiya*

early ра́но *rána*

to earn зараба́тывать/зарабо́тать *zarabátyvat/zarabótat*

earring серьга́ (f), серёжка (f) *sirgá, siryóshka*

earth земля́ (f) *zimlyá*

east восто́к (m) *vastók*

» **eastern** восто́чный *vastóchny*

Easter Па́сха (f) *páskha*

easy лёгкий *lyókhki*

to eat есть/съесть *yest/s-yest*

economy эконо́мия (f) *ekanómiya*

edible съедо́бный *s-yidóbny*

effort уси́лие (n), попы́тка (f) *oosíliye, papýtka*

either... or... и́ли ...и́ли, ли́бо...
  ли́бо *íli ... íli, líba... líba...*
election вы́боры (pl) *výbary*
electrician эле́ктрик (m) *elyéktrik*
electricity электри́чество (n)
  eliktríchistva
electronic электро́нный *elitrónny*
email электро́нная по́чта (f), email
  (m) *eliktrónnaya póchta, i-méíl*
to email писа́ть/написа́ть email *pisát/
  napisát i-méíl*
to embark *(boat)* сади́ться/сесть на
  кора́бль *saditsa/syest na karábl*
embarrassing вызыва́ющий
  смуще́ние *vyzyváyooschi
  smooschéniye*
embassy посо́льство (n) *pasólstva*
emergency крити́ческая ситуа́ция
  (f), кра́йняя необходи́мость (f),
  *kritícheskaya sitooátsiya, kráiniya
  niapkhadímast*
empty пусто́й *poostóї*
end коне́ц (m) *kanyéts*
to end конча́ть/ко́нчить *kanchát/
  kónchit*
energy эне́ргия (f) *enérgiya*
engaged *(to be married)* они́
  помо́лвлены, они́ обручи́лись *aní
  pamólvliny, aní abroochilis*
  » *(toilet/telephone)* за́нято *zánita*
England А́нглия (f) *ángliya*
English *(adj.)* англи́йский *anglíski*
  » *(person)* англича́нин/англича́нка
  (m/f) *anglichánin/anglichánka*
to enjoy наслажда́ться/наслади́ться
  naslazhdátsa/nasladítsa
enough доста́точно *dastátachna*
to enter входи́ть/войти́ *fkhadít/vaití*
entertainment развлече́ние (n)
  razvlichéniye
entrance вход (m) *fkhot*
envelope конве́рт (m) *kanvyért*
environment окружа́ющая среда́ (f)
  akroozháyooschaya sridá

environmentally friendly
  безвре́дный для приро́ды
  bizvryédny dlya priródy
epileptic эпиле́птик (m) *epilyéptik*
equal ра́вный, одина́ковый *rávny,
  adinákavy*
escalator эскала́тор (m) *eskalátar*
especially осо́бенно *asóbino*
essential *(necessary)* необходи́мый
  niapkhadímy
even *(including)* да́же *dázhi*
  » *(not odd)* чётный *chótny*
evening ве́чер (m) *vyéchir*
every ка́ждый, вся́кий *kázhdy, fsyáki*
everyone вся́кий, все *fsyáki, fsye*
everything всё *fsyo*
everywhere везде́ *vizdyé*
exact(ly) ро́вный (ро́вно) *róvny
  (róvna)*
examination *(medical)* осмо́тр (m)
  asmótr
example приме́р (m) *primyér*
  » *for example* наприме́р, к приме́ру
  naprimyér, k primyéroo
excellent отли́чный *atlíchny*
excess baggage переве́с (m) *pirivyés*
to exchange меня́ть/обменя́ть *minyát/
  abminyát*
exchange rate обме́нный курс (m)
  abmyénny koors
exciting увлека́тельный *oovlikátilny*
excursion экску́рсия (f) *ekskóorsiya*
excuse me извини́те *izvinítye*
executive исполни́тельный
  ispalnítilny
exercise упражне́ние (n)
  ooprazhnyéniye
exhibition вы́ставка (f) *výstafka*
exit вы́ход (m) *výkhat*
to expect ждать, ожида́ть *zhdat,
  azhidát*
expensive дорого́й *daragóї*
experience о́пыт (m) *ópyt*
experiment экспериме́нт (m)
  ekspirimyént

expert экспе́рт (m) *ekspyért*

to explain объясня́ть/объясни́ть *ab-yisnyát/ab-yisnít*

explosion взрыв (m) *vzryf*

to export экспорти́ровать, вывози́ть/ вы́везти *ekspartírovat, vyvazít/ vývisti*

exposure (photo) экспози́ция (f), вы́держка (f) *ekspazítsiya, výdirshka*

express сро́чный *sróchny*

extension cable удлини́тель (m) *oodlinítil*

external вне́шний *vnyéshni*

extra дополни́тельный *dapalnítilny*

eyelash ресни́ца (f) *risnítsa*

eyeshadow те́ни (pl) (для век) *tyéni (dlya vyek)*

F

fabric ткань (f) *tkan*

facilities усло́вия (pl), оснаще́ние (n) *oosló viya, asnaschéniye*

fact факт (m) *fakt*

» **in fact** факти́чески, на са́мом де́ле *faktíchiski, na sámam dyéli*

factory фа́брика (f), заво́д (m) *fábrika, zavót*

to fail (exam/test) прова́ливать/ провали́ть *praválivat/pravalít*

failure неуда́ча (f) *nioodácha*

to faint па́дать в о́бморок *pádat v óbmarok*

fair (haired) све́тлый *svyétly*

» (beautiful) прекра́сный, краси́вый *prikrásny, krasívy*

faith ве́ра (f), дове́рие (n) *vyéra, davyériye*

fake подде́лка (f) *paddyélka*

to fall па́дать/упа́сть *pádat/oopást*

false ло́жный, оши́бочный *lózhny, ashíbachny*

familiar знако́мый *znakómy*

family семья́ (f) *sim-yá*

famous знамени́тый *znaminíty*

fan (air) вентиля́тор (m) *vintilyátar*

» (supporter) фана́т (m), боле́льщик (m) *fanát, balyélschik*

fantastic фантасти́ческий *fantastíchiski*

far (away) далеко́ *dalikó*

fare пла́та (f) за прое́зд *pláta za prayést*

farm фе́рма (f) *fyérma*

farmer фе́рмер (m) *fyérmir*

fashion мо́да (f) *móda*

fashionable/in fashion мо́дный, в мо́де *módny, v módye*

fast бы́стрый *býstry*

fat жи́рный *zhírny*

fatal смерте́льный *smirtyélny*

father оте́ц (m) *atyéts*

» (dad) па́па (m) *pápa*

father-in-law (husband's) свёкор (m) *svyókar*

» (wife's) тесть (m) *tyest*

faulty неиспра́вный, с изъя́ном *niisprávny, s iz-yánam*

favourite люби́мый *lyoobímy*

to feel чу́вствовать/почу́вствовать *chóostvavat/pachóostvavat*

» (ill/well) чу́вствовать/ почу́вствовать себя́ пло́хо/ хорошо́ *chóostvavat/pachóostvavat sibyá plókha/kharashó*

female, feminine же́нский *zhénski*

feminist фемини́ст/ка (m/f) *fiminíst/ka*

ferry паро́м (m) *paróm*

festival фестива́ль (m), пра́здник (m) *fistivál, práznik*

fever жар (m), высо́кая температу́ра (f) *zhar, vysókaya timpiratóora*

(a) few не́сколько *nyéskalka*

fiancé(e) жени́х (m), неве́ста (f) *zhiník, nivyésta*

fibre волокно́ (n) *valaknó*

field по́ле (n) *pólye*

fig фи́га (f), инжи́р (m) *fíga, inzhír*

file (computer) файл (m) *faïl*

» *(nail)* пи́лка (f) для ногте́й *pílka dlya naktyéï*

to fill наполня́ть/напо́лнить *napalnyát/napólnit*

filling *(tooth)* пло́мба (f) *plómba*

» *(cake)* начи́нка (f) *nachínka*

film фильм (m) *film*

» *(camera)* плёнка (f) *plyónka*

» **film star** кинозвезда́ (f) *kinazvizdá*

finance фина́нсы (pl), дохо́ды (pl) *finánsy, dakhódy*

to find находи́ть/найти́ *nakhadít/naïtí*

fine *(OK)* хорошо́ *kharashó*

» *(penalty)* штраф (m) *shtraf*

» *(weather)* я́сный, хоро́ший *yásny, kharóshi*

finish фи́ниш (m) *fínish*

fire! пожа́р! (m) *pazhár*

fire alarm пожа́рная трево́га (f) *pazhárnaya trivóga*

fire brigade пожа́рные (pl) *pazhárnyye*

fire extinguisher огнетуши́тель (m) *agnitooshítil*

fireworks фейерве́рк (m) *fiyirvyérk*

firm кре́пкий *kryépki*

» *(company)* фи́рма (f) *fírma*

first aid пе́рвая по́мощь (f) *pyérvaya pómasch*

» **first aid kit** апте́чка (f) *aptyéchka*

to fish/go fishing рыба́чить *rybáchit*

fishing rod у́дочка (f) *óodachka*

fit *(healthy)* здоро́вый *zdaróvy*

to fit приспоса́бливать/приспосо́бить *prispasáblivat/prispasóbit*

» **that fits you well** вам по разме́ру *vam pa razmyéroo*

fitting room приме́рочная (f) *primyérachnaya*

to fix *(mend)* ремонти́ровать/отремонти́ровать *rimantíravat/atrimantíravat*

flag флаг (m) *flak*

flash *(camera)* вспы́шка (f) *fspýshka*

flat *(apartment)* кварти́ра (f) *kvartíra*

flavour арома́т (m), вкус (m) *aramát, fkoos*

flea market барахо́лка (f) *barakhólka*

flight рейс (m) *ryeis*

flippers плавники́ (pl), ла́сты (pl) *plavniкí, lastý*

floor *(bottom)* пол (m) *pol*

» *(level)* эта́ж (m) *etásh*

» **on the first floor** на второ́м этаже́ *na ftaróm etazhé*

» **ground floor** пе́рвый эта́ж *pyérvy etásh*

flour мука́ (f) *mooká*

flower цвето́к (m), цветы́ (pl) *tsvitók, tsvitý*

flu/influenza грипп (m) *grip*

fluent бе́глый *byégly*

fluid жи́дкость (f) *zhítkast*

fly му́ха (f) *móokha*

fly spray аэрозо́ль (m) от мух *aerazól at mookh*

to fly лете́ть, лета́ть *lityét, litát*

foggy тума́нный *toománny*

foil фольга́ (f) *falgá*

folk music наро́дная му́зыка (f) *naródnaya móozyka*

to follow сле́довать/после́довать за *slyédavat/paslyédavat za*

following *(next)* сле́дующий *slyédooyooschi*

food еда́ (f) *yidá*

food poisoning пищево́е отравле́ние (n) *pishchivóye atravlyéniye*

foot ступня́ (f) *stoopnyá*

» **on foot** пешко́м *pishkóm*

football футбо́л (m) *footból*

footpath тропа́ (f), тропи́нка (f) *trapá, trapínka*

for для *dlya*

forbidden запрещено́ *zaprischinó*

foreign иностра́нный *inastránny*

foreigner иностра́нец/иностра́нка (m/f) *inastránits/inastránka*

forest лес (m) *lyes*

to forget забывать/забыть *zabyvát/zabýt*

to forgive прощать/простить *praschát/prastít*

fork вилка (f) *vílka*

form (document) бланк (m) *blank*

forward вперёд *fpiryót*

fountain фонтан (m) *fantán*

fox лиса (f) *lisá*

foyer фойе (n) indecl. *fayé*

fracture перелом (m) *pirilóm*

fragile ломкий, хрупкий *lómki, khróopki*

free свободный *svabódny*

free of charge бесплатно *bisplátna*

freedom свобода (f) *svabóda*

French французский *frantsóoski*

frequent частый *chásty*

fresh свежий *svyézhi*

fridge холодильник (m) *khaladílnik*

fried жареный *zháriny*

friend друг (m), друзья (pl), подруга (f) *drook, drooz-yá, padróoga*

frighten пугать/испугать *poogát/ispoogát*

» I am frightened я боюсь *ya bayóos*

frog лягушка (f) *ligóoshka*

from из *is*

front перёд, передняя сторона *piryód, piryédniya staraná*

» in front of впереди *fpiridí*

frontier граница (f) *granítsa*

frost мороз (m) *marós*

frost bite обморожение (n) *abmarazhéniye*

frozen замёрзший *zamyórshi*

frozen food замороженные продукты *zamarózhennye pradóokty*

fruit фрукт (m) *frookt*

fuel топливо (n) *tópliva*

full полный *pólny*

» full board полный пансион (m) *pólny pansión*

» full up: the hotel is full up свободных номеров нет *svabódnykh namiróf nyet*

to have fun веселиться/повеселиться *visilítsa/pavisilítsa*

» it was fun было весело *býla vyésila*

funeral похороны (pl) *pókharany*

funfair ярмарка (f) *yármarka*

funny (amusing) забавный *zabávny*

» (peculiar) странный *stránny*

fur мех (m) *myekh*

fur coat шуба (f) *shóoba*

G

gallery галерея (f) *galiryéya*

gambling азартные игры (pl) *azártnyye ígry*

game (cards etc) игра (f) *igrá*

» (match) матч *match*

» (meat) дичь (f) *dich*

garage (fuel) заправка (f) *zapráfka*

» (parking) гараж (m) *garásh*

» (repairs) автосервис (m) *aftarsyérvis*

garden сад (m) *sat*

gate ворота (pl) *varóta*

» (airport) выход (m) на посадку *výkhat na pasátkoo*

gay (homosexual) гомосексуалист (m) *gamasiksooalíst*

general общий *ópschi*

» in general вообще *vaapsché*

general practitioner, GP терапевт (m) *tirapyéft*

generous щёдрый *schédry*

gentleman/men джентельмены (m/pl) *dzhintilmyén/y*

gents' toilet мужской туалет (m) *mooshskói tooalét*

genuine подлинный *pódlinny*

German немецкий *nimétski*

to get off (bus) выходить/выйти из *vykhadít/výyti is*

» **to get on** садиться/сесть на *saditsa/syest na*

gift подáрок (m) *padárak*

gin джин (m) *dzhin*

girl *(child)* дéвочка (f) *dyévachka*

» *(young woman)* дéвушка (f) *dyévooshka*

girlfriend подрýга (f) *padróoga*

glass *(material)* стеклó (n) *stikló*

» *(tumbler)* стакáн (m) *stakán*

glasses очки́ (pl) *achkí*

global warming всемúрное потеплéние (n) *vsimírnaye patiplyénie*

gloves перчáтки (pl) *pirchátki*

glue клей (m) *klyeï*

gluten-free без клейкови́ны, без глютéна *byes klyeïkavíny, byes glyooténa*

to go *(on foot)* идти́, ходи́ть *itti, khadít*

» *(in a vehicle)* éхать, éздить *yékhat, yézdit*

» **to go away** уезжáть/уéхать *ooyizhát/ooyékhat*

» **to go down** спускáться/спусти́ться *spooskátsa/spoostítsa*

» **to go in** входи́ть/войти́ *fkhadít/vaïtí*

» **to go out** выходи́ть/вы́йти *vykhadít/vyïti*

» **let's go!** пойдёмте! *païdyómtye*

goal цель (f) *tsel*

God бог (m) *bog*

gold зóлото (n) *zólata*

golf гóльф (m) *golf*

» **golf clubs** клю́шки (pl) для гóльфа *klyóoshki dlya gólfa*

» **golf course** площáдка (f)/пóле (n) для гóльфа *plaschátka/pólye dlya gólfa*

good хорóший *kharóshi*

» **good afternoon** дóбрый день *dóbry dyen*

» **good evening** дóбрый вéчер *dóbry vyéchir*

» **good morning** дóброе ýтро *dóbraye óotra*

» **good night** спокóйной нóчи *spakóïnaï nóchi*

goodbye до свидáния *da svidániya*

government прави́тельство (n) *pravítelstva*

grammar граммáтика (f) *gramátika*

grandchildren внýки (pl) *vnóoki*

grandparents бáбушка и дéдушка *bábooshka i dyédooshka*

grass травá (f) *travá*

greasy жи́рный *zhírny*

green зелёный *zilyóny*

grey сéрый *syéry*

grilled поджáренный на гри́ле *padzhárinny na grílye*

ground земля́ (f) *zimlyá*

» *(football)* стадиóн (n) *stadión*

ground floor пéрвый этáж (m) *pyérvy etásh*

group грýппа (f) *gróopa*

guarantee гарáнтия (f) *garántiya*

guest гость (m) *gost*

guide *(person)* гид (m), экскурсовóд (m) *git, ekskoorsavót*

» **guided tour** экскýрсия (f) *ekskóorsiya*

guidebook путеводи́тель (m) *pootivadítil*

guilty виновáтый *vinaváty*

guitar гитáра (f) *gitára*

gun *(pistol)* пистолéт (m) *pistalyét*

» *(rifle)* ружьё (n) *roozh-yó*

H

hair вóлосы (pl) *vólasy*

hairbrush щётка (f) для волóс *schyótka dlya valós*

haircut стри́жка (f) *stríshka*

hairdresser парикма́хер (m) *parikmákhir*

hairdryer фен (m) *fyen*

half *(adj.)* по́лу-... *póloo-*

half an hour полчаса́ *polchisá*

hand рука́ (f) *rooká*

» **hand luggage** ручна́я кладь (f) *roochnáya klat*

» **hand made** сде́лан(о) вручну́ю *zdyélan(a) vroochnóoyoo*

handbag (да́мская) су́мочка (f) *(dámskaya) sóomachka*

handkerchief носово́й плато́к (m) *nasavói platók*

handle ру́чка (f) *róochka*

to **hang up** *(telephone)* ве́шать/ пове́сить тру́бку *vyéshat/pavyésit tróopkoo*

hangover похме́лье (n) *pakhmyél-ye*

to **happen** случа́ться/случи́ться *sloochátsa/sloochítsa*

happy счастли́вый, дово́льный *schaslívy, davólny*

hard тве́рдый *tvyórdy*

» *(difficult)* тру́дный

hard drive жёсткий диск (m) *zhóski disk*

hat шля́па (f) *shlyápa*

to **hate** ненави́деть *ninavídit*

to **have** име́ть *imyét*

hay fever сенна́я лихора́дка (f) *sinnáya likharátka*

he он *on*

headache головна́я боль (f) *galavnáya bol*

headlight фа́ра (f) *fára*

headphones нау́шники (pl) *naóoshniki*

to **heal** исцеля́ть/исцели́ть *istsilyát/ istsilít*

health здоро́вье (n) *zdaróv-ye*

health food shop магази́н (m) здоро́вой пи́щи *magazín zdaróvaï píschi*

healthy здоро́вый *zdaróvy*

to **hear** слы́шать/услы́шать *slýshat/ ooslýshat*

hearing слух (m) *slookh*

» **hearing aid** слуховой аппара́т (m) *slookhavói aparát*

heart attack серде́чный при́ступ (m) *sirdyéchny prístoop*

heat жара́ (f) *zhará*

heating отопле́ние (n) *ataplyéniye*

heaven не́бо (n) *nyéba*

heavy тяжёлый *tizhóly*

heel *(foot)* пя́тка (f) *pyátka*

» *(shoe)* каблу́к (m) *kablóok*

height высота́ (f) *vysatá*

» *(of person)* рост (m) *rost*

helicopter вертолёт (m) *virtalyót*

hell ад (m) *at*

hello здра́вствуйте *zdrástvooïtye*

» *(answer on phone)* алло́ *alló*

helmet шлем (m) *shlyem*

help по́мощь (f) *pómasch*

» **help!** помоги́те! *pamagítye*

to **help** помога́ть/помо́чь *pamagát/ pamóch*

her её *yivó*

herb трава́ (f) *travá*

herbal tea травяно́й чай *travinói chaï*

here здесь *zdyes*

here is вот... *vot*

hers её *yivó*

high высо́кий *vysóki*

high chair *(child)* де́тский сту́льчик (m) *dyétski stóolchik*

to **hijack** похища́ть/похи́тить *pakhischát/pakhítit*

» *(airplane, car)* угоня́ть/угна́ть *ooganyát/oognát*

hiking экску́рсия (f) пешко́м *ekskóorsiya pishkóm*

hill холм (m) *kholm*

him его́ *yivó*

Hindu хи́нди *khíndi*

to **hire** брать/взять напрока́т *brat/ vzyat naprakát*

his его́ *yivó*

history история (f) *istóriya*
to hitchhike ездить автостопом *yézdit aftastópam*
HIV ВИЧ (m) *vich*
  » **HIV positive** ВИЧ инфицированный *vich infitsíravanny*
hobby хобби (n) *khóbi*
to hold держать *dirzhát*
hole дыра (f) *dyrá*
holiday отпуск *ótpoosk*
  » **on holiday** в отпуске *v ótpooskye*
holidays (school etc.) каникулы (pl) *kaníkooly*
holy священный *svischénny*
home дом (m) *dom*
  » **at home** дома *dóma*
to go home (on foot) идти/пойти домой *itti/paití damóï*
  » **(in a vehicle)** ехать/поехать домой *yékhat/payékhat damóï*
homemade домашний *damáshni*
homeopathic гомеопатический *gamiapatíchiski*
to be homesick скучать по дому *skochát pa dómoo*
homosexual гомосексуальный *gamasiksooálny*
honest честный *chésny*
honeymoon медовый месяц (m) *midóvy myésits*
to hope надеяться *nadyéitsa*
  » **I hope so** я надеюсь *ya nadyéyoos*
horrible ужасный *oozhásny*
horse лошадь (f) *lóshat*
horse riding верховая езда (f) *virkhaváya yizdá*
hose шланг (m) *shlank*
hospital больница (f) *balnítsa*
host хозяин/хозяйка (m/f) *khazyáin/ khazyáïka*
hot горячий *garyáchi*
  (spicy) острый *óstry*
hotel гостиница (f), отель (m) *gastínitsa, atél*

hour час (m) *chas*
house дом (m) *dom*
housework домашняя работа (f) *damáshniya rabóta*
how как *kak*
  » **how far?** как далеко? *kak dalikó*
  » **how long?** как долго? *kak dólga*
  » **how many/much?** сколько? *skólka*
  » **how much does it cost?** сколько это стоит? *skólka éta stóit*
hungry голодный *galódny*
to be hungry хотеть/захотеть есть *khatyét/zakhatyét yest*
to hunt охотиться *akhótitsa*
hurry: to be in a hurry спешить *spishít*
to hurt: it hurts больно *bólna*
husband муж (m) *moosh*
hut хижина (f) *khízhina*
hygienic гигиенический *gigiyiníchiski*

I я *ya*
ice лёд (m) *lyot*
  » **(on roads)** гололёд (m) *galalyót*
  » **with ice** со льдом *sa ldom*
ice cream мороженое (n) *marózhinaye*
ice cream parlour кафе-мороженое (n) *kafé-marózhinaye*
ice cube кубик (m) льда *kóobik lda*
ice rink каток (m) *katók*
iced (coffee) кофе (m) со льдом *kófye sa ldom*
icy ледяной *lidinóï*
idea идея (f) *ídyéya*
if если *yésli*
ill больной *balnóï*
illness болезнь (f) *balyézn*
imagination воображение (n) *vaabrazhéniye*
imitation (leather) искусственный *iskoóstvenny*
  » **(jewellery)** подделка (f) *paddyélka*

important ва́жный *vázhny*
impossible невозмо́жный
  nivazmózhny
in в *v*
in a hurry в спе́шке *f spyéshkye*
in front of впереди́ *fpiridí*
in order to что́бы *shtóby*
included включено́ *fklyoochinó*
independent незави́симый
  nizavísimy
indigestion несваре́ние (n)
  nisvaryéniye
industry индустри́я (f) *indoostríya*
infection инфе́кция (f) *infyéktsiya*
inflamed воспалённый *vaspalyónny*
inflatable надувно́й *nadoovnói*
informal неформа́льный *nifarmálny*
information информа́ция (f)
  infarmátsiya
» information desk/office
  спра́вочная (f) *správachnaya*
injection уко́л (m) *ookól*
to injure повреждать/повредить
  pavrizhdát/pavrídit
  » injured ра́неный,
  травми́рованный *ráneny,
  travmíravanny*
injury ра́на, тра́вма (f) *rána, trávma*
inn гости́ница (f) *gastínitsa*
innocent невино́вный *nivinóvny*
insect насеко́мое (n) *nasikómaye*
  » insect bite уку́с (m) насеко́мого
  ookóos nasikómava
  » insect repellent сре́дство (n) от
  насеко́мых *sryétstva at nasikómykh*
inside внутри́ *vnootrí*
instead of вме́сто *vmyésta*
instructor инстру́ктор (m)
  instróoktar
insulin инсули́н (m) *insoolín*
insult оскорбле́ние (n) *askarblyéniye*
insurance страхо́вка (f) *strakhófka*
intelligent интеллиге́нтный
  intiligyéntny

interested заинтересо́ванный
  zaintirisóvanny
  » I am interested in я интересу́юсь
  ya intirisóoyoos
interesting интере́сный *intiryésny*
international междунаро́дный
  mizhdoonaródny
internet интерне́т (m) *internét*
  » internet café интерне́т-кафе́ (n)
  internét-kafé
  » internet connection интерне́т-
  связь (f) *internét-svyas*
to interpret переводи́ть/перевести́
  pirivadít/pirivistí
interpreter перево́дчик/
  перево́дчица (m/f) *pirivóchik/
  pirivóchitsa*
interview интервью́ (n) *interv-yóo*
  » (job) собесе́дование (n)
  sabisyédavaniye
into в *v*
to introduce представля́ть/
  предста́вить *pritstavlyát/pritstávit*
invitation приглаше́ние (n)
  priglashéniye
to invite приглаша́ть/пригласи́ть
  priglashát/priglasít
Ireland Ирла́ндия (f) *irlándiya*
Irish (adj.) ирла́ндский *irlánski*
  » (people) ирла́ндец/ирла́ндка
  (m/f) *irlándits/irlánka*
iron (for clothes) утю́г (m) *ootyók*
to iron гла́дить/погла́дить *gládit/
  pagládit*
Islam исла́м (m) *islám*
Islamic исла́мский *islámski*
island о́стров (m) *óstraf*
it оно́, это *anó, éta*
itch зуд (m) *zoot*

J

jacket ку́ртка (f) *kóortka*
  » (part of a suit) пиджа́к (m) *pidzhák*
  » (woman's) жаке́т (m) *zhakét*

jam джем (m) *dzhem*

jar банка (f) *bánka*

jaw челюсть (f) *chyélyoost*

jazz джаз (m) *dzhas*

jeans джинсы (pl) *dzhínsy*

jellyfish медуза (f) *midóoza*

jeweller's ювелирный магазин (m) *yoovilírny magazín*

jewellery ювелирные изделия (pl) *yoovilírnyye izdyéliya*

Jewish еврейский *yivryéiski*

job работа (f) *rabóta*

jogging бег (m) трусцой *byek troostsóï*

joke шутка (f) *shóotka*

journalist журналист/ка (m/f) *zhoornalíst/ka*

journey путешествие (n) *pootishéstviye*

judge судья (m) *sood-yá*

jug кувшин (m) *koofshín*

juice сок (m) *sok*

to jump прыгать/прыгнуть *prýgat/ prýgnoot*

jumper джемпер (m) *dzhémpir*

just (only) только *tólka*

K

to keep держать *dirzhát*

keep the change сдачи не надо *zdáchi ni náda*

kettle чайник (m) *cháïnik*

key ключ (m) *klyooch*

to key in one's PIN number вводить/ввести пин-код *vvadít/ vvistí pin-kot*

to kill убивать/убить *oobivát/oobít*

kind (generous) добрый *dóbry*

» (type) род (m) *rot*

king король (m) *karól*

kiss поцелуй (m) *patsilóoï*

to kiss целовать/поцеловать *tsilavát/ patsilavát*

kitchen кухня (f) *kóokhnya*

knickers трусы, трусики (pl) *troosý, tróosiki*

knife нож (m) *nosh*

to knock at the door стучаться/ постучаться в дверь *stoochátsa/ pastoochátsa v dvyer*

to knock down сбивать/сбить *zbivát/ zbit*

» she's been knocked down by a car её сбила машина *iyó zbíla mashína*

knot узел (m) *óozil*

to know знать *znat*

» I don't know я не знаю *ya ni znáyoo*

L

label этикетка (f) *etikyétka*

lace кружево (n) *króozhiva*

ladder лестница (f) *lyésnitsa*

lady леди (f) *lyédi*

ladies' toilet женский туалет (m) *zhénski tooalyét*

lager светлое пиво (n) *svyétlaye píva*

lake озеро (n) *ózira*

lamp лампа (f) *lámpa*

lamp post уличный фонарь (m) *óolichny fanár*

land земля (f) *zimlyá*

language язык (m) *yizýk*

laptop ноутбук (m) *no ootbóok*

large большой *balshóï*

last последний *paslyédni*

to last длиться/продлиться *dlítsa/ pradlítsa*

late поздний *pózni*

to laugh смеяться/засмеяться *smiyátsa/zasmiyátsa*

launderette прачечная (f) самообслуживания *práchishnaya samaapslóozhivaniya*

laundry (clothes) бельё (n) *bil-yó*

law закон (m) *zakón*

lawyer юрист (m) *yooríst*

lazy ленивый *linívy*

lead-free без свинца, неэтилированный *bes svintsá, nietilíravanny*

leaf лист (m) *list*

leaflet брошюра (f) *brashóora*

least: at least по крайней мере *pa kráini myéri*

leather кожа (f) *kózha*

to leave
» *(go away, on foot)* уходить/уйти *ookhadít/ooití*
» *(go away, in a vehicle)* уезжать/уехать *ooyizhát/ooyékhat*
» *(forget smthg.)* забывать/забыть *zabyvát/zabýt*

lecture лекция (f) *lyéktsiya*

left левый, налево *lyévy, nalyéva*

left luggage office камера (f) хранения *kámira khranyéniya*

legal законный *zakónny*

leisure досуг (m) *dasóok*

to lend давать/дать взаймы *davát/dat vzaïmý*

length длина (f) *dliná*

lens *(contact)* линза (f) *línza*
» *(camera)* объектив *ab-yektíf*

lentil чечевица (f) *chichivítsa*

lesbian лесбиянка (f) *lisbiyánka*

less меньше *myénshe*

lesson урок (m) *oorók*

to let *(allow)* позволять/позволить *pazvalyát/pazvólit*
» *(rent)* сдавать/сдать *zdavát/zdat*

letter *(to someone)* письмо (n) *pismó*
» *(of alphabet)* буква (f) *bookva*

library библиотека (f) *bibliatyéka*

licence *(driving)* права (pl) *pravá*
» *(fishing etc.)* разрешение (n) *razrishéniye*

lid крышка (f) *krýshka*

to lie down ложиться/лечь *lazhítsa/lyech*

life жизнь (f) *zhizn*

lifeboat спасательная лодка (f) *spasátilnaya lótka*

lifeguard спасатель (m) *spasátil*

lifejacket спасательный жилет (m) *spasátilny zhilyét*

lift лифт (m) *lift*

to lift поднимать/поднять *padnimát/padnyát*
» **could you give me a lift?** вы не могли бы меня подвезти? *vy ni maglí by minyá padvistí*

light свет (m) *svyet*

light bulb лампочка (f) *lámpachka*

light *(colour)* светлый *svyétly*
» *(weight)* лёгкий *lyókhki*

to light освещать/осветить *asvischát/asvitít*

lighter зажигалка (f) *zazhigálka*

lightning молния (f) *mólniya*

to like любить *lyóobit*

line линия (f) *líniya*

lion лев (m) *lyef*

lipstick помада (f) *pamáda*

liqueur ликёр (m) *likyór*

liquid жидкость (f) *zhítkast*

list список (m) *spísak*

to listen *(to)* слушать/послушать *slóoshat/paslóoshat*

litter мусор (m) *móosar*

little маленький *málinki*
» **just a little, thanks** чуть-чуть, спасибо *choot-choot, spasíba*

to live жить *zhit*

loan заём (m), ссуда (f) *zayóm, ssóoda*

local местный *myésny*

to lock запирать/запереть *zapirát/zapiryét*

locker *(for luggage)* автоматическая камера хранения *aftamatícheskaya kámira khranyéniya*

lonely одинокий *adinóki*

long длинный *dlíny*

to look *(at)* смотреть/посмотреть *smatryét/pasmatryét*

» **to look for** иска́ть/найти́ *iskát/naití*

loose *(dress etc)* свобо́дный *svabódny*

lorry грузови́к (m) *groozavík*

to lose теря́ть/потеря́ть *tiryát/patiryát*
» *(in a contest, game)* прои́грывать/ проигра́ть *práigryvat/praigrát*

lost поте́рянный *patyérinny*
» **lost property office** бюро́ (n) нахо́док *byooró nakhódak*

a lot *(of)* мно́го, мно́гие *mnóga, mnógiye*

lotion лосьо́н (m) *lasión*

lottery лотере́я (f) *lateryéya*

loud гро́мкий *grómki*

lounge фойе́ (n) *fayé*

to love люби́ть/полюби́ть *lyoobít/ palyoobít*

to be in love *(with)* (m/f) быть влюблённым/влюблённой в *byt vlyooblyónnym/vlyooblyónnaï v*

low ни́зкий *níski*

low-fat нежи́рный *nizhírny*

lucky: he is lucky ему́ везёт *yimóo vizyót*

luggage бага́ж (m) *bagásh*

lump кусо́к (m) *koosók*

lunch ланч (m) *lanch*

M

machine маши́на (f) *mashína*

mad сумасше́дший *soomashédshi*

magazine журна́л (m) *zhoornál*

mail по́чта (f) *póchta*

main гла́вный *glávny*
» **main station** вокза́л (m) *vagzál*

to make де́лать/сде́лать *dyélat/zdyélat*

make-up косме́тика (f) *kasmyétika*

male мужско́й *mooshskóï*

manager ме́неджер (m) *myénidzher*

managing director управля́ющий дире́ктор (m) *oopravlyáyooschi diryéktar*

many мно́го *mnóga*

» **not many** немно́го *nimnóga*

map ка́рта (f) *kárta*

market ры́нок (m) *rýnak*

married (m/f) жена́т/за́мужем *zhinát/zámoozhim*
» **to get married** жени́ться *zhinítsa* (m), выходи́ть/вы́йти за́муж (f) *vykhadít/výyti zámoosh*

mask *(diving)* ма́ска (f) *máska*

matches спи́чки (pl) *spíchki*

material материа́л (m) *matiriál*

mathematics матема́тика (f) *matimátika*

matt *(finish)* ма́товый *mátavy*

matter: it doesn't matter не ва́жно *ni vázhna*
» **what's the matter?** в чём де́ло? *f chom dyéla*

mattress матра́с (m) *matrás*
» **air mattress** надувно́й матра́ц (m) *nadoovnóï matráts*

mature зре́лый *zryély*

me меня́ *minyá*

meal еда́ (f) *yidá*

mean: what does this mean? что э́то зна́чит? *shto éta znáchit*

meanwhile тем вре́менем *tyem vryéminim*

measles корь (f) *kor*
» **German measles** красну́ха (f) *krasnóokha*

to measure измеря́ть/изме́рить *izmiryát/izmyérit*

meat мя́со (n) *myása*

mechanic меха́ник (m) *mikhánik*

medical медици́нский *miditsínski*

medicine *(drug)* лека́рство (n) *likárstva*
» *(subject)* медици́на (f) *miditsína*

medieval средневеко́вый *sryednivikóvy*

medium *(size)* сре́дний *sryédni*
» *(steak)* уме́ренно прожа́ренный *oomyérina prazhárinny*

meeting встре́ча (f) *fstryécha*

meeting place ме́сто (для) встре́чи *myésta (dlya) fsryéchi*

member член (m) *chlyen*

memory па́мять (f) *pámit*

memory card ка́рта (f) па́мяти *kárta pámiti*

to **mend** чини́ть/почини́ть *chinít/ pachinít*

menu меню́ (n) *minyóo*

message сообще́ние (n) *saapschéniye*

metal мета́лл (m) *mitál*

microwave oven микроволно́вка (f) *mikravalnófka*

midday по́лдень (m) *póldyen*

middle середи́на (f) *siridína*

» **(adj.)** сре́дний *sryédni*

middle-aged сре́дних лет *sryédnikh lyét*

midnight по́лночь *pólnach*

migraine мигре́нь (f) *migryén*

mild мя́гкий *myákhki*

mind: do you mind if…? вы не про́тив, е́сли…? *vy ni prótif, yésli*

» **I don't mind** я не про́тив *ya ni prótif*

mine (of me) мой *moï*

minibus микроавто́бус (m) *mikraaftóboos*

minute (time) мину́та (f) *minóota*

mirror зе́ркало (n) *zyérkala*

miscarriage вы́кидыш (m) *výkidysh*

to **miss** (bus etc.) опа́здывать/ опозда́ть на *apázdyvat/apazdát na*

» **(nostalgia)** скуча́ть по *skoochát pa*

mist тума́н (m) *toomán*

mistake оши́бка (f) *ahípka*

» **to make a mistake** ошиба́ться/ ошиби́ться *ashibátsa/ashibítsa*

mixed сме́шанный *smyéshanny*

mobile phone моби́льный телефо́н (m), моби́льник (m, coll.) *mabílny tilifón, mabílnik*

model моде́ль (f) *madél*

modem моде́м (m) *madém*

modern совреме́нный *savrimyénny*

moisturiser увлажня́ющий крем (m) *oovlazhnyáyooschi kryem*

moment моме́нт (m) *mamyént*

money де́ньги (pl) *dyéngi*

month ме́сяц (m) *myésits*

monthly ежеме́сячно *yezhimyésichna*

monument па́мятник (m) *pámitnik*

moon луна́ (f) *looná*

moped мопе́д (m) *mapyét*

more бо́льше *bólshe*

» **no more** бо́льше не(т) *bólshe nye(t)*

morning у́тро (n) *óotra*

mortgage ипоте́ка (f) *ipatyéka*

mosque мече́ть (f) *michét*

mosquito кома́р (m) *kamár*

most (of) о́чень, бо́льше всего́ *óchen, bólshe fsivó*

mother мать (f) *mat*

» **(mom)** ма́ма (f) *máma*

mother-in-law (wife's mother) тёща (f) *tyóscha*

» **(husband's mother)** свекро́вь (f) *svikróf*

motor мото́р (m) *matór*

motorbike мотоци́кл (m) *matatsíkl*

motorboat мото́рная ло́дка (f) *matórnaya lótka*

motorway шоссе́ (n) *shassé*

» **(in Great Britain)** автостра́да (f) *aftastráda*

mountain гора́ (f) *gará*

mountaineering альпини́зм (m) *alpinízm*

to **move** дви́гать *dvígat*

» **to move house** переезжа́ть/ перее́хать *piriyizhát/piriyékhat*

MP3-player MP-три́шка (f, coll.) em pi tríshka*

Mr господи́н (m) *gaspadín*

Mrs госпожа́ (f) *gaspazhá*

much мно́го *mnóga*

» **not much** немно́го *nimnóga*

mug *(cup)* кру́жка (f) *króoshka*
museum музе́й (m) *moozyéi*
music му́зыка (f) *móozyka*
musical мю́зикл (m) *myóozikl*
musician музыка́нт (m) *moozykánt*
Muslim *(adj.)* мусульма́нский *moosoolmánski*
» *(people)* мусульма́нин/ мусульма́нка (m/f) *moosoolmánin/ moosoolmánka*
must: you must ты до́лжен/должна́ (m/f) *ty dólzhin/dalzhná*
my мой мои́
mystery та́йна (f) *táina*

N

nail clippers/scissors но́жницы (pl) для ногте́й *nózhnitsy dlya naktyéi*
nail file (m) для ногте́й *lak dlya naktyéi*
nail polish remover жи́дкость (f) для сня́тия ла́ка *zhítkast dlya snyátiya láka*
naked го́лый *góly*
name и́мя (n) *ímya*
» my name is... меня́ зову́т... *minyá zavóot*
» what is your name? как вас/тебя́ зову́т? *kak vas/tibyá zavóot*
napkin салфе́тка (f) *salfyétka*
nappy подгу́зник (m) *padgóoznik*
national национа́льный *natsianálny*
nationality национа́льность (f) *natsianálnast*
natural(ly) есте́ственный (есте́ственно) *yistyéstvinny (yistyéstvinna)*
naughty непослу́шный *nipaslóoshny*
nausea тошнота́ (f) *tashnatá*
navy морско́й *marskói*
navy blue тёмно-си́ний *tyómna-síni*
near бли́зко *blíska*
» nearby побли́зости *pablízasti*
nearest ближа́йший *blizháishi*
nearly почти́ *pachtí*

necessary необходи́мый *niapkhadímy*
necklace ожере́лье (n) *azhiryélye*
to need нужда́ться в *noozhdátsa v*
» we need to... нам на́до... *nam náda*
needle иго́лка (f) *igólka*
negative *(photo)* негати́в (m) *nigatíf*
neighbour сосе́д/ка (m/f) *sasyét/ka*
neither ... nor ни..., ни... *ni ni*
nephew племя́нник (m) *plimyánik*
nervous не́рвный *nyérvny*
net се́тка (f) *syétka*
never никогда́ *nikagdá*
new но́вый *nóvy*
» New Year's Day Но́вый год *nóvy got*
news но́вости (pl) *nóvasti*
newspaper газе́та (f) *gazyéta*
newspaper kiosk газе́тный кио́ск (m) *gazyétny kiosk*
next сле́дующий *slyédooschi*
» next week на сле́дующей неде́ле *na slyédooschi nidyélye*
» next month/year в сле́дующем ме́сяце/году́ *v slyédooschem myésitse/gadóo*
next to ря́дом с *ryádam s*
nice прия́тный, ми́лый *priyátny, míly*
niece племя́нница (f) *plimyánitsa*
night ночь (f) *noch*
nightclub ночно́й клуб (m) *nachnói kloop*
no нет *nyet*
no longer/no more бо́льше нет *bólshe nyet*
nobody никто́ *niktó*
noise шум (m) *shoom*
non-alcoholic безалкого́льный *bizalkagólny*
none никто́ *niktó*
non-smoking некуря́щий *nikooryáschi*
normal норма́льный, обы́чный *narmálny, abýchny*

» **normally** обы́чно *abýchna*

north се́вер (m) *syévir*

» *(adj.)* се́верный *syévirny*

nosebleed кровь (f) из но́са *krof iz nósa*

not не *nye*

nothing ничто́ *nishtó*

» **nothing else** бо́льше ничего́ *bólshe nichivó*

now сейча́с *sichás*

nowhere нигде́ *nigdyé*

number *(figure)* число́ (n) *chisló*

» *(room, telephone etc)* но́мер (m) *nómyer*

nurse (m/f) медбра́т, медсестра́ *myetbrát, mitsistrá*

nursery *(children)* де́тский сад (m) *dyétski sat*

nursery slope спуск (m) для начина́ющих лы́жников *spoosk dlya nachináyooschikh lýzhnikof*

nut оре́х (m) *aryékh*

O

oar весло́ (n), вёсла (pl) *visló, vyósla*

occasionally поро́й *paróï*

occupied *(seat)* за́нято *zánita*

odd стра́нный *stránny*

» *(not even)* нечётный *nichótny*

of course коне́чно *kanyéshna*

off *(tv, light)* вы́ключено *výklyoochina*

» *(milk)* проки́сло *prakísla*

offer предложе́ние (n) *pridlazhéniye*

» **special offer** специа́льное предложе́ние (n) *spitsiálnaye pridlazhéniye*

office о́фис (m) *ófis*

official официа́льный *afitsálny*

often ча́сто *chásta*

» **how often?** как ча́сто? *kak chásta*

oil ма́сло (n) *másla*

OK хорошо́! *kharashó*

old ста́рый *stáry*

old-fashioned старомо́дный *staramódny*

olive оли́вка (f) *alívka*

» **olive oil** оли́вковое ма́сло (n) *alífkavaye másla*

on включен *fklyóochin*

once одна́жды, оди́н раз *adnázhdy, adín ras*

one-way street у́лица (f) с односторо́нним движе́нием *óolitsa s adnastaróním dvizhéniyem*

one-way ticket биле́т (m) в одну́ сто́рону *bilyét v adnóo stóranoo*

only то́лько *tólka*

open откры́тый *atkrýty*

to **open** открыва́ть/откры́ть *atkryvát/ atkrýt*

opera о́пера (f) *ópira*

operation опера́ция (f) *apirátsiya*

opinion мне́ние (n) *mnyéniye*

» **in my opinion** по-мо́ему *pa-móyimoo*

opposite противополо́жный *prativapalózhny*

optician о́птик (m) *óptik*

or и́ли *íli*

orange *(colour)* ора́нжевый *aránzhivy*

orchestra орке́стр (m) *arkyéstr*

to **order** зака́зывать/заказа́ть *zakázyvat/zakazát*

ordinary обы́чный *abýchny*

organic food экологи́чески чи́стые проду́кты (pl) *ekalagíchiski chístyye pradóokty*

to **organise** организо́вывать/ организова́ть *arganizóvyvat/ arganizavát*

original(ly) первонача́льный (первонача́льно) *pirvanachálny (pirvanachálna)*

» **original language film** фильм (m) без перево́да *film byes pirivóda*

Orthodox правосла́вный *pravaslávny*

other другой *droogói*

others другие *droogíye*

our/ours наш *nash*

out of order не работает *ni rabótait*

outdoor(s)/outside на улице *na óolitse*

over: over here вот здесь *vot zdyes*

» **over there** вон там *von tam*

owe: how much do I owe (you)? сколько я вам должен/ должна? (m/f) *skólka ya vam dólzhin/dalzhná*

owner владелец (m) *vladyélits*

ozone-friendly не разрушающий слой озона *ni razrooshááyooschi sloí azóna*

ozone layer озонный слой (m) *azónny sloí*

P

pacemaker ритмизатор (m) сердца *ritmizátar syértsa*

package посылка (f) *pasýlka*

package holiday организованный отдых (m) *arganizóvanny óddyk*

packet (*of cigarettes etc.*) пачка (f) *páchka*

padlock висячий замок (m) *visyáchi zamók*

painful болезненный *balyézninny*

painkiller болеутоляющее (n) *boliootalyáyooscheye*

painting картина (f) *kartína*

pair пара (f) *pára*

palace дворец (m) *dvaryéts*

pale бледный *blyédny*

paper бумага (f) *boomága*

» (*newspaper*) газета (f) *gazyéta*

paralysed парализованный *paralizóvanny*

parcel посылка (f) *pasýlka*

pardon? простите? *prastíte*

parents родители (pl) *radítili*

park парк (m) *park*

to park парковаться/припарковаться *parkavátsa/priparkavátsa*

parking стоянка (f) *stayánka*

parking meter паркомат (m) *parkamát*

parliament парламент (m) *parlámint*

part часть (f) *chast*

particular: in particular в частности *f chásnasti*

partly частично *chistíchna*

partner партнёр (m) *partnyór*

party вечеринка (f), парти (n) *vichirínka, párti*

» (*political*) партия (f) *pártiya*

to pass (*salt etc.*) передавать/передать *piridavát/piridát*

» (*exam, test*) сдавать/сдать *zdavát/zdat*

passenger пассажир (m) *passazhír*

passport паспорт (m) *páspart*

» **passport control** паспортный контроль (m) *páspartny kantról*

past прошлый *próshly*

» **in the past** в прошлом *f próshlam*

pasta макароны (pl) *makaróny*

pastry выпечка (f) *výpichka*

path тропа (f), тропинка (f) *trapá, trapínka*

patient (*adj.*) терпеливый *tirpilívy*

» (*hospital*) пациент (m) *patsiént*

pavement тротуар (m) *tratooár*

to pay платить/заплатить *platít/zaplatít*

» **Can I pay, please?** можно заплатить? *mózhna zaplatít*

peach персик (m) *pyérsik*

peanut земляной орех (m) *zimlinói aryékh*

pedal педаль (f) *pidál*

pedestrian пешеход (m) *prishikhót*

pen ручка (f) *róochka*

pencil карандаш (m) *karandásh*

penfriend друг (m) по переписке *drook pa piripískye*

penicillin пенициллин (m) *pinitsilín*

pension пéнсия (f) *pyénsiya*

pensioner пенсионéр/ка (m/f) *pinsionyér/ka*

people люди (pl) *lyóodi*

pepper пéрец (m) *pyérits*

peppermint пéречная мя́та (f) *pyérichnaya myáta*

perfect идеáльный *idiálny*

performance представлéние (n) *pritstavlyéniye*

perfume духи́ (pl) *dookhí*

perhaps возмóжно *vazmózhna*

period (menstrual) мéсячные (pl), менструáция (f) *myésichnyye, minstrooátsiya*

» period pains бóли (pl) при менструáции *bóli pri minstrooátsii*

perm перманéнт (m) *pirmanyént*

permit разрешéние (n) *razrishéniye*

to permit разрешáть/разреши́ть *razrishát/razrishít*

person человéк (m) *chilavyék*

personal ли́чный *líchny*

petrol бензи́н (m) *binzín*

petrol station (áвто)запрáвка (f) *(áfta)zapráfka*

pharmacy аптéка (f) *aptyéka*

phone card телефóнная кáрточка (f) *tilifónnaya kártachka*

photocopy кóпия (f), ксéрокс (m) *kópiya, ksyéraks*

photo фотогрáфия (f), фóто (n) *fatagráfiya, fóta*

photographer фотóграф (m) *fatógraf*

phrase book разговóрник (m) *razgavórnik*

piano фортепиáно (n), пиани́но (n) *fartepiána, pianína*

to pick (choose) выбирáть/вы́брать *vybirát/výbrat*

» (flowers etc.) собирáть/собрáть *sabirát/sabrát*

picnic пикни́к (m) *pikník*

picture карти́на (f) *kartína*

piece кусóк (m) *koosók*

pill таблéтка (f) *tablyétka*

» the pill противозачáточные таблéтки (pl) *prativazachátachnye tablyétki*

pillow подýшка (f) *padóoshka*

pillowcase нáволочка (f) *návalachka*

pilot пилóт (m), лётчик (m) *pilót, lyótchik*

pin булáвка (f) *booláfka*

pink рóзовый *rózavy*

pipe (drain) трубá (f) *troobá*

» (smoking) трýбка (f) *tróopka*

pity: it's a pity жаль *zhal*

place мéсто (n) *myésta*

plain простóй *prastóï*

plaster плáстырь (m) *plástyr*

plastic (adj.) пластмáссовый *plasmássavy*

plastic bag полиэтилéновый пакéт (m) *palietilyénavy pakyét*

plate тарéлка (f) *taryélka*

platform платфóрма (f) *platfórma*

play (theatre) пьéса (f) *p-yésa*

please пожáлуйста *pazhálsta*

pleased to meet you óчень прия́тно *óchen priyátna*

plumber водопровóдчик (m), сантéхник (m) *vadapravóchik, santyékhnik*

pocket кармáн (m) *karmán*

poisonous ядови́тый *yidavíty*

police поли́ция (f) *palítsiya*

» (in Russia) мили́ция (f) *milítsiya*

polish (for shoes) крем для óбуви *kryem dlya óboovi*

polite вéжливый *vyézhlivy*

political полити́ческий *palitíchiski*

politician поли́тик (m) *palítik*

politics поли́тика (f) *palítika*

polluted загрязнённый *zagriznyónny*

pollution загрязнéние (n) *zagriznyéniye*

pool (swimming) бассéйн (m) *bassyéïn*

poor *(not rich)* бе́дный *byédny*

pop music поп-му́зыка (f) *pop-móozyka*

Pope Па́па Ри́мский *pápa rímski*

popular популя́рный *papoolyárny*

portable переносно́й *pirinasnói*

portion по́рция (f) *pórtsiya*

portrait портре́т (m) *partryét*

positive позити́вный, положи́тельный *pazitívny, palazhítilny*

possible возмо́жный *vazmózhny*

possibly возмо́жно *vazmózhna*

post по́чта (f) *póchta*

to post отправля́ть/отпра́вить по по́чте *atpravlyát/atprávit pa póchtye*

postbox почто́вый я́щик (m) *pachtóvy yáschik*

postcard откры́тка (f) *atkrýtka*

poster афи́ша (f), плака́т (m) *afísha, plakát*

postgraduate аспира́нт/ка (m/f) *aspiránt/ka*

postman почтальо́н (m) *pachtalión*

post office по́чта (f) *póchta*

to postpone откла́дывать/отложи́ть *atkládyvat/atlazhít*

pottery кера́мика (f) *kirámika*

potty *(child's)* де́тский горшо́к (m) *dyétski garshók*

pound *(sterling)* фунт (m) *foont*

to pour лить *lit*

power *(electricity)* электри́чество (n) *eliktríchistva*
   » *(strength)* си́ла (f) *síla*

power cut отключе́ние (n) электри́чества *atklyoochéniye eliktríchistva*

power point розе́тка (f) *razétka*

pram де́тская коля́ска (f) *dyétskaya kalyáska*

to prefer предпочита́ть/предпоче́сть *pritpachitát/pritpachyést*

pregnant бере́менная (f) *biryéminnaya*

prescription реце́пт (m) *ritsépt*

present *(gift)* пода́рок (m) *padárak*

press *(newspapers)* пре́сса (f) *pryéssa*

to press нажима́ть/нажа́ть *nazhimát/ nazhát*

pressure давле́ние (n) *davlyéniye*

pretty краси́вый *krasívy*

price цена́ (f) *tsiná*

priest свяще́нник (m) *svischénnik*

prime minister премье́р-мини́стр (m) *prim-yér minístr*

prince принц (m) *prints*

princess принце́сса (f) *printséssa*

prison тюрьма́ (f) *tyoormá*

private ча́стный *chásny*

private bathroom отде́льная ва́нная *atdyélnaya vánnaya*

prize приз (m), награ́да (f) *pris, nagráda*

probably вероя́тно *virayátna*

problem пробле́ма (f) *prablyéma*

product проду́кт (m) *pradóokt*

profession профе́ссия (f) *prafyéssiya*

professor профе́ссор (m) *prafyésar*

profit при́быль (f) *príbyl*

programme програ́мма (f) *pragráma*

prohibited запрещено́ *zaprischinó*

to promise обеща́ть/пообеща́ть *abischát/paabischát*

to pronounce произноси́ть/ произнести́ *praiznasít/praiznistí*

properly как сле́дует *kak slyédooit*

property со́бственность (f) *sópstvinost*

public *(adj.)* обще́ственный *apschéstvinny*
   » *(people)* пу́блика (f) *póoblika*

public holiday пра́здник (m) *práznik*

to pull тяну́ть/потяну́ть *tinóot/patinóot*

to pump up нака́чивать/накача́ть *nakáchivat/nakachát*

puncture проко́л (m) *prakól*

pure чи́стый *chísty*

purple фиоле́товый *fialyétavy*

purse *(for money)* кошелёк (m) *kashilyók*

» *(handbag)* су́мочка (f) *sóomachka*

to push толка́ть/толкну́ть *talkát/talknóot*

push-chair коля́ска (f) *kalyáska*

to put down опуска́ть/опусти́ть *apooskát/apoostít*

to put on надева́ть/наде́ть *nadivát/nadyét*

pyjamas пижа́ма (f) *pizháma*

Q

quality ка́чество (n) *káchistva*

quarter че́тверть (f) *chyétvirt*

question вопро́с (m) *vaprós*

queue о́чередь (f) *óchiryet*

quick(ly) бы́стрый (бы́стро) *býstry (býstra)*

quiet ти́хий *tíkhi*

quiet! ти́ше! *tíshe*

quite дово́льно *davólna*

R

rabbi равви́н (m) *ravín*

rabbit кро́лик (m) *królik*

rabies бе́шенство (n) *byéshinstva*

racecourse ипподро́м (m) *ipadróm*

racket *(tennis)* раке́тка (f) *rakyétka*

radiator *(in room)* батаре́я (f) *bataryéya*

radio ра́дио (n) *rádia*

radioactive радиоакти́вный *radiaaktívny*

radio station радиоста́нция (f) *radiastántsiya*

railway station железнодоро́жная ста́нция (f), вокза́л (m) *zhilizndarózhnaya stántsiya, vagzál*

rain дождь (m) *dosht*

» **it's raining** идёт дождь *idyót dosht*

to rape наси́ловать/изнаси́ловать *nasílavat/iznasílavat*

rare ре́дкий *ryétki*

» *(steak)* с кро́вью *s króv-yoo*

rash сыпь (f) *syp*

rate *(exchange)* курс (m) *koors*

raw сырой *syróï*

razor бри́тва (f) *brítva*

razor blade ле́звие (n) *lyézviye*

to reach достига́ть/дости́гнуть *dastigát/dastígnoot*

to read чита́ть/прочита́ть *chitát/prachitát*

reading чте́ние (n) *chtyéniye*

ready гото́вый *gatóvy*

real *(authentic)* настоя́щий *nastayáschi*

really действи́тельно *distvítilna*

receipt квита́нция (f) *kvitántsiya*

recipe реце́пт (m) *ritsépt*

to recognise узнава́ть/узна́ть *ooznavát/ooznát*

to recommend рекомендова́ть/ порекомендо́вать *rikamindavát/ parikamindavát*

record за́пись (f) *zápis*

to record запи́сывать/записа́ть *zapísyvat/zapisát*

to recover поправля́ться/попра́виться *papravlyátsa/paprávitsa*

red кра́сный *krásny*

» **Red Cross** Кра́сный Крест (m) *krásny kryest*

refugee бе́женец/бе́женка (m/f) *byézhinits/byézhinka*

region о́бласть (f) *óblast*

to register регистри́ровать/ зарегистри́ровать *rigistríravat/ zarigistríravat*

religion рели́гия (f) *rilígiya*

to remain остава́ться/оста́ться *astavátsa/astátsa*

to remember запомина́ть/запо́мнить *zapaminát/zapómnit*

to remove убира́ть/убра́ть *oobirát/oobrát*

to rent *(a flat)* снимáть/снять (квартúру) *snimát/snyat (kvartíroo)*

to repair ремонтúровать/ отремонтúровать *rimantíravat/ atrimantíravat*

to repeat повторя́ть/повторúть *paftaryát/paftarít*

report доклáд (m) *daklát*

to rescue спасáть/спастú *spasát/spastí*

to reserve заказывать/заказáть *zakázyvat/zakazát*

reserved закáзанный *zakázanny*

to rest отдыхáть/отдохнýть *addykhát/ addakhnóot*

restaurant рестóран (m) *ristarán*

restaurant-car вагóн-рестóран (m) *vagón-ristarán*

result результáт (m) *rizooltát*

retired на пéнсии *na pyénsii*

to return возвращéние (n) *vazvraschéniye*

» *(ticket)* обрáтный билéт (m) *abrátny bilyét*

to return возвращáть(ся)/вернýть(ся) *vazvraschát(sa)/virnóot(sa)*

reverse-charge call звонóк (m) за счёт вызывáемого абонéнта *zvanók za schot vyzyváimava abanyénta*

rich *(person)* богáтый *bagáty*

» *(food)* жúрный *zhírny*

to ride *(bike, horse)* éздить, éхать на *yézdit, yékhat na*

right прáвый *právy*

» *(correct)* прáвильный *právilny*

ring *(jewellery)* кольцó (n) *kaltsó*

ripe спéлый *spyély*

risk риск (m) *risk*

river рекá (f) *riká*

road дорóга (f) *daróga*

roadworks дорóжные рабóты (pl) *darózhnyye rabóty*

roast жаркóе (n) *zharkóye*

to rob грáбить/огрáбить *grábit/agrábit*

robbery ограблéние (n) *agrablyéniye*

rock climbing скалолáзание (n) *skalalázaniye*

roof крыша (f) *krýsha*

roll *(bread)* бýлочка (f) *bóolachka*

room кóмната (f) *kómnata*

room service обслýживание (n) в нóмере *apslóozhivaniye v nómirye*

rope верёвка (f) *viryófka*

rose рóза (f) *róza*

rotten гнилóй *gnilói*

rouble рубль (m) *roobl*

rough *(sea)* бýрный, неспокóйный *bóorny, nispakóiny*

» *(surface)* нерóвный *niróvny*

round крýглый *króogly*

row *(theatre etc.)* ряд (m) *ryat*

to row грестú *gristí*

royal королéвский *karalyéfski*

rubbish *(nonsense)* чепухá (f) *chipookhá*

» *(poor quality)* барахлó (n) *barakhló*

» *(waste)* мýсор (m) *móosar*

rucksack рюкзáк (m) *ryookzák*

rude грýбый *gróoby*

ruins развáлины (pl) *razváliny*

ruler *(for measuring)* линéйка (f) *linyéika*

to run бежáть, бéгать *bizhát, byégat*

rush hour час-пик (m) *chas-pik*

Russia Россúя (f) *rasíya*

Russian *(adj.)* рýсский *róoski*

» *(people)* рýсский/рýсская (m/f) *róoski/róoskaya*

rusty ржáвый *rzhávy*

S

sad грýстный *gróosny*

safe *(strongbox)* сейф (m) *syeif*

safe безопáсный *bizapásny*

safety belt ремéнь (m) безопáсности *rimén bizapásnasti*

safety pin англúйская булáвка (f) *anglíiskaya boolófka*

sail пáрус (m) *pároos*

sailing па́русный спорт (m) *pároosny sport*

sailor моря́к (m) *maryák*

saint свято́й *svitói*

salad сала́т (m) *salát*

sale *(bargains)* распрода́жа (f) *raspradázha*

salt соль (f) *sol*

salty солёный *salyóny*

same: the same то же са́мое *tó zhe sámoye*

sample образе́ц (m) *abrazyéts*

sand песо́к (m) *pisók*

sandals санда́лии (pl) *sandálii*

sandwich бутербро́д (m) *bootirbrót*

sanitary towels гигиени́ческие прокла́дки (pl) *gigiyiníchiskiye praklátki*

satisfied дово́льный *davólny*

sauce со́ус (m) *só oos*

saucepan кастрю́ля (f) *kastryóolya*

sauna са́уна (f) *sáoona*

to say говори́ть/сказа́ть *gavarít/skazát*

to scald ошпа́ривать/ошпа́рить *ashpárivat/ashpárit*

scales весы́ (pl) *visý*

scarf шарф (m) *sharf*

school шко́ла (f) *shkóla*

science нау́ка (f) *naóoka*

scissors но́жницы (pl) *nózhnitsy*

score: what's the score? счёт (m): како́й счёт? *schot: kakói schot*

Scotland Шотла́ндия (f) *shatlándiya*

Scottish *(adj.)* шотла́ндский *shatlánski*

» *(people)* шотла́ндец/шотла́ндка (m/f) *shatlándits/shatlánka*

screw винт (m), шуру́п (m) *vint, shooróop*

sculpture скульпту́ра (f) *skoolptóora*

sea мо́ре (n) *mórye*

seafood морепроду́кты (pl) *móripradóokty*

seasick: I am seasick меня́ ука́чивает *minyá ookáchivait*

season сезо́н (m) *sizón*

seat ме́сто (n) *myésta*

seatbelt (привязно́й) реме́нь (m) *(priviznói) rimyén*

secret секре́т (m) *sikryét*

secretary секрета́рь (m) *sikritár*

to see ви́деть/уви́деть *vídyet/oovídyet*

to seem каза́ться/показа́ться *kazátsa/pakazátsa*

self-service/self-catering самообслу́живание (n) *samaapslóozhivaniye*

to sell продава́ть/прода́ть *pradavát/pradát*

to send посыла́ть/посла́ть *pasylát/paslát*

senior citizen пенсионе́р/ка (m/f) *pinsianyér/ka*

sensible (благо)разу́мный *(blaga)razóomny*

sentence предложе́ние (n) *pridlazhéniye*

separate отде́льный *addyélny*

separated: we are separated мы разошли́сь *my razashlís*

serious серьёзный *siryózny*

to serve обслу́живать/обслужи́ть *apslóozhivat/apsloozhít*

service charge пла́та (f) за обслу́живание *plata za apslóozhivaniye*

several не́сколько *nyéskalka*

to sew шить/сшить *shit/s-shit*

sewing шитьё (n) *shit-yó*

sex *(gender)* пол (m) *pol*

» *(intercourse)* секс (m) *seks*

shade: in the shade в тени́ *f tíni*

shadow тень (f) *tyen*

shampoo шампу́нь (m) *shampóon*

sharp о́стрый *óstry*

shave бритьё (n) *brit-yó*

to shave бри́ться *brítsa/pabrítsa*

shaving cream/foam крем (m)/ пе́на (f) для бритья́ *kryem/pyéna dlya brit-yá*

shaving point розе́тка (f) для электробри́твы *razétka dlya elyektrabrítvy*

she она́ *aná*

sheep овца́ (f) *aftsá*

sheet *(for bed)* простыня́ (f) *prastynyá*

» *(paper)* лист (m) *list*

shelf по́лка (f) *pólka*

shell *(egg, nut)* скорлупа́ (f) *skarloopá*

shelter укры́тие (n) *ookrýtiye*

shiny блестя́щий *blistyáschi*

ship кора́бль (m) *karábl*

shirt руба́шка (f) *roobáshka*

shock: I got an electric shock меня́ уда́рило то́ком *minyá oodárila tókam*

shock *(emotional)* шок (m) *shok*

shocked в шо́ке *f shókye*

shoe(s) ту́фель (m), ту́фли (pl) *tóofil, tóofli*

shoelaces шнурки́ (pl) *shnoorkí*

shoe repairer's ремо́нт (m) о́буви *rimónt óboovi*

shoe shop обувно́й магази́н (m) *aboovnói magazín*

shoe size разме́р (m) о́буви *razmyér óboovi*

shop магази́н (m) *magazín*

shop assistant продаве́ц (m) *pradavyéts*

shopping: to go shopping де́лать/сде́лать поку́пки *dyélat/zdyélat pakóopki*

shopping centre торго́вый центр (m) *targóvy tsentr*

short коро́ткий *karótki*

» *(of posture)* невысо́кого ро́ста *nivysókava rósta*

shorts шо́рты (pl) *shórty*

shout крик (m) *krik*

show шо́у (n), представле́ние (n) *shó oo, pritstavlyéniye*

to show пока́зывать/показа́ть *pakázyvat/pakazát*

shower душ (m) *doosh*

to shower принима́ть/приня́ть душ *prinimát/prinyát doosh*

to shrink: the sweater has shrunk сади́ться/сесть: сви́тер сел *sadítsa/syest: svíter syel*

shut закры́тый *zakrýty*

shutter *(camera)* затво́р (m) *zatvór*

sick больно́й *balnói*

» **to feel sick: I feel sick** меня́ тошни́т *minyá tashnít*

» **I was sick** меня́ вы́рвало *minyá výrvala*

side сторона́ (f) *staraná*

sieve си́то (n) *síta*

sight *(vision)* зре́ние (n) *zryéniye*

» **long-sighted** дальнозо́ркий *dalnazórki*

» **short-sighted** близору́кий *blizaróoki*

» *(tourist)* вид (m) *vit*

sightseeing осмо́тр (m) достопримеча́тельностей *asmótr dastaprimichátilnastyeĭ*

sign знак (m) *znak*

to sign подпи́сывать/подписа́ть *patpísyvat/patpisát*

signal сигна́л (m) *signál*

signature по́дпись (f) *pótpis*

silent ти́хий *tíkhi*

silk шёлк (m) *sholk*

» *(adj.)* шёлковый *shólkavy*

silver серебро́ (n) *siribró*

SIM card сим-ка́рта (f) *sim-karta*

similar похо́жий *pakhózhi*

simple просто́й *prastóĭ*

since с, с тех пор *s, s tyekh por*

» **since Monday** с понеде́льника *s panidyélnika*

to sing петь/спеть *pyet/spyet*

single *(room)* одноме́стный но́мер (m) *adnamyésny nómir*

» *(ticket)* биле́т (m) в оди́н коне́ц *bilyét v adín kanyéts*

» *(unmarried)* нежена́тый/не за́мужем (m/f) *nizhináty/ni zámoozhim*

sink ра́ковина (f) *rákavina*

sister сестра́ (f) *sistrá*

sister-in-law *(brother's wife)* неве́стка (f) *nivyéstka*

» *(husband's sister)* золо́вка (f) *zalófka*

» *(wife's sister)* своя́чница (f) *svayáchnitsa*

to sit *(down)* сади́ться/сесть *sadítsa/syest*

size разме́р (m) *razmyér*

skates *(ice)* конькй (pl) *kankí*

» *(roller)* ро́ликовые конькй (pl) *rólikavye kankí*

to skate ката́ться на конька́х *katátsa na kankákh*

ski лы́жи (pl) *lýzhi*

to ski ката́ться на лы́жах *katátsa na lýzhakh*

ski boots лы́жные боти́нки (pl) *lýzhnyye batínki*

skiing лы́жный спорт (m) *lýzhny sport*

» **cross-country skiing** ходьба́/бег (f/m) на лы́жах *khadbá/byek na lýzhakh*

» **downhill skiing** го́рные лы́жи (pl) *górnyye lýzhi*

ski-lift подъёмник (m) *pad-yómnik*

ski pole лы́жная па́лка (f) *lýzhnaya pálka*

ski-run лыжня́ (f) *lyzhná*

skimmed milk обезжи́ренное молоко́ (n) *abizhírinaye malakó*

skin ко́жа (f) *kózha*

skirt ю́бка (f) *yóopka*

sky не́бо (n) *nyéba*

to sleep спать *spat*

sleeper/sleeping-car спа́льный ваго́н (m) *spálny vagón*

sleeping bag спа́льный мешо́к (m) *spálny mishók*

sleeve рука́в (m) *rookáf*

slice кусо́к (m) *koosók*

sliced поре́занный *paryézanny*

slim то́нкий *tónki*

slippery ско́льзкий *skólski*

slow(ly) ме́дленный (ме́дленно) *myédlinny (myédlinna)*

small ма́ленький *mályenki*

smell за́пах (m) *zápakh*

to smell ню́хать/поню́хать *nyóokhat/ panyóokhat*

to smell of: па́хнуть *pákhnoot*

» **it smells of gas** па́хнет га́зом *pákhnit gázam*

smile улы́бка (f) *oolýpka*

to smile улыба́ться/улыбну́ться *oolybátsa/oolybnóotsa*

smoke дым (m) *dym*

to smoke кури́ть *koorít*

» **I don't smoke** я не курю́ *ya ni kooryóo*

smooth гла́дкий *glátki*

to sneeze чиха́ть/чихну́ть *chikhát/ chikhnóot*

snow снег (m) *snyek*

to snow: it's snowing идёт снег *idyót snyek*

snow chains цепь (m) (противоскольже́ния) *tsep (prativaskalzhéniya)*

snowfall снегопа́д (m) *snigapát*

snowflake снежи́нка (f) *snizhínka*

snowman снегови́к (m) *snigavík*

snowplough снегоочисти́тель (m) *snyégaachistítil*

snowstorm мете́ль (f) *mityél*

so так *tak*

» *(therefore)* поэ́тому *paétamoo*

soap мы́ло (n) *mýla*

sober тре́звый *tryézvy*

socialism социали́зм (m) *satsializm*

socialist *(adj.)* социалисти́ческий *satsialistíchiski*

sock носо́к (m), носки́ (pl) *nasók, naskí*

socket розе́тка (f) *razyétka*

soft мя́гкий *myákhki*

soft drink безалкого́льный напи́ток (m) *bizalkagólny napítak*

software програ́ммное обеспече́ние (n) *pragrámnaye abispichéniye*

soldier солда́т (m) *saldát*

sold out про́дано *pródana*

solicitor адвока́т (m) *advakát*

solid твёрдый *tvyórdy*

some не́который *nyékatary*

somehow ка́к-то, ка́к-нибудь *kák-ta, kák-niboot*

someone кто́-то *któ-ta*

something что́-нибудь *shtó-niboot*

sometimes иногда́ *inagdá*

somewhere где́-то, где́-нибудь *gdyé-ta, gdyé-niboot*

son сын (m), сыновья́ (pl) *syn, synav-yá*

song пе́сня (f) *pyésnya*

son-in-law зять (m) *zyat*

soon ско́ро *skóra*

» **as soon as possible** как мо́жно скоре́е *kak mózhna skaryéye*

sore: it's sore боли́т *balít*

sorry: I'm sorry прости́те *prastítye*

sort сорт (m) *sort*

sound звук (m) *zvook*

sour ки́слый *kísly*

south юг (m) *yook*

» **(adj.)** ю́жный *yóozhny*

souvenir сувени́р (m) *soovinír*

space простра́нство (n) *prastránstva*

spare запасно́й *zapasnóї*

to **speak** говори́ть/сказа́ть *gavarít/skazát*

special специа́льный *spitsiálny*

specialist специали́ст (m) *spitsialíst*

speciality осо́бенность (f) *asóbinast*

spectacles очки́ (pl) *achkí*

speed ско́рость (f) *skórast*

speed limit ограниче́ние (f) ско́рости *agranichéniye skórasti*

spell: how do you spell it? Как э́то пи́шется по бу́квам? *kak éta píshetsa pa boókvam*

to **spend** (money) тра́тить/потра́тить *trátit/patrátit*

» **(time)** проводи́ть/провести́ *pravadít/pravistí*

spice спе́ция (f) *spétsiya*

spicy о́стрый *óstry*

splinter зано́за (f) *zanóza*

to **spoil** по́ртить/испо́ртить *pórtit/ispórtit*

spoon ло́жка (f) *lóshka*

sport спорт (m) *sport*

spot пятно́ (n) *pitnó*

» **(place): on the spot** ме́сто (n): на ме́сте *myésta: na myéstye*

to **sprain** растя́гивать/растяну́ть *rastyágivat/rastinóot*

spray спрей (m) *spreï*

square пло́щадь (f) *plóschat*

» **(shape)** квадра́т (m) *kvadrát*

stadium стадио́н (m) *stadión*

stain пятно́ (n) *pitnó*

stainless steel нержаве́ющая сталь (f) *nirzhavyéyooschiya stal*

stairs ле́стница (f) *lyésnitsa*

stalls (theatre) парте́р (m) *partér*

stamp (postage) ма́рка (f) *márka*

stand (stadium) трибу́на (f) *tribóona*

to **stand** стоя́ть *stayát*

to **stand up** встава́ть/встать *fstavát/fstat*

stapler сте́плер (m) *stéplir*

star звезда́ (f) *zvizdá*

start нача́ло (n), старт (m) *nachála, start*

to **start** начина́ть/нача́ть *nachinát/nachát*

starter (food) заку́ска (f) *zakóoska*

station ста́нция (f) *stántsiya*

statue ста́туя (f) *státooya*

to stay (live) остана́вливаться/
остановиться *astanávlivatsa/
astanavítsa*
» (remain) остава́ться/оста́ться
astavátsa/astátsa

to steal красть/укра́сть *krast/ookrást*

steam пар (m) *par*

steel сталь (f) *stal*

steep круто́й *krootóï*

step (footstep) шаг (m) *shak*
» (stairs) ступе́нь(ка) (f)
stoopyén(ka)

step-brother сво́дный брат (m)
svódny brat

step-children сво́дные де́ти (pl)
svódnyye dyéti

step-father о́тчим (m) *ótchim*

step-mother ма́чеха (f) *máchikha*

step-sister сво́дная сестра́ (f)
svódnaya sistrá

sterling: pound sterling сте́рлинг
(m): фунт сте́рлингов *styérlink:
foont styérlingaf*

stick па́лка (f) *pálka*

to stick: it's stuck застря́ло *zastryála*

sticky ли́пкий *lípki*

stiff жёсткий *zhóski*

still (yet) ещё *yischó*
» (non-fizzy) без га́за *biz gáza*
» **Keep still!** Не дви́гайтесь! *ni
dvígaïtyes*

sting жа́ло (n) *zhála*

stock exchange би́ржа (f) *bírzha*

stockings чулки́ (pl) *choolkí*

stomach ache: I have stomach ache
у меня́ боли́т живо́т *oo minyá
balít zhivót*

stomach upset расстро́йство (n)
желу́дка *rasstróïstva zhilóotka*

stone ка́мень (m) *kámin*

stop (bus) остано́вка (f) *astanófka*

to stop остана́вливаться/
остановиться *astanávlivatsa/
astanavítsa*
» **stop!** стоп! *stop*

story исто́рия (f) *istóriya*

stove плита́ (f) *plitá*

straight прямо́й *primóï*

straight on пря́мо *pryáma*

strange стра́нный *stránny*

stranger (m/f) незнако́мец/
незнако́мка (m/f) *niznakómits/
niznakómka*

strap реме́нь (m) *rimyén*

straw (drinking) соло́минка (f)
salóminka

street у́лица (f) *óolitsa*

stretcher носи́лки (pl) *nasílki*

strike забасто́вка (f) *zabastófka*
» **on strike** бастова́ть *bastavát*

string верёвка (f) *viryófka*

stripe полоса́ (f) *palasá*
» **striped** в поло́ску, полоса́тый
f palóskoo, palasáty

strong си́льный *sílny*

student (m/f) студе́нт/ка (m/f)
stoodyént/ka

to study учи́ться *oochítsa*

stupid глу́пый *glóopy*

style стиль (m) *stil*

subtitles субти́тры (pl) *sooptítry*

suburb при́город (m) *prígarat*

to succeed добива́ться/доби́ться
успе́ха *dabivátsa/dabítsa
oospyékha*

success успе́х (m) *oospyékh*

such тако́й *takóï*

suddenly вдруг *vdrook*

sugar са́хар (m) *sákhar*

suit (man's) костю́м (m) *kastyóom*

suitcase чемода́н (m) *chimadán*

sun со́лнце (n) *sóntse*

to sunbathe загора́ть/загоре́ть
zagarát/zagaryét

sunburn со́лнечный ожо́г (m)
sólnichny azhók

sunglasses очки́ (pl) от со́лнца *achkí
at sóntsa*

sunny со́лнечный *sólnichny*

sunshade зо́нтик (m) от со́лнца *zóntik at sóntsa*

sunstroke со́лнечный уда́р (m) *sólnichny oodár*

suntan зага́р (m) *zagár*

suntan lotion крем (m) для зага́ра *kryem dlya zagára*

supermarket суперма́ркет (m) *soopirmárkit*

supper у́жин (m) *óozhin*

supplement надба́вка (f), допла́та (f) *nadbáfka, dapláta*

to support подде́рживать/ поддержа́ть *paddyérzhivat/ paddirzhát*
» *(sport)* боле́ть за *balyét za*

suppose: I suppose so/not наве́рное/наве́рное, нет *navyérnaye/navyérnaye nyet*

suppository суппозито́рий (m), све́чка (f) *soopazitóri, svyéchka*

to surf *(internet)* ла́зить/пола́зить в интерне́те *lázit/palázit v internétye*

surface пове́рхность (f) *pavyérkhnast*

surname фами́лия (f) *famíliya*

surprise сюрпри́з (m) *syoorprís*

surprised удивлённый *oodivlyónny*

surrounded by окружённый *akroozhónny*

to sweat поте́ть/вспоте́ть *patyét/ fspatyét*

sweater сви́тер (m) *svíter*

sweet сла́дкий *slátki*

sweetener замени́тель (m) са́хара *zaminítil sákhara*

sweets конфе́ты (pl) *kanfyéty*

swelling о́пухоль (f) *ópookhal*

to swim пла́вать *plávat*

swimming пла́вание (n) *plávaniye*

swimming pool бассе́йн (m) *bassyéin*

swimming trunks/swimsuit пла́вки (pl)/купа́льник (m) *pláfki/ koopálnik*

switch выключа́тель (m) *vyklyoochátil*

to switch off выключа́ть/вы́ключить *vyklyoochát/výklyoochit*

to switch on включа́ть/включи́ть *fklyoochát/fklyoochít*

swollen опу́хший *apóokhshi*

symptom симпто́м (m) *simptóm*

synagogue синаго́га (f) *sinagóga*

synthetic синтети́ческий *sintetíchiski*

system систе́ма (f) *sistyéma*

T

table стол (m) *stol*
» *(restaurant)* сто́лик (m) *stólik*

to take брать/взять *brat/vzyat*

to take a photo фотографи́ровать/ сфотографи́ровать *fatagrafíravat/ sfatagrafíravat*

to take time дли́ться/продли́ться *dlítsa/pradlítsa*

taken *(seat)* за́нято *zánita*

to take off *(clothes)* снима́ть/снять *snimát/snyat*
» *(plane)* взлета́ть/взлете́ть *vzlitát/ vzlitét*

talcum powder тальк (m) *talk*

to talk разгова́ривать *razgavárivat*

tall высо́кий *vysóki*

tampon тампо́н (m) *tampón*

tap кран (m) *kran*

tape *(adhesive)* ли́пкая ле́нта (f) *lípkaya lyénta*
» *(cassette)* плёнка (f), за́пись (f) *plyónka, zápis*

tape measure сантиме́тр (m) *santimyétr*

taste вкус (m) *fkoos*

to taste: can I taste it? мо́жно попро́бовать? *mózhna papróbavat*

tax нало́г (m) *nalók*

taxi такси́ (n) *taksí*

taxi rank стоя́нка (f) такси́ *stayánka taksí*

tea чай (m) *chái*

teabag чáйный пакéтик (m) *cháiny pakyétik*

to teach учи́ть/научи́ть *oochít/ naoochít*

teacher учи́тель (m) *oochítil*

team кома́нда (f) *kamánda*

teapot ча́йник (m) *cháinik*

tear *(rip)* дыра́ (f) *dyrá*

tear *(cry)* слеза́ (f), слёзы (pl) *slizá, slyózy*

» **in tears** в слеза́х *f slizákh*

teaspoon ча́йная ло́жка (f) *cháinaya lóshka*

teat *(for baby's bottle)* со́ска (f) *sóska*

tea-towel ку́хонное полоте́нце (n) *kóokhannaye palatyéntse*

technical техни́ческий *tikhnichiski*

technology техноло́гия (f) *tikhnalógiya*

teenager подро́сток (m), подро́стки (pl) *padróstak, padróstki*

telephone телефо́н (m) *tilifón*

to telephone звони́ть/позвони́ть *zvanít/pazvanít*

telephone box телефо́нная бу́дка (f) *tilifónnaya bóotka*

telephone card телефо́нная ка́рточка (f) *tilifónnaya kártachka*

telephone directory телефо́нный спра́вочник (m) *tilifónny správachnik*

television телеви́дение (n) *tilivídiniye*

to tell расска́зывать/рассказа́ть *rasskázyvat/rasskazát*

temperature температу́ра (f) *timpiratóora*

» **I have a temperature** у меня́ температу́ра *oo minyá timpiratóora*

temporary вре́менный *vryéminny*

tender не́жный *nyézhny*

tennis те́ннис (m) *ténis*

tennis court те́ннисный корт (m) *ténisny kort*

tent пала́тка (f) *palátka*

» **tent peg** ко́лышек (m) *kólyshik*

» **tent pole** шест (m) для пала́тки *shest dlya palátki*

terminal *(airport)* термина́л (m) *tirminál*

terminus коне́чный пункт (m) *kanyéchny poonkt*

terrace терра́са (f) *tirása*

terrible ужа́сный *oozhásny*

terrorist террори́ст (m) *tiraríst*

to text посыла́ть/посла́ть SMS *pasylát/ paslát es em és*

text message SMS, SMS-ка (f, *coll.*) *es em és, es em éska*

than чем *chem*

thank you *(very much)* спаси́бо (большо́е) *spasíba (balshóye)*

that *(one)* тот *tot*

theatre теа́тр (m) *tiátr*

their, theirs их *ikh*

them их, им *ikh, im*

then: if.... then е́сли ..., то... *yésli...to*

» *(later)* пото́м *patóm*

there там *tam*

there is/are э́то...; вот... *éta... vot...*

these э́ти *éti*

they они́ *aní*

thick то́лстый *tólsty*

thief вор (m) *vor*

thin то́нкий *tónki*

thing вещь (f) *vyesch*

to think ду́мать/поду́мать *dóomat/ padóomat*

thirsty: to be thirsty хоте́ть/ захоте́ть пить *khatyét/zakhatyét pit*

this *(one)* э́тот *état*

those те *tye*

thread нить (f) *nit*

through че́рез *chyéris*

to throw броса́ть/бро́сить *brasát/brósit*

to throw away выбра́сывать/ вы́бросить *vybrásyvat/výbrasit*

thunder гром (m) *grom*

ticket билет (m) *bilyét*

ticket office билетная касса (f) *bilyétnaya kássa*

tide *(high/low)* прилив (m)/отлив (m) *prilif/atlif*

tidy опрятный *apryátny*

tie галстук (m) *gálstook*

tight *(clothes)* тесный *tyésny*

tights колготки (pl) *kalgótki*

till *(cashier)* касса (f) *kássa*

time время (n) *vryémya*

» *(once etc.)* раз (m) *ras*

timetable *(train)* расписание (n) *raspisániye*

tin консервная банка (f) *kansyérvnaya bánka*

tin foil фольга (f) *falgá*

tin opener консервный нож (m) *kansyérvny nosh*

tip *(in restaurant)* чаевые (pl) *chiyivýye*

tired усталый *oostály*

tissues бумажные носовые платки (pl) *boomázhnyye nasavýye platki*

toast *(drinking)* тост (m) *tost*

tobacco табак (m) *tabák*

tobacconist's табачная лавка (f) *tabáchnaya láfka*

toboggan сани (pl) *sáni*

today сегодня *sivódnya*

toilet paper туалетная бумага (f) *tooalyétnaya boomága*

toiletries туалетные принадлежности (pl) *tooalyétnyye prinadlyézhnasti*

toilets туалет (m) *tooalyét*

toll пошлина (f) *póshlina*

tomorrow завтра *záftra*

tonight сегодня вечером *sivódnya vyéchirom*

too тоже *tózhe*

» *(as well)* также *tákzhe*

tool инструмент (m) *instroomyént*

toothache зубная боль (f) *zoobnáya bol*

toothbrush зубная щётка (f) *zoobnáya schótka*

toothpaste зубная паста (f) *zoobnáya pásta*

toothpick зубочистка (f) *zoobachístka*

top *(mountain)* вершина (f) *virshína*

» **on top of** наверху *navirkhoó*

top floor верхний этаж *vérkhni etázh*

torch фонарь (m) *fanár*

torn порванный *pórvanny*

total итого, всего *itavó, fsivó*

totally совершенно *savirshénna*

to touch трогать/тронуть *trógat/trónoot*

tough *(meat)* жёсткий *zhóski*

tour экскурсия (f) *ekskóorsiya*

tour guide (m/f) экскурсовод (m) *ekskoorsavót*

to tour совершать/совершить экскурсию *savirshát/savirshít ekskóoriyoo*

tourism туризм (m) *toorízm*

tourist турист (m) *tooríst*

tourist office турагенство (n) *tooragyénstva*

towards к *k*

towel полотенце (n) *palatyéntse*

tower башня (f) *báshnya*

town город (m) *górat*

town centre центр (m) города *tsentr górada*

town hall мэрия (f), ратуша (f) *mériya, rátoosha*

toy игрушка (f) *igróoshka*

tracksuit спортивный костюм (m) *spartívny kastyúom*

trade union профсоюз (m) *prafsayóos*

traditional традиционный *traditsiónny*

traffic движение (n) *dvizhéniye*

traffic jam пробка (f) *própka*

traffic light светофор (m) *svitafór*

train поезд (m) *póist*

» **by train** по́ездом *póizdam*

trainers кроссо́вки (pl) *krasófki*

tram трамва́й (m) *tramváï*

tranquilliser транквилиза́тор (m) *trankvilizátar*

to **translate** переводи́ть/перевести́ *pirivadít/pirivistí*

translation перево́д (m) *pirivót*

to **travel** путеше́ствовать *pootishéstvavat*

travel agency бюро́ (n) путеше́ствий *byooró pootishéstvi*

traveller's cheque доро́жный/ тури́стский чек (m) *darózhny/ tooríssti chek*

travel sickness: he/she suffers from travel sickness его́/её́ ука́чивает *yivó/yiyó ookáchivayet*

tray подно́с (m) *padnós*

treatment лече́ние (n) *lichéniye*

tree де́рево (n), дере́вья (pl) *dyériva, diryév-ya*

trip пое́здка (f) *payéstka*

trolley-bus тролле́йбус (m) *tralyéboos*

trousers брюки (pl) *bryóoki*

true ве́рно *vyérna*

» **that's true** э́то пра́вда *éta právda*

to **try** про́бовать/попро́бовать *próbavat/paróbavat*

to **try on** примеря́ть/приме́рить *primiryát/primyérit*

T-shirt футбо́лка (f), ма́йка (f) *footbólka, máïka*

tube *(pipe)* труба́ (f) *troobá*

» *(underground)* метро́ (n) *mitró*

tunnel тонне́ль (m) *tanél*

turn: it's my turn моя́ о́чередь *mayá óchiryet*

to **turn** повора́чивать/поверну́ть *pavaráchivat/pavirnóot*

to **turn off** закрыва́ть/закры́ть *zakryvát/zakrýt*

turning *(side road)* поворо́т (m) *pavarót*

twice два́жды *dvázhdy*

twin beds две односпа́льные крова́ти *dvyé adnaspálnyye kraváti*

twins близнецы́ (pl) *bliznitsý*

to **twist** *(ankle)* подвора́чивать/ подверну́ть *padvaráchivat/ padvirnóot*

type *(sort)* тип (m) *tip*

to **type** печа́тать/напеча́тать *pichátat/ napichátat*

typical типи́чный *tipíchny*

U

ugly некраси́вый *nikrasívy*

ulcer я́зва (f) *yázva*

umbrella зонт (m) *zont*

uncle дя́дя (m) *dyádya*

uncomfortable неудо́бный *nioodóbny*

under под *pod*

undergraduate *(student)* студе́нт/ка (m/f) *stoodyént/ka*

underpants трусы́ (pl) *troosý*

to **understand** понима́ть/поня́ть *panimát/panyát*

underwear ни́жнее бельё (n) *nízhniye bil-yó*

to **undress** раздева́ться/разде́ться *razdivátsa/razdyétsa*

unemployed безрабо́тный (m) *bizrabótny*

unfortunately к сожале́нию *k sazhilyéniyoo*

unhappy несча́стный *nischásny*

uniform *(clothing)* фо́рма (f) *fórma*

university университе́т (m) *oonivirsityét*

unleaded petrol неэтили́рованный бензи́н (m), бензи́н (m) без свинца́ *nietilíravanny binzín, binzín byes svintsá*

to **unpack** распако́вываться/ распакова́ться *raspakóvyvatsa/ raspakavátsa*

unpleasant неприя́тный *nipriyátny*

to unscrew отви́нчивать/отвинти́ть *atvínchivat/atvintít*

until до *do*

unusual необы́чный *niabýchny*

unwell нездоро́вый *nizdaróvy*

» **I feel unwell** мне не здоро́виться *mnye ni zdaróvitsa*

up вверх, наве́рх *vvyerkh, navyérkh*

uphill в го́ру *v góroo*

upper ве́рхний *vyérkhni*

upstairs наверху́, наве́рх *navirkhóo, navyérkh*

up-to-date совреме́нный *savrimyénny*

urgent сро́чный *sróchny*

urine моча́ (f) *machá*

us нас *nas*

USB lead ка́бель (m) USB *kábyel yoo es bi*

USB stick ка́рта (f) па́мяти USB флёшка (f, coll.) *kárta pámiti yoo es bi, fléshka*

to use употребля́ть/употреби́ть *oopatriblyát/oopatribít*

useful поле́зный *palyézny*

useless бесполе́зный *bispalyézny*

V

vacant *(unoccupied)* свобо́дный, неза́нятый *svabódny, nizánity*

vaccinate де́лать/сде́лать приви́вку *dyélat/zdyélat privífkoo*

vacuum cleaner пылесо́с (m) *pylisós*

valid действи́тельный *distvítilny*

valley доли́на (f) *dalína*

valuable це́нный *tsénny*

valuables це́нности (pl) *tsénnasti*

van (а́вто)фурго́н (m) *(áfta)foorgón*

vanilla вани́ль (f) *vanil*

vase ва́за (f) *váza*

VAT НДС (m) *en de es*

vegan стро́гий вегетариа́нец (m) *strógi vigitariánits*

vegetables о́вощи (pl) *óvaschi*

vegetarian *(adj.)* вегетариа́нский *vigitariánski*

» (m/f) вегетариа́нец/вегетариа́нка (m/f) *vigitariánits/vigitariánka*

vehicle тра́нспортное сре́дство (n) *tránspartnaye sryétstva*

very о́чень *óchen*

vest ма́йка (f) *máika*

vet ветерина́р (m) *vitirinár*

via че́рез *chyéris*

video ви́део (n) *vídia*

view вид (m) *vit*

village дере́вня (f) *diryévnya*

vinegar у́ксус (m) *óoksoos*

vineyard виногра́дник (m) *vinagrádnik*

virgin де́вственница/де́вственник (f/m) *dyéfstvinitsa/dyéfstvinik*

» **Virgin Mary** Де́ва Мари́я, Богоро́дица *dyéva maríya, bagaróditsa*

visa ви́за (f) *víza*

visit визи́т (m), посеще́ние (n) *vizít, pasischéniye*

to visit посеща́ть/посети́ть *pasischát/pasitít*

visitor гость (m), посети́тель (m) *gost, pasitítil*

vitamin витами́н (m) *vitamín*

voice го́лос (m) *gólas*

volleyball волейбо́л (m) *valiból*

voltage напряже́ние (n) *naprizhéniye*

to vomit: he vomited его́ вы́рвало/рвало́ *yivó výrvala/rvaló*

to vote голосова́ть/проголосова́ть *galasavát/pragalasavát*

W

wage зарпла́та (f) *zarpláta*

to wait *(for)* ждать *zhdat*

waiter/waitress официа́нт/ка (m/f) *afitsánt/ka*

waiting room *(at the doctor's)* приёмная (f) *priyómnaya*

» *(station)* зал ожида́ния *zal azhidániya*

wake-up call телефо́нный буди́льник *tilifónny boodílnik*

Wales Уэ́льс (m) *ooéls*

walk *(excursion)* прогу́лка (f) *pragóolka*

to walk, go for a walk ходи́ть пешко́м, гуля́ть *khadít pishkóm, goolyát*

wall стена́ (f) *stiná*

wallet бума́жник (m) *boomázhnik*

to want хоте́ть/захоте́ть *khatyét/ zakhatyét*

I (don't) want я (не) хочу́ *ya (ni) khachóo*

war война́ (f) *vaïná*

warm тёплый *tyóply*

to wash *(hands)* мыть/помы́ть, вы́мыть *myt/pamýt, výmyt*

» *(clothes)* стира́ть/постира́ть *stirát/pastirát*

washable мо́ющийся *móyooschïïsya*

wash-basin ра́ковина (f) *rákavina*

washing machine стира́льная маши́на (f) *stirálnaya mashína*

washing powder стира́льный порошо́к (m) *stirálny parashók*

washing-up liquid сре́дство (f) для мытья́ посу́ды *sryétstva dlya mytyá pasóody*

to wash-up мыть/вы́мыть посу́ду *myt/výmyt pasóodoo*

wastepaper basket корзи́на (f) для бума́ги *karzína dlya boomági*

watch *(clock)* часы́ (pl) *chisý*

to watch смотре́ть/посмотре́ть *smatryét/pasmatryét*

watch out! осторо́жно! *astarózhna*

water вода́ (f) *vadá*

water heater кипяти́льник (m) *kipitílnik*

waterfall водопа́д (m) *vadapát*

waterproof непромока́емый *nipramakáyimy*

wave волна́ (f) *valná*

wax воск (m) *vosk*

way *(path)* доро́га (f), путь (m) *daróga, poot*

» **this way** сюда́ *syoodá*

» **that way** туда́ *toodá*

we мы *my*

weather пого́да (f) *pagóda*

weather forecast прогно́з (m) пого́ды *prognós pagódy*

web *(internet)* интерне́т (m) *internét*

wedding сва́дьба (f) *svádba*

wedding ring обруча́льное кольцо́ (n) *abroochálnaye kaltsó*

week неде́ля (f) *nidyélya*

weekday бу́дний/рабо́чий день (m) *bóodni/rabóchi dyen*

weekend выходны́е (pl) *vykhadnýye*

weekly еженеде́льно *yezhinidyélna*

to weigh взве́шивать/взве́сить *vzvyéshivat/vzvyésit*

weight вес (m) *vyes*

well *(good)* хорошо́ *kharashó*

» *(oil)* нефтяна́я сква́жина (f) *niftináya skvázhina*

well-done *(meat)* хорошо́ прожа́ренный *kharashó prazhárinny*

well done! молоде́ц! *maladyéts*

Welsh *(adj.)* валли́йский, уэ́льский *valíski, ooélski*

» *(people)* валли́ец/валли́йка (m/f) *valíyits/valíïka*

west за́пад (m) *západ*

western *(adj.)* за́падный *západny*

» *(film)* ве́стерн (m) *vyéstern*

wet мо́крый *mókry*

wetsuit гидрокостю́м (m) *gidrakastyóom*

what? что? *shto*

what's that? что э́то? *shto eta*

wheel колесо́ (n), колёса (pl) *kalisó, kalyósa*

wheelchair кре́сло-коля́ска (n) *kryésla-kalyáska*

when когда́ *kagdá*

when? когда? *kagdá*

where где *gdye*

where? где? *gdye*

which который (m), которая (f), которое (n), которые (pl) *katóry, katóraya, katóraye, katóryye*

which? который (m), которая (f), которое (n), которые (pl) *katóry, katóraya, katóraye, katóryye*

while пока; в то время, как *paká; f to vryémya, kak*

white белый *byély*

white coffee кофе (m) с молоком *kófye s malakóm*

who кто *kto*

who? кто? *kto*

whole целый, весь *tsely, vyes*

why? почему? *pachimóo*
» *(what for)* зачем? *zachém*

wide широкий *shiróki*

widow вдова (f) *vdavá*

widower вдовец (m) *vdavyéts*

wife жена (f), жёны (pl) *zhiná, zhóny*

wild дикий *díki*

to win выигрывать/выиграть *výigryvat/výigrat*
» **who won?** кто выиграл? *kto výigral*

wind ветер (m) *vyétir*
» **windy: it's windy** ветрено *vyétrina*

window окно (n) *aknó*

window *(shop)* витрина (f) *vitrína*

windsurfing виндсёрфинг (m) *vint-syérfink*

wine вино (n) *vinó*
» **wine tasting** дегустация (f) вин *digoostátsiya vin*

wing крыло (n), крылья (pl) *kryló, krýl-ya*

wireless беспроводной *bispravadnóï*

with с *s*

without без *byes*

woman женщина (f) *zhénchsina*

wonderful чудесный *choodyésny*

wood *(adj.)* деревянный *dirivyánny*

wool шерсть (f) *sherst*

word слово (n), слова (pl) *slóva, slavá*

work работа (f) *rabóta*

to work *(job, function)* работать *rabótat*

world (noun) мир (m) *mir*
» *(adj.)* мировой *miravóï*
» **World War One** первая мировая война (f) *pyérvaya miraváya vaïná*
» **World War Two** вторая мировая война (f) *ftaraya miraváya vaïná*

worry: don't worry не беспокойтесь *ni bispakóïtis*

worse худший, хуже *khóotshi, khóozhe*

worth: it's worth это стоит *éta stóit*
» **it's not worth it** это не стоит того *éta ni stóit tavó*

wound рана (f) *rána*

to wrap заворачивать/завернуть *zavaráchivat/zavirnóot*
» **could you wrap it?** заверните, пожалуйста *zavirnítye, pazhálsta*

to write писать/написать *pisát/napisát*
» **could you write it down** напишите, пожалуйста *napishítye, pazhálsta*

writer писатель (m) *pisátil*

writing pad блокнот (m) *blaknót*

writing paper писчая бумага (f) *píschaya boomága*

wrong неправильный, ошибочный *niprávilny, ashibáchny*
» **what's wrong?** в чём дело? *f chom dyéla*

X

X-ray рентген (m) *rintgyén*

Y

yacht яхта (f) *yákhta*

to yawn зевать/зевнуть *zivát/zivnóot*

year год (m), лет (pl) *got, lyet*

» **leap year** високо́сный год
  visakósny got
yellow жёлтый *zhólty*
yes да *da*
yesterday вчера́ *fchirá*
yet ещё *yischó*
yoghurt йо́гурт (m) *yógoort*
you *(informal)* ты *ty*
  (pl *and formal* s) вы/Вы *vy*
young молодо́й *maladóï*
your *(informal)* твой *tvoï*
  (plural and formal singular) ваш/
  Ваш *vash*
youth молодёжь (f) *maladyósh*
youth hostel молодёжное
  общежи́тие (n) *maladyózhnaye*
  apschizhitiye

Z

zero нуль (m) *nool*
» **below zero** ни́же нуля́ *nízhe noolyá*
zip мо́лния (f) *mólniya*
zoo зоопа́рк (m) *zaapárk*

Russian – English Dictionary

А

a *a* while, and, but

аварийная служба (f) *avaríinaya slóozhba* breakdown service

авария (f) *aváriya* accident, emergency

ávia(почта) (f) *ávia(póchta)* air mail

австралиец/австралийка (m/f) *afstralíyits/afstralíka* Australian (people)

австралийский *afstralíski* Australian (adj.)

автобус (m) *aftóboos* bus, coach
» автобусом *aftóboosam* by bus

автобусная станция (f) *aftóboosnaya stántsiya* bus station

автовокзал (m) *aftavagzál* bus station

автоматический *aftamatíchiski* automatic

автомобиль (m) *aftamabíl* car

автоответчик (m) *aftaatvyéchik* answering machine

áвтор (m) *áftar* author

автосервис (m) *aftarsyérvis* garage (for repairs)

автостоп (m) *aftastóp* hitchhiking

адаптер (m) *adápter* adaptor

адвокат (m) *advakát* solicitor

áдрес (m) *ádris* address
» áдрес для пересылки почты *ádris dlya pirisýlki póchty* forwarding address

азáртные игры (pl) *azártnyye ígry* gambling

алкоголик (m) *alkagólik* alcoholic (person)

алкоголь (m) *alkagól* alcohol

аллергический *alirgíchiski* allergic

алмáз (m) *almás* diamond

американец/американка (m/f) *amirikánits/amirikánka* American (people)

американский *amirikánski* American (adj.)

английский *anglíski* English (adj.)

англичанин/англичанка (m/f) *anglichánin/anglichánka* English (people)

Ánглия (f) *ángliya* England

антибиотик (m) *antibiótik* antibiotics

антракт (m) *antrákt* interval (theatre)

аптéкарь (m) *aptyékar* pharmacist

аптéчка (f) *aptyéchka* first aid kit

арéнда (f) *aryénda* hire
» арéнда автомобилей *aryénda aftamabílyeï* car hire

арéст (m): под арéстом *pad aryéstam* arrest: under arrest

ármия (f) *ármiya* army

аромáт (m) *aramát* scent

архитéктор (m) *arkhityéktar* architect

аэрозоль (m) от мух *aerazól at mookh* fly spray

аэропóрт (m) *aerapórt* airport

Б

бакалéя (f) *bakalyéya* grocer's

балéт (m) *balyét* ballet

балкóн (m) *balkón* balcony (theatre etc.)

банкнóт (m) *banknót* banknote

банкомáт (m) *bankamát* cashpoint

бáня (f) *bánya* Russian baths

бар (m) *bar* bar

барахóлка (f) *barakhólka* flea market

бассéйн (m) *bassyéin* swimming pool

бастовáть *bastavát* to be on strike

бéгать, бежáть *byégat, bizhát* to run

бéглый *byégly* **fluent**

бéженец/бéженка (m/f) *byézhinits/ byézhinka* **refugee**

без *byes* **without**

безалкогóльный *bizalkagólny* **non-alcoholic**

» безалкогóльный напúток (m) *bizalkagólny napítak* **soft drink**

безрабóтный (m) *bizrabótny* **unemployed**

бéлый *byély* **white**

бельё (n) *bil-yó* **(bed)linen**

беспла́тно *bisplátna* **free of charge**

беспокóить/побеспокóить *bispakóit/pabispakóit* **to disturb**

» не беспокóить *ni bispakóit* **do not disturb**

бúзнес (m) *bíznis* **business**

бизнесмéн/ка (m/f) *biznismyén/ biznismyénka* **businessman/woman**

билéт (m) *bilyét* **ticket**

» билéт в одúн конéц *bilyét v adín kanyéts* **one way ticket**

» входнóй билéт *fkhadnóï bilyét* **entrance ticket**

» обра́тный билéт *abrátny bilyét* **return ticket**

билéтная кácса (f) *bilyétnaya kássa* **ticket office**

бинт (m) *bint* **bandage**

блúзко *blíska* **near**

блондúн/ка (m/f) *blandín/ka* **blonde**

блýзка (f) *blóoska* **blouse**

блюдо (n) *blyóoda* **dish**

блюдце (n) *blyóotse* **saucer**

бокáл (m) *bakál* **glass (wine)**

болéзненный *balyézninny* **painful**

болéзнь (f) *balyézn* **illness**

болéть/заболéть *balyét/zabalyét* **to be unwell**

болеутоля́ющее *bólïootalyayooschiye* **painkiller**

боль (f) *bol* **ache, pain**

» бóли (pl) при менструáции *bóli pri minstrooátsii* **period pains**

больнúца (f) *balnítsa* **hospital**

бóльно *bólna* **it hurts**

больнóй *balnóï* **ill, sore**

бóльше *bólshe* **more**

большóй *balshóï* **big, large**

боя́ться *bayátsa* **to be afraid**

» не бóйтесь *ni bóïtis* **don't be afraid**

брат (m) *brat* **brother**

брать/взять *brat/vzyat* **to take**

» брать/взять напрокáт *brat/vzyat naprakát* **to hire**

британец/британка (m/f) *británits/ británka* **British (people)**

британский *británski* **British (adj.)**

брошю́ра (f) *brashóora* **leaflet**

брю́ки (pl) *bryóoki* **trousers**

будúльник (m) *boodílnik* **alarm clock**

бýква (f) *bookva* **letter (of alphabet)**

бумáжник (m) *boomázhnik* **wallet**

бумáжные носовы́е платкú (pl) *boomázhnyye nasavýye platkí* **tissues**

буты́лка (f) *bootýlka* **bottle**

буфéт (m) *boofyét* **buffet**

бюрó (n) *byooró* **office**

» бюрó нахóдок *byooró nakhódak* **lost property office**

» бюрó путешéствий *byooró pootishéstvi* **travel agency**

В

в *v* **in, at, into, to (destination)**

вагóн (m) *vagón* **carriage (train)**

валлúец/валлúйка (m/f) *valíyits/ valíïka* **Welsh (people)**

валлúйский *valíïski* **Welsh (adj.)**

валю́та (f) *valyoota* **currency**

ванúль (f) *vanil* **vanilla**

ва́нна (f) *vánna* **bath, bathtub**

ва́нная (кóмната) (f) *vánnaya* **bathroom**

вáта (f) *váta* **cotton wool**

ваш/Ваш *vash* **your (pl and formal s)**

Ва́ше здоро́вье! *váshe zdaróv-ye* **Cheers!**

вегетариа́нец/вегетариа́нка (m/f) *vigitariánits/vigitariánka* **vegetarian**

» стро́гий вегетариа́нец (m) *strógi vigitariánits* **vegan**

вегетариа́нский *vigitariánski* **vegetarian (adj.)**

век (m) *vyek* **century**

Великобрита́ния (f) *vilikabritániya* **Great Britain**

велосипе́д (m) *vilasipyét* **bicycle**

ве́ник (m) *vyénik* **birch twigs (Russian bath)**

вентиля́тор (m) *vintilyátar* **fan (air)**

ве́рный *vyérny* **true**

ве́тер (m) *vyétir* **wind**

» ве́трено *vyétrinna* **windy: it's windy**

ве́чер (m) *vyéchir* **evening**

» ве́чером *vyéchiram* **in the evening**

ве́щи (pl) *vyéschi* **things, belongings**

взро́слый (m) *vzrósly* **adult**

взрыв (m) *vzryf* **explosion**

взя́тка (f) *vzyátka* **bribe**

ви́деть/уви́деть *vídyet/oovídyet* **to see**

ви́за (f) *víza* **visa**

визи́т (m) *vizít* **visit**

ви́нный магази́н (m) *víny magazín* **wine and spirits shop**

вино́ (n) *vinó* **wine**

винова́тый *vinaváty* **guilty**

витри́на (f) *vitrína* **window (shop)**

ВИЧ (m) *vich* **HIV**

» ВИЧ инфици́рованный *vich infitsíravanny* **HIV positive**

включа́ть/включи́ть *fklyoochát/ fklyoochít* **to switch on**

включено́ *fklyoochinó* **included**

вкус (m) *fkoos* **taste**

вку́сный *fkóosny* **delicious**

владе́лец (m) *vladyélits* **owner**

вла́жный *vlázhny* **damp**

вме́сте *vmyésti* **together**

вме́сто *vmyésta* **instead of**

вне́шний *vnyéshni* **external**

внизу́ *vnizóo* **below, downstairs**

внук (m) *vnook* **grandson**

» вну́ки (pl) *vnóoki* **grandchildren**

внутри́ *vnootrí* **inside**

вну́чка (f) *vnóochka* **granddaughter**

во вре́мя *va vryémya* **during**

во́время *vóvryemya* **on time**

вода́ (f) *vadá* **water**

води́тельские права́ (pl) *vadítilskiye pravá* **driving licence**

водосто́йкий *vadastóiki* **waterproof**

возбуждённый *vazboozhdyónny* **excited**

возвраща́ть(ся)/верну́ть(ся) *vazvraschát(sa)/virnóot(sa)* **to return**

» возвраща́ть/верну́ть де́ньги *vazvraschát/virnóot dyéngi* **to refund**

возду́шный шар (m) *vazdóoshny shar* **balloon**

возмо́жно *vazmózhna* **perhaps**

возмо́жный *vazmózhny* **possible**

война́ (f) *vawashá* **war**

» пе́рвая мирова́я война́ *pyérvaya miraváya vaïná* **World War One**

» втора́я мирова́я война́ *ftaráya miraváya vaïná* **World War Two**

» Вели́кая Оте́чественная война́ *vilíkaya atyéchistvinnaya vaïná* **The Great Patriotic War**

вокза́л (m) *vagzál* **main station**

во́лосы (pl) *vólasy* **hair**

вопро́с (m) *vaprós* **question**

вор (m) *vor* **thief**

воспалённый *vaspalyónny* **inflamed**

восто́к (m) *vastók* **east**

» восто́чный *vastóchny* **eastern**

вот *vot* **here is/are**

вот и всё *vot i fsyo* **that's all**

вот, пожа́луйста *vot, pazhálsta* **here you are**

впереди́ *fpiridí* **in front of**

врач (m) *vrach* doctor *(med.)*

вред (m) *vryet* damage

вредный *vryédny* harmful

временный *vryéminny* temporary

время (n) *vryémya* time

» время отправления *vryémya atpravlyéniya* departure time

все *fse* everyone, all

всё *fsyo* everything

» всё вместе *fsyo vmyéstye* altogether

» всё в порядке *fsyo f paryátkye* all right *(OK)*

всегда *fsigdá* always

вспышка (f) *fspýshka* flash *(camera)*

встреча (f) *fstryécha* meeting

встречать/встретить *fstrichát/ fstryétit* to meet

вход (m) *fkhot* entrance

» вход воспрещён *fkhot vasprischón* no admittance

» вход свободный *fkhot svabódny* admission free

» входить/войти *fkhadít/vaïtí* to come in

» Входите! *fkadítye* come in!

» без вызова не входить *byez výzava ni fkhadít* do not enter without being called

входная плата (f) *fkhadnáya pláta* admission charge

вчера *fchirá* yesterday

вы/Вы *vy* you

выбирать/выбрать *vybirát/výbrat* to choose

выборы (pl) *výbary* election

выключать/выключить *vyklyoochát/ výklyoochit* to switch off

выключен *výklyoochin* off *(tv, light)*

вылет (m) *výlyet* departure

вылечивать/вылечить *vylyéchivat/ výlichit* to cure

выпечка (f) *výpichka* pastry

высокий *vysóki* high, tall

высота (f) *vysatá* height

выставка (f) *výstafka* exhibition

выход (m) *výkhat* exit

» выход на посадку *výkhat na pasátkoo* gate *(airport)*

выходить/выйти *vykadít/výiti* to go out, to get off *(bus)*

выходить/выйти замуж *vykhadít/ výiti zámoosh* to get married *(woman)*

выходной (m) *vykhadnói* holiday, day off

газета (f) *gazyéta* newspaper

газированный *gaziróvanny* fizzy

галстук (m) *gálstook* tie

гардероб (m) *gardiróp* cloakroom

где *gdye* where, where?

где-нибудь *gdyé-niboot* anywhere

где-то *gdyé-ta* somewhere

гигиенический *gigiyiníchiski* hygienic

» гигиенический пакет (m) *gigiyiníchiski pakyét* sick bag

» гигиенические прокладки (pl) *gigiyiníchiskiye praklátki* sanitary towels

гид (m) *git* guide *(person)*

гидрокостюм (m) *gidrakastyóom* wetsuit

гинеколог (m) *ginikólak* gynaecologist

гладить/погладить *gládit/pagládit* to iron

глубина (f) *gloobiná* depth

глухой *glookhói* deaf

говорить/сказать *gavarít/skazát* to say, to speak

год (m), лет (pl) *got, lyet* year

годовщина (f) *gadafshhína* anniversary

головная боль (f) *galavnáya bol* headache

голо́дный *galódny* hungry

гололёд (m) *galalyót* ice *(on roads)*

го́лос (m) *gólas* voice

голосова́ть/проголосова́ть *galasavát/pragalasavát* to vote

го́лый *góly* naked

гомосексуа́льный *gomasiksooálny* homosexual

гонора́р (m) *ganarár* fee

горе́ть/сгоре́ть *garyét/zgaryét* to burn

го́рничная (f) *górnichnaya* maid, cleaner

го́рные лы́жи (pl) *górnyye lýzhi* downhill skiing

го́род (m) *górat* city, town

го́рький *górki* bitter

горя́чий *garyáchi* hot

господи́н (m) *gaspadín* Mr

госпожа́ (f) *gaspazhá* Mrs

гости́ница (f) *gastínitsa* hotel

гость (m) *gost* guest, visitor

госуда́рство (n) *gasoodárstva* state

гото́вить/пригото́вить *gatóvit/ prigatóvit* to cook

гото́вый *gatóvy* ready

гра́дус (m) *grádoos* degree *(temperature)*

грани́ца (f) *granitsa* border *(frontier)*
» за грани́цей *za granítseï* abroad

гро́мкий *grómki* loud

гру́бый *gróoby* rude

гря́зный *gryázny* dirty

гудо́к (m) *goodók* dialling tone

гуля́ть *goolyát* to go for a walk

Д

да *da* yes

дава́ть/дать *davát/dat* to give
» дава́ть/дать взаймы́ *davát/dat vzaïmý* to lend

далеко́ *dalikó* far *(away)*

дальнозо́ркий *dalnazórki* long-sighted

дальто́ник (m) *daltónik* colour-blind

да́та (f) *dáta* date *(day)*

движе́ние (n) *dvizhéniye* traffic
» односторо́нние движе́ние *adnastaróniye dvizhéniye* one-way traffic

двойно́й *dvaïnóï* double

дворе́ц (m) *dvaryéts* palace

дежу́рный/дежу́рная (m/f) *dizhóorny/dizhóornaya* concierge, receptionist

дезинфици́рующее сре́дство (n) *dezinfitsírooyooschiye sryétstva* disinfectant

дезодора́нт (m) *dezadaránt* deodorant

действи́тельный *distvítilny* valid

де́лать/сде́лать *dyélat/zdyélat* to do, to make

де́лать/сде́лать поку́пки *dyélat/ zdyélat pakóopki* shopping, to go shopping

делика́тный *dilikátny* delicate

де́ло (n) *dyéla* business, affair(s)
» по де́лу *pa dyéloo* on business
» как ва́ши дела́? *kak váshi dilá* how are you doing?

день (m), дни (pl) *dyen, dni* day(s)

день рожде́ния *dyen razhdyéniya* birthday
» с днём рожде́ния *s dnyom razhdyéniya* Happy Birthday!

де́ньги (pl) *dyéngi* money

дере́вня (f) *diryévnya* village

де́рево (n) *dyéreva* tree, wood

де́ти (pl) *dyéti* children

дешёвый *dishóvy* cheap
» деше́вле *dishévli* cheaper

диабе́тик (m) *diabyétik* diabetic

диаре́я (f) *diaryéya* diarrhoea

дивиди́ (m) *dividí* DVD
» дивиди́-пле́ер (m) *dividí-pléyer* DVD-player

дие́та (f) *diyéta* diet

дизайнер (m) *dizáinir* designer

диплом (m) *diplóm* degree (*university*)

дипломат (m) *diplamát* diplomat

диск (m) *disk* disc (*computer*)

диск-жокей (m) *disk-zhakyéi* disk jockey

дискотека (f) *diskatyéka* disco

дислексия (f) *dislyéksiya* dyslexia

дичь (f) *dich* game (*wild fowl*)

длина (f) *dliná* length

длинный *dlíny* long

длиться/продлиться *dlítsa/pradlítsa* to last

для некурящих *dlya nikooryáshchikh* non-smoking

до *do* until

до свидания *da svidániya* goodbye

добиваться/добиться успеха *dabivátsa/dabítsa oospyékha* to succeed

добрый *dóbry* kind (*generous*)

» доброе утро *dóbraye óotra* good morning

» добрый вечер *dóbry vyéchir* good evening

» добрый день *dóbry dyen* good day

добро пожаловать *dabró pazhálavat* welcome!

довольный *davólny* pleased, satisfied

договариваться/договориться *dagavárivatsa/dagavarítsa* to arrange

» договорились! *dagavarílis* agreed!

договор (m) *dagavór* contract

дождь (m) *dosht* rain

доктор (m) *dóktar* doctor

документ (m) *dakoomyént* document

долг (m) *dolk* debt

доллар (m) *dólar* dollar

домашний *damáshni* homemade

домашняя работа (f) *damáshniya rabóta* housework

дорога (f) *daróga* road, way

дорогой *daragói* expensive, darling

доставлять/доставить *dastavlyát/dastávit* to deliver

доступный *dastóopny* affordable

дочь (f), дочери (pl) *doch, dóchiri* daughter(s)

друг (m), друзья (pl) *drook, drooz-yá* friend(s)

дублёнка (f) *dooblyónka* sheepskin coat

думать/подумать *dóomat/padóomat* to think

духи (pl) *dookhí* perfume

духовка (f) *dookhófka* oven

душ (m) *doosh* shower

дышать *dyshát* to breathe

дядя (m) *dyádya* uncle

Е

еврейский *ivryéiski* Jewish

Европа *yevrópa* Europe

европейский *yevrapyéiski* european

его *yivó* his, him

ему *yimóo* him

еда (f) *yedá* food

её *iyó* hers, her

ежедневный *yezhidnyévny* daily

ежемесячный *yezhimyésichny* monthly

еженедельный *yezhinidyélny* weekly

ей *yeí* to her

если *yésli* if

» если ...то *yésli...to* if... then

естественный *istyéstvinny* natural

есть...? *yest* is there...?

есть/съесть *yest/s-yest* to eat

ехать, ездить *yékhat, yézdit* to go (*in a vehicle*), to ride (*bike, horse*)

» ездить автостопом *yézdit aftastópam* to hitchhike

ехать/поехать домой *yékhat/payékhat damói* to go home (*in a vehicle*)

ещё *yischó* still (*yet*)

Ж

жа́лоба (f) *zháloba* complaint
жар (m) *zhar* fever
жара́ (f) *zhará* heat
жа́реный *zháriny* fried
жа́ркий *zhárki* hot
» жа́рко *zhárka* (it's) hot *(weather)*
жва́чка (f) *zhváchka* chewing gum
ждать *zhdat* to wait (for)
железнодоро́жная ста́нция (f)
 zhiliznadaróznaya stántsiya railway
 station
железнодоро́жный перее́зд (m)
 zhiliznadarózhny piriyést level
 crossing
жена́ (f), жёны (pl) *zhiná, zhóny* wife
жена́т *zhinát* married *(man)*
жени́ться *zhinítsa* to get married
 (man)
жени́х (m) *zhiníkh* bridegroom
же́нский *zhénski* female, feminine
же́нский туале́т (m) *zhénski tooalyét*
 ladies
же́нщина (f) *zhénschina* woman
жёсткий *zhóski* stiff, tough *(meat)*
жёсткий диск (m) *zhóski disk* hard
 drive
живо́тное (n) *zhivótnaye* animal
жильё (n) *zhil-yó* accommodation
жи́рный *zhírny* fat, greasy
журна́л (m) *zhoornál* magazine
журнали́ст/ка (m/f) *zhoornalíst/ka*
 journalist

3

за *za* behind
заба́вный *zabávny* funny *(amazing)*
забасто́вка (f) *zabastófka* strike
забира́ть/забра́ть *zabirát/zabrát*
 to pick up
заболева́ть/заболе́ть *zabalivát/
 zabalyét* to fall sick
забыва́ть/забы́ть *zabyvát/zabýt* to
 forget

заве́дующий (m) *zavyédooschi*
 manager
заво́д (m) *zavót* factory
за́втра *záftra* tomorrow
за́втрак (m) *záftrak* breakfast
зага́р (m) *zagár* suntan
загора́ть/загоре́ть *zagarát/zagaryét*
 to sunbathe
загружа́ть/загрузи́ть *zagroozhát/
 zagroozít* download
загрязне́ние (n) *zagriznyéniye*
 pollution
заде́ржка (f) *zadyérshka* delay
зажига́лка (f) *zazhigálka* lighter
заинтересо́ванный *zaintirisóvanny*
 interested
зака́з (m) *zakás* reservation
зака́занный (зара́нее) *zakázanny
 (zarániye)* reserved
зако́нный *zakónny* legal
закры́то *zakrýta* closed
заку́ски (pl) *zakóoski* starters *(food)*
зал (m) ожида́ния *zal azhidániya*
 departure lounge
зало́г (m) *zalók* deposit
замёрзший *zamyórshi* frozen
за́мок (m) *zámak* castle
замо́к (m) *zamók* lock
занаве́ска (f) *zanavyéska* curtain
за́мужем *zámoozhim* married
 (woman)
за́нято *zánita* taken, occupied
за́нятый, занято́й *zányaty, zanitóï*
 busy
за́пад (m) *západ* west
» за́падный *západny* western
запасно́й вы́ход (m) *zapasnóï výkhot*
 emergency exit
за́пах (m) *západh* scent, smell
запира́ть/запере́ть *zapirát/zapiryét*
 to lock
заполня́ть/запо́лнить *zapalnyát/
 zapólnit* to fill in
запра́вка (f) *zapráfka* petrol station

зарегистри́роваться *zarigistríravatsa* **to register**

зарезерви́рованный *zarizirvíravanny* **reserved**

зарпла́та (f) *zarpláta* **wage**

застрахо́ванный *zastrakhóvany* **insured**

» Вы застрахо́ваны? *vy zastrakhóvany* **are you insured?**

заче́м? *zachém* **why?**

звать *zvat* **to call**

» как Вас зову́т? *kak vas zavóot* **what is your name?**

» меня́ зову́т *minyá zavóot* **my name is**

звони́ть/позвони́ть *zvaníť/pazvaníť* **to telephone**

звук (m) *zvook* **sound**

зда́ние (n) *zdániye* **building**

здесь *zdyes* **here**

здоро́вье (n) *zdaróv-ye* **health**

» За (Ва́ше) здоро́вье! *za (váshe) zdaróvye* **Cheers!**

зе́ркало (n) *zyérkala* **mirror**

знак (m) *znak* **sign**

знамени́тый *znaminíty* **famous**

знать *znat* **to know**

» я не зна́ю *ya ni znáyoo* **I don't know**

зна́чить *znáchit* **to mean**

» что э́то зна́чит? *shto éta znáchit* **what does this mean?**

зонт (m) *zont* **umbrella**

зубно́й

» зубна́я боль (f) *zoobnáya bol* **toothache**

» зубна́я па́ста (f) *zoobnáya pasta* **toothpaste**

» зубна́я щётка (f) *zoobnáya schótka* **toothbrush**

» зубно́й врач (m) *zoobnóï vrach* **dentist**

» зубно́й проте́з (m) *zoobnóï pratés* **denture**

зубочи́стка (f) *zoobachístka* **toothpick**

И

и *i* **and**

игла́ (f) *iglá* **needle**

игра́ (f) *igrá* **game** *(match)*

идёт: идёт дождь/снег *idyót dosht/ snyek* **it's raining/snowing**

идти́, ходи́ть *ittí, khadíť* **to go** *(on foot)*

идти́/пойти́ домо́й *ittí/païtí damóï* **to go home** *(on foot)*

из *is* **from**

изве́стный *izvyésny* **well-known**

извини́те *izviníte* **excuse me**

ико́на *ikóna* **icon**

и́ли …и́ли *íli … íli* **either… or…**

име́ть *imyét* **to have**

и́мя (n) *ímya* **name**

инвали́д (m) *invalít* **disabled**

инвали́дное кре́сло (n) *invalídnaye kryésla* **wheelchair**

индустри́я (f) *indoostríya* **industry**

иногда́ *inagdá* **sometimes**

иностра́нец/иностра́нка (m/f) *inastránits/inastránka* **foreigner**

иностра́нный *inastránny* **foreign**

инстру́кция (f) *instróoktsiya* **instructions, manual**

инструме́нт (m) *instroomyént* **tool**

инсули́н (m) *insoolín* **insulin**

интеллиге́нтный *intiligyéntny* **intelligent**

интерва́л (m) *intervál* **interval** *(of time)*

интервью́ (n) *interv-yóo* **interview**

интере́сный *intiryésny* **interesting**

интересова́ться/заинтересова́ться *intirisavátsa/zaintirisavátsa* **to be interested in**

» я интересу́юсь *ya intirisóoyoos* **I am interested in**

интерне́т (m) *internét* **web** *(internet)*

» интерне́т-кафе́ (n) *internét-kafé* **internet café**

» интернéт-свя́зь (f) *internét-svyas* internet connection

инфéкция (f) *infyéktsiya* infection

информáция (f) *infarmátsiya* information

ипотéка (f) *ipatyéka* mortgage

ипподрóм (m) *ipadróm* racecourse

ирлáндец/ирлáндка (m/f) *irlándits/ irlánka* Irish (people)

Ирлáндия (f) *irlándiya* Ireland

ирлáндский *irlánski* Irish (adj.)

искáть/найтú *iskát/naïtí* to look for

исключéние (n) *isklyoochéniye* exception

» за исключéнием *za isklyoochéniem* except

искýсственный *iskóostviny* artificial

искýсство (n) *iskóostva* art

ислáм (m) *islám* Islam

ислáмский *islámski* Islamic

исполнúтельный *ispalnítilny* executive

испóльзовать *ispólzavat* to use

испóрченный *ispórchyenny* faulty, rotten

истóрия (f) *istóriya* history, story

их *ikh* their, theirs

Й

йóгурт (m) *yógoort* yoghurt

йод (m) *yot* iodine

К

кáбель (m) USB *kábyel yoo es bi* USB lead

каблýк (m) *kablóok* heel (shoe)

кáждый *kázhdy* each, every

как *kak* how

» как Вас/тебя́ зовýт? *kak vas/tíbya zavóot* what is your name?

» как Вы сказáли? *kak vy skazáli* pardon?

» как делá? *kak dilá?* how are you doing?

какóй *kakóï* what?, which?

кáмера (f) хранéния *kámira khranyéniya* left luggage office

карандáш (m) *karandásh* pencil

кармáн (m) *karmán* pocket

кáрта (f) *kárta* map

кáрта (f) пáмяти *kárta pámiti* memory card

» кáрта (f) пáмяти USB *kárta pámiti yoo es bi* USB stick

картóфель (m), картóшка (f) *kartófil, kartóshka* potato

картóфельные чúпсы (pl) *kartófilnyye chípsy* potato crisps

катáться

» катáться на конькáх *katátsa na kankákh* to skate

» катáться на лóдке *katátsa na lótkye* to go boating

» катáться на лы́жах *katátsa na lýzhakh* to ski

» катáться на сáнках *katátsa na sánkakh* to sleigh

катóк (m) *katók* ice rink

катóлик/католúчка (m/f) *katólik/ katalíchka* Catholic (people)

католúческий *katalíchiski* Catholic (adj.)

кафé (n) *kafé* café

» кафé-морóженое (n) *kafé-marózhinaye* ice cream parlour

кáчество (n) *káchistva* quality

кáшлять/кашлянýть *káshlit/ kashlinóot* to cough

квитáнция (f) *kvitántsiya* receipt

кéмпинг (m) *kyémpink* camping

керáмика (f) *kirámika* pottery

кинó (n) *kinó* cinema

кинозвездá (f) *kinazvizdá* film star

кипятúльник (m) *kipitílnik* water heater

кипятúть/вскипятúть *kipitít/vskipitít* to boil

кипятóк (m) *kipitók* boiling water

ки́слый *kísly* sour

кла́дбище (n) *kládbische* cemetery

класси́ческий *klassíchiski* classical

» класси́ческая му́зыка (f)
klassíchiskaya móozyka classical
music

клаустрофо́бия (f) *klaoostrafóbiya*
claustrophobia

кли́ника (f) *klínika* clinic

клуб (m) *kloop* club

ключ (m) *klyooch* key

кни́га (f) *kníga* book

кни́жный магази́н (m) *knízhny
magazín* bookshop

когда́ *kagdá* when, when?

код (m) *kot* dialling code

кокте́йль (m) *kaktél* cocktail

коли́чество (n) *kalíchistva* amount

колле́га (m/f) *kallyéga* colleague

колле́дж (m) *kalyédsh* college

кольцо́ (n) *kaltsó* ring *(jewellery)*

коля́ска (f) *kalyáska* push-chair

кома́нда (f) *kamánda* team

командиро́вка (f) *kamandirófka*
business trip

коми́ссия (f) *kamíssiya* commission

комме́рческий *kamyérchiski*
commercial

ко́мната (f) *kómnata* room

компа́кт-диск (m) *kampákt-disk* CD

компа́ния (f) *kampániya* company

компози́тор (m) *kampazítar*
composer

компью́тер (m) *kampyóoter*
computer

коне́чно *kanyéshna* of course

коне́чная ста́нция (f) *kanyéchnaya
stántsiya* terminus

ко́нсульство (n) *kónsoolstva*
consulate

конта́ктные ли́нзы (pl) *kantáktnyye
línzy* contact lens

контине́нт (m) *kantinyént* continent

контрацепти́в (m) *kantratsiptíf*
contraceptive

контро́ль (m) *kantról* control
(passport)

контролёр (m) *kantralyór* ticket
inspector

конфере́нция (f) *kanfiryéntsiya*
conference

конфе́та (f) *kanfyéta* sweet,
chocolate

» коро́бка (f) конфе́т *karópka
kanfyét* box of sweets/chocolates

конце́рт (m) *kantsért* concert

конце́ртный зал (m) *kantsértny zal*
concert hall

копе́йка (f) *kapyéika* kopeck

короле́ва (f) *karalyéva* queen

короле́вский *karalyéfski* royal

коро́ль (m) *karól* king

коро́ткий *karótki* short

кото́рый (m)/кото́рая (f)/кото́рое
(n)/кото́рые (pl) *katóry, katóraya,
katóraye, katóryye* which, which?

ко́фе (m) *kófye* coffee

» ко́фе без кофеи́на *kófye byes
kafiína* decaffeinated coffee

» ко́фе с молоко́м *kófye s malakóm*
white coffee

» раствори́мый ко́фе *rastvarímy
kófye* instant coffee

кран (m) *kran* tap

креди́тная ка́рта (f) *kridítnaya kárta*
credit card

кре́сло-коля́ска (n) *kryésla-kalyáska*
wheelchair

крова́ть (f) *kravát* bed

» односпа́льная крова́ть
adnaspálnaya kravát single bed

» двуспа́льная крова́ть
dvoospálnaya kravát double bed

кто *kto* who, who?

кто-нибу́дь *któ-nibood* anyone

кто́-то *któ-ta* someone

кувши́н (m) *koofshín* jug

ку́пол (m) *kóopal* dome

купа́льная ша́почка (f) *koopálnaya shápachka* bathing cap
купа́льник (m) *koopálnik* swimsuit
кури́ть *koorít* to smoke
курс (m) *koors* course *(lessons)*
курс валю́ты (m) *koors valyóoty* exchange rate
кусо́к (m) *koosók* piece, slice, lump
» кусо́к са́хара *koosók sákhara* sugar lump
» кусо́к хле́ба *koosók khlýeba* slice of bread

Л

ла́мпа (f) *lámpa* lamp
ла́мпочка (f) *lámpachka* light bulb
ланч (m) *lanch* lunch
ле́вый *lyévy* left
лёд (m) *lyot* ice
ле́ди (f) *lyédi* lady
лека́рство (n) *likárstva* medicine *(drug)*
ле́кция (f) *lyéktsiya* lecture
лени́вый *linívy* lazy
лес (m) *lyes* forest
лесбия́нка (f) *lisbiyánka* lesbian
ле́стничная кле́тка (f) *lyésnichnaya klyétka* staircase
лет: ско́лько Вам лет? *lyet : skólka vam lyet* years: how old are you?
лече́ние (n) *lichéniye* treatment
ли́бо… ли́бо… *líba… líba…* either… or…
лимона́д (m) *limanát* lemonade
ли́ния (f) *líniya* line
» ли́ния метро́ *líniya mitró* underground line
литр (m) *litr* litre
лить *lit* to pour
лифт (m) *lift* lift
ли́фчик (m) *lífchik* bra
лицо́ (n) *litsó* face
ли́чный *líchny* personal
ложи́ться/лечь *lazhítsa/lyech* to lie down

ло́жка (f) *lóshka* spoon
лома́ть/слома́ть *lamát/slamát* to break
ло́мтик (m) *lómtik* slice
лу́чше *lóochshe* better
лу́чший *lóochshi* best
лы́жи (pl) *lýzhi* ski, cross-country skiing
» го́рные лы́жи *górnyye lýzhi* downhill skiing
» ката́ться на лы́жах *katátsa na lýzhakh* to ski
» лы́жная па́лка (f) *lýzhnaya pálka* ski pole
» лы́жные боти́нки (pl) *lýzhnyye batínki* ski boots
» лы́жный куро́рт (m) *lýzhny koorórt* ski resort
льго́та (m) *lgóta* concession
люби́мый *lyoobímy* favourite
люби́ть/полюби́ть *lyoobít/palyoobít* to love, to like
лю́ди (pl) *lyóodi* people

М

магази́н (m) *magazín* shop
ма́ленький *málinki* little, small
ма́льчик (m) *málchik* boy
ма́рка (f) *márka* stamp *(postage)*
маршру́т (m) *marshróot* route, itinerary
маршру́тка (f) *marshróotka* minibus
ма́сло (n) *másla* butter, oil
материа́л (m) *matiriál* material
матери́к (m) *matirík* mainland
матра́ц (m) *matráts* mattress
матрёшка (f) *matryóshka* Russian doll
матч (m) *mach* match *(game)*
мать (f), ма́ма (f) *mat, máma* mother, mum
маши́на (f) *mashína* car, machine
» на маши́не *na mashíne* by car
ме́бель (f) *myébil* furniture
медици́нский *miditsínski* medical

междугоро́дный звоно́к (m)
mizhdoogaródny zvanók **long-distance call**

междунаро́дный *mizhdoonaródny*
international

ме́лочь (f) *myélach* **change** *(coins)*

ме́неджер (m) *myénidzher* **manager**

менструа́ция (f) *minstrooátsiya*
period *(menstrual)*

ме́ньше *myénshe* **less**

меню́ (n) *minyóo* **menu**

меня́ *minyá* **me**

мёртвый *myórtvy* **dead**

ме́сса (f) *myéssa* **mass** *(church)*

ме́стный *myésny* **local**

ме́сто (n) *myésta* **place, seat**

» на ме́сте *na myéstye* **on the spot**

ме́сто для купа́ния (n) *myésta dlya koopániya* **bathing area**

ме́сто для куре́ния (n) *myésta dlya kooryéniya* **smoking area**

ме́сяц (m) *myésits* **month**

ме́сячные (pl) *myésichnyye* **period** *(menstrual)*

мета́лл (m) *mitál* **metal**

меха́ник (m) *mikhánik* **mechanic**

мили́ция (f) *milítsiya* **police** *(in Russia)*

милице́йская маши́на (f) *militséiskaya mashína* **police car**

милиционе́р (m) *militsianyér*
policeman

ми́лый *míly* **dear** *(loved)*

мир (m) *mir* **world, peace**

младе́нец (m) *mladyénits* **baby**

мно́го *mnóga* **many, much**

мно́гие *mnógiye* **a lot** *(of)*, **many**

мно́жество *mnózhistva* **plenty** *(of)*

мобильный телефо́н (m),
моби́льник (m) *mabílny tilifón, mabilnik* **mobile phone**

мо́да (f) *móda* **fashion**

моде́ль (f) *madél* **model**

моде́м (m) *madém* **modem**

мой *moí* **my, mine** *(of me)*

мо́лния (f) *mólniya* **lightning, zip**

молодо́й *maladói* **young**

молоко́ (n) *malakó* **milk**

молото́к (m) *malatók* **hammer**

моло́чные проду́кты (pl)
malóchnyye pradóokty **dairy products**

мо́ре (n) *mórye* **sea**

морепроду́кты (pl) *móripradóokty*
seafood

моро́женое (n) *marózhinaye* **ice cream**

мост (m) *most* **bridge**

мотоци́кл (m) *matatsíkl* **motorbike**

моча́ (f) *machá* **urine**

мочь/смочь *moch/smoch* **can** *(to be able)*

мо́ющее сре́дство (n) *móyooschiye sryétstva* **detergent**

мо́ющийся *móyooschiísya* **washable**

мра́мор (m) *mrámar* **marble**

муж (m) *moosh* **husband**

мужско́й *mooshkói* **male**

мужско́й туале́т (m) *mooshkói tooalyét* **gents**

музе́й (m) *moozyéi* **museum**

му́зыка (f) *móozyka* **music**

му́сор (m) *móosar* **litter, rubbish**

мы *my* **we**

мы́ло (n) *mýla* **soap**

мыть/помы́ть, вы́мыть *myt/pamýt, výmyt* **to wash**

мышь, мы́шка (f) *mysh, myshka*
mouse

мя́со (n) *myása* **meat**

мяч (m) *myach* **ball**

Н

на́бережная (f) *nábirizhnaya* **quay**

набира́ть/набра́ть но́мер *nabirát/ nabrát nómir* **to dial**

наве́рх *navyérkh* **up, upstairs**

наверху́ *navirkhoó* **above, on top of**

на вы́нос *navýnas* to take away

надева́ть/наде́ть *nadivát/nadyét* to put on

надёжный *nadyozhny* safe, reliable

на́до *náda* it is necessary

» мне на́до *mnye náda* I need to

» не на́до *ni náda* don't (do that)

нажима́ть/нажа́ть *nazhimát/nazhát* to press

назначе́ние (n) *naznachéniye* appointment, prescription

» пункт назначе́ния *poonkt naznachéniya* destination

накладна́я (f) *nakladnáya* invoice

нале́во *nalyéva* to the left

нали́чные (pl) *nalíchnyye* cash

нало́г (m) *nalók* tax

нам *nam (to) us*

напада́ть/напа́сть на *napadát/ napást na* to attack, to assault

напи́ток (m) *napítak* drink

напра́во *napráva* to the right

направле́ние (n) *napravlyéniye* direction

наприме́р *naprimyér* for example

напро́тив *naprótif* across (opposite)

напряже́ние (n) *naprizhéniye* voltage

» высо́кое напряже́ние *vysokaye naprizhéniye* high voltage

нарко́з (m) *narkós* anaesthetic

» ме́стный/о́бщий *myésny/ópschi* local/general

наркома́н (m) *narkamán* drug addict

нарко́тик (m) *narkótik* drug

наро́дная му́зыка (f) *naródnaya móozyka* folk music

нас *nas* us

на себя́ *na sibyá* pull

насеко́мое (n) *nasikómaye* insect

наско́лько: наско́лько я зна́ю *naskólka: naskólka ya znáyoo* as far as I know

наслажда́ться/наслади́ться *naslazhdátsa/nasladítsa* to enjoy

насто́льный те́ннис (m) *nastólny ténnis* table tennis

настоя́щий *nastayáschi* real (authentic)

нау́шники (pl) *naóoshniki* headphones

находи́ть/найти́ *nakhadít/naití* to find

национа́льность (f) *natsianálnast* nationality

национа́льный *natsianálny* national

начина́ть/нача́ть *nachinát/nachát* to begin, to start

наш *nash* our/ours

НДС (m) *en de es* VAT

не *nye* not

» не кури́ть *nye koorít* no smoking

» не рабо́тает *nye rabótayet* out of order, closed

» не фотографи́ровать *nye fatagrafíravat* no photography

неве́ста (f) *nivyésta* bride, fiancé(e)

невино́вный *nivinóvny* innocent

невозмо́жный *nivazmózhny* impossible

неде́ля (f) *nidyélya* week

недоста́ток (m) *nidastátak* fault

нежена́тый/не за́мужем (m/f) *nizhináty/nizámoozhim* unmarried (m/f)

нежи́рный *nizhírny* low-fat

незави́симый *nizavísimy* independent

нездоро́вый *nizdaróvy* unwell

незнако́мец/незнако́мка (m/f) *niznakómits/niznakómka* stranger

не́кто *nyékta* someone

ненави́деть *ninavídit* to hate

необходи́мый *niapkhadímy* necessary

необы́чный *niabýchny* unusual

непло́хо *niplókha* (it's) not bad

непослу́шный *nipaslóoshny* naughty

непра́вильный *niprávilny* wrong

неприя́тный *nipriyátny* unpleasant

непромока́емый *nipramakáyimy* waterproof

не́рвный *nyérvny* nervous

неро́вный *niróvny* uneven *(surface)*

несваре́ние (n) *nisvaryéniye* indigestion

не́сколько *nyéskalka* (a) few, several

несча́стный *nischásny* unhappy

» несча́стный слу́чай (m) *nischásny slóochaï* accident

нет *nyet* no

неуда́ча (f) *nioodácha* failure

неуда́чный *nioodáchny* unsuccessful

неудо́бный *nioodóbny* uncomfortable

неформа́льный *nifarmálny* informal

нечётный *nichótny* odd *(not even)*

не́что *nyéchta* something

неэтилли́рованный *nietilíravanny* lead-free

ни... ни... *ni... ni...* neither... nor...

нигде́ *nigdyé* nowhere

ни́жнее бельё (n) *nízhniye bil-yó* underwear

ни́жний *nízhni* lower

ни́зкий *níski* low

» низкокалори́йный *niskakalaríiny* low-calorie

никогда́ *nikagdá* never

никто́ *niktó* nobody, none

ни́тки (pl) *nítki* cotton *(thread)*

ничто́ *nishtó* nothing

но *no* but

но́вости (pl) *nóvasti* news

но́вый *nóvy* new

» но́вый год *nóvy got* New Year's Day

» С Но́вым го́дом! *s nóvym gódam* Happy New Year!

но́жницы (pl) *nózhnitsy* scissors

носи́ть/нести́ *nasít/nistí* to carry

носово́й плато́к (m) *nasavóï platók* handkerchief

ноутбу́к (m) *no-oot bóok* laptop

ночно́й клуб (m) *nachnóï kloop* nightclub

ночь (f) *noch* night

нра́виться *nrávitsa* to like

» мне нра́вится *mne nrávitsa* I like

нужда́ться *noozhdátsa* to need

ну́жно *nóozhna* to have to

» Вам ну́жно... *vam nóozhna* you have to...

ну́жный *nóozhny* necessary

ню́хать/поню́хать *nyóokhat/ panyóokhat* to smell

ня́ня (f) *nyánya* nanny, babysitter

О

о, об *a, ab* about *(relating to)*

о́ба (m/n)/о́бе (f) *óba/óbe* both

обвиня́ть/обвини́ть *abvinyát/abvinít* to accuse

обе́д (m) *abyét* lunch, dinner

обе́дать/пообе́дать *abyédat/ paabyédat* to have lunch, dinner

обе́денный переры́в *abyédinny pirirýf* lunch break

обезжи́ренный *abizhírinny* low-fat

обеща́ть/пообеща́ть *abischát/ paabischát* to promise

оби́женный *abízhinny* offended

о́бласть (f) *óblast* region

областно́й *ablasnóï* regional

о́блачный *óblachny* cloudy

обме́нивать/обменя́ть *abmyénivat/ abminyát* to change *(money)*

обме́нный курс (m) *abmyénny koors* exchange rate

обмороже́ние (n) *abmarazhéniye* frost bite

обра́тный биле́т (m) *abrátny bilyét* return ticket

обслу́живание (n) номеро́в *apslóozhivaniye namiróf* room service

обслу́живать/обслужи́ть *apslóozhivat/apsloozhít* to serve

обы́чно *abýchna* normally

обы́чный *abýchny* ordinary

обяза́тельный *abizátilny* compulsory

о́вощи (pl) *óvaschi* vegetables

огнетуши́тель (m) *agnitooshítil* fire
  extinguisher

ого́нь (m) *agón* fire

ограбле́ние (n) *agrablyéniye* robbery

ограниче́ние (n) ско́рости
  agranichéniye skórasti speed limit

ограни́ченный *agraníchiny* limited

оде́жда (f) *adyézhda* clothes

одна́жды *adnázhdy* once

озо́нный слой (m) *azónny sloї* ozone
  layer

окно́ (n) *aknó* window

окра́ина (f) *akráina* outskirts

окружа́ющая среда́ (f)
  akroozháyooschaya sridá
  environment

окружённый *akroozhónny*
  surrounded by

оку́рки *akóorki* cigarette ends

оле́нь (m) *alyén* deer

он *on* he

она́ *aná* she

они́ *aní* they

оно́ *anó* it

опа́здывать/опозда́ть *apázdyvat/
  apazdát* to be late

опа́сность (f) *apásnast* danger

опа́сный *apásny* dangerous

опу́хший *apóokhshi* swollen

о́пыт (m) *opyt* experience

опя́ть *apyat* again

организо́ванный *arganizóvanny*
  organised

оре́х (m) *aryékh* nut

осмо́тр (m) *asmótr* examination,
  check-up

» осмо́тр достопримеча́тельностей
  asmótr dastaprimichátilnastyeї
  sightseeing

осо́бенность (f) *asóbinnast* speciality

остава́ться/оста́ться *astavátsa/
  astátsa* to remain

остана́вливаться/останови́ться
  astanávlivatsa/astanavítsa to stay
  (live), to stop

остано́вка (f) *astanófka* stop (bus)

осторо́жно! *astarózhna* watch out!

осторо́жно! Зла́я соба́ка!
  astarózhna, zláya sabáka Beware
  of the dog!

осторо́жно! Окра́шено! *astarózhna,
  akráshina* wet paint

осторо́жный *astarózhny* careful

о́стров (m) *óstraf* island

о́стрый *óstry* sharp, spicy

отбе́ливатель (m) *atbyélivatyel*
  bleach

отва́ливаться/отвали́ться
  atválivatsa/atvalítsa to come off

отве́т (m) *atvyét* answer

отделе́ние (n) *addilyéniye* branch
  (bank)

» отделе́ние мили́ции *addilyéniye
  milítsii* police station

оте́ль (m) *atél* hotel

оте́ц (m) *atyéts* father

откла́дывать/отложи́ть *atkládyvat/
  atlazhít* to postpone

отклоне́ние (n) *atklanyéniye*
  diversion

отключа́ть/отключи́ть *atklyoochát/
  atklyoochít* to cut (power)

открыва́ть/откры́ть *atkryvát/atkrýt*
  to open

откры́тка (f) *atkrýtka* postcard

откры́тый *atkrýty* open

отменя́ть/отмени́ть *atminyát/
  atminít* to cancel

отопле́ние (n) *ataplyéniye* heating

отправле́ние (n) *atpravlyéniye*
  departure

отправля́ть/отпра́вить по по́чте
  atpravlyát/atprávit pa póchtye
  to post

о́тпуск (m) *ótpoosk* holiday

отравле́ние (n) *atravlyéniye* food
  poisoning

отста́вка (f) *atstáfka* **resignation, retirement**

» в отста́вке *v atstáfkye* **retired**

официа́льный *afitsiálny* **official**

официа́нт/ка (m/f) *afitsiánt/ka* **waiter/waitress**

охо́титься *akhótitsa* **to hunt**

охра́нник (m) *akhránnik* **security guard**

о́чень *óchen* **very**

о́чередь (f) *óchiryet* **queue**

» стоя́ть в о́череди *stayát v óchiridi* **to queue (for)**

очки́ (pl) *achkí* **spectacles**

» очки́ от со́лнца *achkí at sóntsa* **sunglasses**

ошиба́ться/ошиби́ться *ashibátsa/ ashibítsa* **to make a mistake**

оши́бка (f) *ashípka* **mistake**

оши́бочный *ashíbachny* **faulty**

ошпа́ривать/ошпа́рить *ashpárivat/ ashpárit* **to scald**

П

па́дать/упа́сть *pádat/oopást* **to fall**

паке́т (m) *pakyét* **packet, carrier bag**

пала́тка (f) *palátka* **tent**

» жить в пала́тке *zhit f palátkye* **to camp**

пала́точный городо́к (m) *palátachny garadók* **campsite**

пальто́ (n) *paltó* **coat**

па́мятник (m) *pámitnik* **monument**

па́мять (f) *pámit* **memory**

пансио́н (m) *pansión* **guest house**

» по́лный пансио́н (m) *pólny pansión* **full board**

» полупансио́н (m) *poloopansión* **half board**

па́па (m) *pápa* **dad**

Па́па Ри́мский *pápa rímski* **Pope**

па́пка (f) *pápka* **file** *(documents)*

пари́лка (f), парна́я (f) *parílka, parnáya* **steam-room** *(Russian bath)*

па́риться/попа́риться *páritsa/ papáritsa* **to steam, sweat out** *(Russian bath)*

парово́й котёл (m) *paravói katyól* **boiler**

па́ра (f) *pára* **couple, pair**

парализо́ванный *paralizóvanny* **paralysed**

парикма́хер (m) *parikmákhir* **hairdresser**

парикма́херская (f) *parikmákhirskaya* **barber's**

парк (m) *park* **park**

» парк культу́ры и о́тдыха *park kooltóory i ódykha* **theme park**

паркова́ться/припаркова́ться *parkavátsa/priparkavátsa* **to park**

парла́мент (m) *parlámint* **parliament**

па́ртия (f) *pártiya* **party** *(political)*

па́русный спорт (m) *pároosny sport* **sailing**

па́спорт (m) *páspart* **passport**

па́спортный контро́ль (m) *páspartny kantról* **passport control**

пассажи́р (m) *passazhír* **passenger**

Па́сха (f) *páskha* **Easter**

» пасха́льное яйцо́ *paskhálnaye ïitsó* **Easter egg**

пеницили́н (m) *pinitsilín* **penicillin**

пенсионе́р/ка (m/f) *pinsianyér/ka* **pensioner**

пе́пельница (f) *pyépilnitsa* **ashtray**

пе́рвая по́мощь (f) *pyérvaya pómasch* **first aid**

переводи́ть/перевести́ *pirivadít/ pirivistí* **to interpret, to translate**

перево́дчик/перево́дчица (m/f) *pirivóchik/pirivóchitsa* **interpreter, translator**

переезжа́ть/перее́хать *piriyizhát/ piriyékhat* **to move house**

переносно́й *pirinasnói* **portable**

перепо́лненный *piripólniny* **crowded**

перо́ (n), пе́рья (pl) *piró, pyér-ya* **feather**

перча́тки (pl) *pirchátki* **gloves**

пе́сня (f) *pyésnya* **song**

песо́к (m) *pisók* **sand**

петь/спеть *pyet/spyet* **to sing**

печа́тать/напеча́тать *pichátat/napichátat* **to print, to type**

пешко́м *pishkóm* **on foot**

пиани́но (n) *pianína* **piano**

пивно́й бар (m) *pivnói bar* **bar, beer cellar, pub**

пи́во (n) *píva* **beer**

ПИН код *pin kot* **PIN number**

писа́ть/написа́ть *pisát/napisát* **to write**

» писа́ть/написа́ть e-má́il *pisát/napisát i-méil* **to email**

пить/вы́пить *pit/výpit* **to drink**

питьева́я вода́ (f) *pit-yeváya vadá* **drinking water**

пла́вание (n) *plávaniye* **swimming**

пла́вать *plávat* **to swim**

пла́вки (pl) *pláfki* **swimming trunks**

пластма́ссовый *plasmássavy* **plastic (adj.)**

пла́стырь (m) *plástyr* **plaster**

пла́та (f) *pláta* **fee**

» пла́та за обслу́живание *pláta za apslóozhivaniye* **service charge**

» пла́та за прое́зд *pláta za prayést* **fare**

плати́ть/заплати́ть *platít/zaplatít* **to pay**

» плати́ть/заплати́ть нали́чными *platít/zaplatít nalíchnymi* **to pay cash**

платфо́рма (f) *platfórma* **platform**

плащ (m) *plasch* **raincoat**

племя́нник (m) *plimyánik* **nephew**

племя́нница (f) *plimyánitsa* **niece**

пло́мба (f) *plómba* **filling (tooth)**

плохо́й *plakhói* **bad**

площа́дка (f) *plaschátka* **ground**

пло́щадь (f) *plóschat* **square, area (measurement)**

пляж (m) *plyásh* **beach**

повора́чивать/поверну́ть *pavaráchivat/pavirnóot* **to turn**

повторя́ть/повтори́ть *paftaryát/paftarít* **to repeat**

пого́да (f) *pagóda* **weather**

под *pod* **under**

пода́рок (m) *padárak* **gift, present**

подпи́сывать/подписа́ть *patpísyvat/patpisát* **to sign**

по́дпись (f) *pótpis* **signature**

подро́сток (m) *padróstak* **teenager**

подру́га (f) *padróoga* **friend (female), girlfriend**

подтвержда́ть/подтверди́ть *pattvirzhdát/pattvirdít* **to confirm**

поду́шка (f) *padóoshka* **cushion, pillow**

пожа́луйста *pazhálsta* **please**

пожа́р (m) *pazhár* **fire**

пожа́рные (pl) *pazhárnyye* **fire brigade**

по́здний *pózni* **late**

» по́зже *pózzhe* **later**

поздравля́ю! *pazdravlyáyoo* **congratulations!**

пойдёмте! *païdyómtye* **let's go!**

пока́з (m) *pakás* **demonstration**

пока́зывать/показа́ть *pakázyvat/pakazát* **to show**

покупа́тель (m) *pakoopátil* **customer**

покупа́ть/купи́ть *pakoopát/koopít* **to buy**

поли́тик (m) *palítik* **politician**

поли́тика (f) *palítika* **politics**

полиэтиле́новый паке́т (m) *palietilyénavy pakyét* **plastic bag**

полови́на (f) *palavína* **half**

полоте́нце (n) *palatyéntse* **towel**

помога́ть/помо́чь *pamagát/pamóch* **to help**

» помоги́те! *pamagítye* **help!**

по-мо́ему *pa-móyimoo* **in my opinion**

понима́ть/поня́ть *panimát/panyát* to understand

поно́с (m) *panós* diarrhoea

поп (m) *pop* priest *(Orthodox)*

поп-му́зыка (f) *pop-móozyka* pop music

по́рванный *pórvanny* torn

поре́занный на куски́ *paryézanny na kooskí* sliced

поре́заться *paryézatsa* to cut oneself

посети́тель (m) *pasitítil* visitor

посеща́ть/посети́ть *pasischát/pasitít* to visit

по́сле *pósli* after

после́дний *paslyédni* last

послеза́втра *poslizáftra* day after tomorrow

посо́льство (n) *pasólstva* embassy

посыла́ть/посла́ть *pasylát/paslát* to send

» посыла́ть/посла́ть SMS *pasylát/paslát es em es* to text

посы́лка (f) *pasýlka* parcel

поте́рянный *patyérinny* lost

поте́ть/вспоте́ть *patyét/fspatyét* to sweat

пото́м *patóm* afterwards, then

потому́ что *patamóo shta* because

похища́ть/похи́тить *pakhischát/pakhítit* to hijack, kidnap

похме́лье (n) *pakhmyél-ye* hangover

по́хороны (pl) *pókharany* funeral

поцелу́й (m) *patsilóoï* kiss

почему́? *pachimóo* why?

пра́вда (f) *právda* truth

» э́то пра́вда *éta právda* that's true

пра́вильный *právilny* correct

прави́тельство (n) *pravítilstva* government

правосла́вный *pravaslávny* Orthodox

пра́вый *právy* right

» Вы (не) пра́вы *vy (ni) právy* you are (not) right

» с пра́вой стороны́ *s právaï staraný* right-hand side

представле́ние (n) *pritstavlyéniye* performance

представля́ть/предста́вить *pridstavlyát/pritstávit* to introduce

предупрежда́ть/предупреди́ть *pridooprizhdát/pridoopridít* to warn

презервати́в (m) *prizirvatíf* condom

президе́нт (m) *prizidyént* president

прекра́сный *prikrásny* beautiful

премье́р-мини́стр (m) *prim-yér minístr* prime minister

пре́сса (f) *pryéssa* press *(newspapers)*

приблизи́тельно *priblizítilna* approximately

прибыва́ть/прибы́ть *pribyvát/pribýt* to arrive

при́быль (f) *príbyl* profit

прибы́тие (n) *pribytíye* arrival

приве́т *privyét* hello

приви́вка (f) *privífka* vaccination, jab

привлека́тельный *privlikátilny* attractive

приглаша́ть/пригласи́ть *priglashát/priglasít* to invite

приглаше́ние (n) *priglashéniye* invitation

при́город (m) *prígarat* suburb

приме́р (m) *primyér* example

» к приме́ру *k primyéroo* for example

прия́тный *priyátny* nice

» прия́тного аппети́та! *priyátnava apitíta* enjoy your meal!

пробива́ться/проби́ться *prabivátsa/prabítsa* to get through *(phone)*

про́бка (f) *própka* plug *(sink)*, cork, traffic jam

пробле́ма (f) *prablyéma* problem

продава́ть/прода́ть *pradavát/pradát* to sell

про́дано *pródana* sold out

произноси́ть/произнести́ *praiznasít/praiznistí* to pronounce

прока́т (m) *prakát* rental, hire

прóпуск (m) *própoosk* pass, hotel card

проспéкт (m) *praspyékt* brochure, avenue

простúте *prastítye* I'm sorry

простýда (f) *prastóoda* cold

простывáть/простыть *prastyvát/prastýt* to have a cold, to get cold

» я простыл/а (m/f) *ya prastýl/a* I've caught a cold

простыня́ (f) *prastynyá* sheet (for bed)

прóсьба (f) *prósba* request

протестáнтский *pratistánski* Protestant (adj.)

протестáнтка (m/f) *pratistántka* Protestant (people)

профéссия (f) *prafyéssiya* profession

профéссор (m) *prafyésar* professor

профсою́з (m) *prafsayóos* trade union

прóшлый *próshly* past

» в прóшлом *f próshlam* in the past

пря́мо *pryáma* straight on

пугáть/испугáть *poogát/ispoogát* to frighten

пýговица (f) *póogavitsa* button

пустóй *poostóï* empty

путеводúтель (m) *pootivadítil* guidebook

путешéствие (n) *pootishéstviye* journey

путешéствовать *pootishéstvavat* to travel

пыль (f) *pyl* dust

пы́льный *pýlny* dusty

пытáться/попытáться *pytátsa/papytátsa* to try

пьéса (f) *p-yésa* play (theatre)

пья́ный *p-yány* drunk

пятнó (n) *pitnó* spot, stain

пятновыводúтель (m) *pyátnavyvadítil* stain remover

Р

рабóта (f) *rabóta* job, work

рабóтать *rabótat* to work (job, function)

» не рабóтает *ni rabótait* closed, out of order

рабóчий день (m) *rabóchi dyen* weekday

раввúн (m) *ravín* rabbi

рáвный *rávny* equal

рáд/а познакóмиться (m/f) *rád/a paznakómitsa* pleased to meet you

радиáтор (m) *radiátar* radiator

рáдио (n) *rádia* radio

радиоактúвный *radiaaktívny* radioactive

радиостáнция (f) *radiastántsiya* radio station

разведённый *razvidyónny* divorced

развлечéние (n) *razvlichéniye* entertainment

развора́чиваться/развернýться *razvaráchivatsa/razvirnóotsa* to reverse (car)

разгова́ривать *razgavárivat* to talk

разгово́рник (m) *razgavórnik* phrase book

разме́р (m) *razmyér* size

» разме́р óбуви *razmyér óboovi* shoe size

рáзный *rázny* different

разрешéние (n) *razrishéniye* permit, licence (fishing etc.)

райóн (m) *rayón* district

рак (m) *rak* cancer

рáно *rána* early

рáньше *ránshe* before, earlier

расписáние (n) *raspisániye* timetable (train)

распродáжа (f) *raspradázha* sale (bargains)

расскáзывать/рассказáть *rasskázyvat/rasskazát* to tell

расстоя́ние (n) *rastayániye* distance

рвота (f) *rvóta* vomiting
» рвать, вы́рвать *rvat, výrvat* to vomit, to be sick
» меня́ вы́рвало *minyá vývrala* I was sick
ребёнок (m) *ribyónak* child
регио́н (m) *rigión* region
региона́льный *rigianálny* regional
регистрату́ра (f) *rigistratóora* reception
регистрацио́нная сто́йка (f) *rigistratsiónnaya stóïka* check-in (desk)
регистри́роваться/зарегистри́роваться *rigistírovatsa/zarigistírovatsa* to check-in
ре́зать *ryézat* to cut
результа́т (m) *rizooltát* result
рейс (m) *ryeïs* flight
река́ (f) *riká* river
рекла́ма (f) *rikláma* advertisement, advertising
рекомендова́ть/порекомендова́ть *rikamindavát/parokamindavát* to recommend
рели́гия (f) *rilígiya* religion
ремонти́ровать/отремонти́ровать *rimantírovat/atrimantírovat* to repair
рентге́н (m) *ringyén* X-ray
рестора́н (m) *ristarán* restaurant
реце́пт (f) *ritsépt* prescription, recipe
реша́ть/реши́ть *rishát/rishít* to decide
ржа́вый *rzhávy* rusty
ро́вный *róvny* even, flat
роди́тели (pl) *radítili* parents
роди́ться *radítsya* to be born
рожде́ственская ёлка (f) *razhdyéstvinskaya yólka* Christmas tree
Рождество́ (n) *razhdistvó* Christmas
» С Рождество́м! *s razhdistvóm!* Merry Christmas!

разливно́е пи́во (n) *razlivnóye píva* draught beer
Росси́я (f) *rasíya* Russia
рост (m) *rost* height *(of person)*
рубль (m) *roobl* rouble
ружьё (n) *roozh-yó* gun
рука́ми не тро́гать *rookámi nye trógat* do not touch
ру́сский *róoski* Russian *(adj.)*
ру́сский/ру́сская (m/f) *róoski/róoskaya* Russian *(people)*
ры́нок (m) *rýnak* market
рюкза́к (m) *ryookzák* rucksack
рю́мка (f) *ryóomka* wine glass
ря́дом *ryádam* close, next to

С

с *s* with
сад (m) *sat* garden
сади́ться/сесть *sadítsa/syest* to sit *(down)*
салфе́тка (f) *salfyétka* napkin
самова́р (m) *samavár* samovar
са́ни (pl) *sáni* toboggan, sledge, sleigh
са́уна (f) *sáoona* sauna
са́хар (m) *sákhar* sugar
сва́дьба (f) *svádba* wedding
све́жий *svyézhi* fresh
светофо́р (m) *svitafór* traffic light
свяще́нный *svischénny* holy
сгни́вший *zgnífshi* rotten
сде́лан(о) вручну́ю *zdyélan(a) vroochnóoyoo* hand made
сде́лка (f) *zdyélka* bargain *(deal)*
се́вер (m) *syévir* north
» се́верный *syévirny* northern
сего́дня *sivódnya* today
» сего́дня ве́чером *sivódnya vyéchirom* tonight
сезо́н (m) *sizón* season
сейча́с *sichás* now
секрета́рь (m) *sikritár* secretary
секс (m) *seks* sex *(intercourse)*

секу́нда (f) sikóonda **second** *(time period)*

се́льская ме́стность (f) syélskaya myésnast **countryside**

семья́ (f) sim-yá **family**

серде́чный при́ступ (m) sirdyéchny prístoop **heart attack**

серебро́ siribró **silver**

» сере́бряный siryébryany **silver** *(adj.)*

сза́ди zzádi **behind**

сига́ра (f) sigára **cigar**

сигаре́та (f) sigaryéta **cigarette**

сиди́ (m) sidí **CD**

» сидиро́м sidiróm **CD-Rom**

сим-ка́рта (f) sim-karta **SIM card**

синаго́га (f) sinagóga **synagogue**

ско́льзкий skólski **slippery**

ско́лько? skólka **how many/much?**

» ско́лько э́то сто́ит? skólka éta stóit **how much does it cost?**

ско́рая по́мощь (f) skóraya pómasch **ambulance**

скуча́ть skoochát **to miss** *(nostalgia)*

» скуча́ть по до́му skochát pa dómoo **to be homesick**

сла́дкое slátkaye **dessert**

сле́довать/после́довать slyédavat/paslyédavat **to follow**

сле́дующий slyédooyooschi **next**

слепо́й slipóï **blind**

сли́шком slíshkam **too**

» сли́шком до́рого slíshkam dóraga **too expensive**

слова́рь (m) slavár **dictionary**

сло́во (n) slóva **word**

сло́манный slómanny **broken**

слухово́й аппара́т (m) slookhavóï aparát **hearing aid**

случа́йно sloochaïna **by chance**

слу́шать/послу́шать slóoshat/paslóoshat **to listen** *(to)*

слы́шать/услы́шать slýshat/ooslýshat **to hear**

смерте́льный smirtyélny **fatal**

смерть (f) smyert **death**

смех (m) smyekh **laugh**

сме́шанный smyéshanny **mixed**

смо́кинг (m) smókink **dinner jacket**

смотре́ть/посмотре́ть smatryét/pasmatryét **to watch, to look** *(at)*

смуща́ть/смути́ть smooschát/smootít **to embarrass, to confuse**

снару́жи snaróozhi **outside**

снег (m) snyek **snow**

снегови́к (m) snigavík **snowman**

снегоочисти́тель (m) snyégaachistítil **snowplough**

снегопа́д (m) snigapát **snowfall**

снежи́нка (f) snizhínka **snowflake**

сниже́ние (n) snizhéniye **cut** *(reduction)*

снима́ть/снять snimát/snyat **to take off** *(clothes)*

» снима́ть/снять (кварти́ру) snimát/snyat (kvartíroo) **to rent** *(a flat)*

сно́ва snóva **again**

соба́ка (f) sabáka **dog**

собесе́дование (n) sabisyédavaniye **interview** *(job)*

собо́р (m) sabór **cathedral**

совеща́ние (n) savischániye **conference, meeting**

совреме́нный savrimyénny **modern, up-to-date**

сожале́ние: к сожале́нию sazhilyéniye: k sazhilyéniyoo **unfortunately**

сок (m) sok **juice**

солда́т (m) saldát **soldier**

соле́ный salyóny **salty**

со́лнечный sólnichny **sunny**

» со́лнечный ожо́г (m) sólnichny azhók **sunburn**

» со́лнечный уда́р (m) sólnichny oodár **sunstroke**

со́лнце (n) sóntse **sun**

соло́минка (f) *salóminka* straw *(drinking)*

соль (f) *sol* salt

сообще́ние (n) *saapschéniye* message

сосе́д/ка (m/f) *sasyét/ka* neighbour

сосе́дний *sasyédni* nearby

социалисти́ческий *satsialistíchiski* socialist *(adj.)*

социали́зм (m) *satsialízm* socialism

спа́льня (f) *spálnya* bedroom

спаса́ть/спасти́ *spasát/spastí* to rescue

спаси́бо (большо́е) *spasíba (balshóye)* thank you (very much)

спать *spat* to sleep

спекта́кль (m) *spiktákl* performance *(theatre)*

специали́ст (m) *spitsialist* specialist

специа́льный *spitsiálny* special

» специа́льное предложе́ние (n) *spitsiálnaye pridlazhéniye* special offer

спеши́ть *spishít* to be in a hurry

» в спе́шке *f spyéshkye* in a hurry

СПИД (m) *spit* AIDS

спиртно́е (n) *spirtnóye* spirits *(alcohol)*

спорт (m) *sport* sport

спра́вочный стол (m) *správachny stol* information desk

сра́зу же *srázoo zhe* at once

сре́дний *sryédni* medium *(size)*

сре́дних лет *sryédnikh lyét* middle-aged

срок го́дности (m) *srok gódnasti* expiry date

сро́чный *sróchny* urgent, express

стадио́н (m) *stadión* stadium

стака́н (m) *stakán* glass *(tumbler)*

сталь (f) *stal* steel

ста́нция (f) *stántsiya* station

старт (m) *start* start

ста́рше *stárshe* older

ста́рый *stáry* old

ста́туя (f) *státooya* statue

стекло́ (n) *stikló* glass *(substance)*

» стекля́нный *stiklyánny* glass *(adj.)*

стена́ (f) *stiná* wall

сте́рлинг (m): фунт сте́рлингов *styérlink: foont styérlingaf* sterling: pound sterling

стира́ть/постира́ть *stirát/pastirát* to wash *(clothes)*

сто́имость (f) *stóimast* charge, cost

сто́ить *stóit* to cost

» э́то сто́ит *éta stóit* it's worth

» э́то не сто́ит того́ *éta ni stóit tavó* it's not worth it

стол (m) *stol* table

столи́ца (f) *stalítsa* capital *(city)*

столо́вая (f) *stalóvaya* dining room, canteen

столо́вые прибо́ры (pl) *stalóvyye pribóry* cutlery

стомато́лог (m) *stamatólok* dentist

стоп! *stop!* stop!

стоя́нка (f) *stayánka* car park

» стоя́нка (f) такси́ *stayánka taksí* taxi rank

стоя́ть *stayát* to stand

страна́ (f) *straná* country

страхо́вка (f) *strakhófka* insurance

стри́жка (f) *stríshka* haircut

студе́нт/ка (m/f) *stoodyént/ka* undergraduate *(student)* (m/f)

стул (m) *stul* stool chair

субти́тры (pl) *sooptítry* subtitles

сувени́р (m) *soovinír* souvenir

сугро́б (m) *soogróp* snowdrift

суд (m) *soot* court *(law)*

су́дорога (f) *sóodaraga* cramp

судья́ (m) *sood-yá* judge

су́мочка (f) *sóomachka* hand bag

США *se-she-a* USA

съедо́бный *s-yidóbny* edible

сын (m), сыновья́ (pl) *syn, synav-yá* son(s)

сыпь (f) *syp* **rash**

сырóй *syróï* **raw**

сюдá *syoodá* **this way**

Т

таблéтка (f) *tablyétka* **tablet, pill**

так *tak* **so**

тáкже *tákzhe* **also, as well**

таксú (n) *taksí* **taxi**

тамóжня (f) *tamózhnya* **customs**

тамóженная декларáция (f)
tamózhennaya diklarátsiya **customs declaration form**

тамóженный контрóль *tamózheny kantról* **customs inspection**

тампóн (m) *tampón* **tampon**

тáнец (m) *tánits* **dance**

тарéлка (f) *taryélka* **plate**

те *tye* **those**

теáтр (m) *tiátr* **theatre**

телевúдение (n) *tilivídiniye* **television**

телефóн (m) *tilifón* **telephone**

тёмные очкú (pl) *tyómnyye achkí* **goggles, sun glasses**

тёмный *tyómny* **dark**

температýра (f) *timpiratóora* **temperature**

тéннис (m) *ténis* **tennis**

тéннисный корт (m) *ténisny kort* **tennis court**

терапéвт (m) *tirapyéft* **GP**

терминáл (m) *tirminál* **terminal** *(airport)*

терпелúвый *tirpilívy* **patient** *(adj.)*

террáса (f) *tirása* **terrace**

террорúст (m) *tiraríst* **terrorist**

терять/потерять *tiryát/patiryát* **to lose**

тётя (f) *tyótya* **aunt**

технолóгия (f) *tikhnalógiya* **technology**

течéние (n) *tichéniye* **stream**

тип (m) *tip* **type** *(sort)*

типúчный *tipíchny* **typical**

тúхий *tíkhi* **quiet, silent**

ткань (f) *tkan* **fabric**

толпá (f) *talpá* **crowd**

тóлстый *tólsty* **thick, fat**

тóлько *tólka* **only, just**

тóнкий *tónki* **thin, slim**

тоннéль (m) *tanél* **tunnel**

тонýть/утонýть *tanóot/ootanóot* **to drown**

тóпливо (n) *tópliva* **fuel**

тошнúть *tashnít* **to feel sick**

» меня тошнúт *minyá tashnít* **I feel sick**

традициóнный *traditsiónny* **traditional**

трамвáй (m) *tramvái* **tram**

трáнспортное срéдство (n) *tránspartnaye sryétstva* **vehicle**

тревóга (f) *trivóga* **alarm**

трёзвый *tryézvy* **sober**

трéнер (m) *tryénir* **coach** *(instructor)*

трóгать/трóнуть *trógat/trónoot* **to touch**

тротуáр (m) *tratoár* **pavement**

трýдный *tróodny* **difficult**

туалéт (m) *tooalyét* **toilet**

туалéтная бумáга (f) *tooalyétnaya boomága* **toilet paper**

туалéтные принадлéжности (pl) *tooalyétnyye prinadlyézhnastí* **toiletries**

тумáн (m) *toomán* **fog**

тургрýппа (f) *toorgróopa* **tour group**

турúзм (m) *toorízm* **tourism**

турúст (m) *tooríst* **tourist**

туристúческое агéнство (n) *tooristíchiskaye agyénstva* **tourist office**

тýфель (m), тýфли (pl) *tóofil, tóofli* **shoe(s)**

тяжёлый *tizhóly* **heavy**

тянýть/потянýть *tinóot/patinóot* **to pull**

у

у *oo* at, by, near
убива́ть/уби́ть *oobivát/oobít* to kill
убира́ть/убра́ть *oobirát/oobrát* to take away, to clean
у́гол (m) *óogal* corner
удаля́ть/удали́ть *oodalyát/oodalit* to remove
удивлённый *oodivlyónny* surprised
уда́ча *oodácha* luck
» уда́чи! *oodáchi* Good luck!
удлини́тель (m) *oodlinítil* extension lead
удо́бный *oodóbny* comfortable
удово́льствие *oodavólstviye* pleasure
» с удово́льствием *s oodavólstviyem* delighted to
удостовере́ние (n) ли́чности *oodastaviryéniye líchnasti* proof of identity
у́дочка (f) *óodachka* fishing rod
ужа́сный *oozhásny* awful, terrible
уже́ *oozhé* already
у́зкий *óoski* tight, narrow
уко́л (f) *ookól* injection
уку́с (m) насеко́мого *ookóos nasikómava* insect bite
у́лица (f) *óolitsa* street
» на у́лице *na óolitse* outdoor(s)/ outside
улыба́ться/улыбну́ться *oolybátsa/ oolybnóotsa* to smile
у́мный *óomny* clever
универма́г (m) *oonivirmák* department store
университе́т (m) *oonivirsityét* university
употребля́ть/употреби́ть *oopatriblyát/oopatribít* to use
управля́ющий дире́ктор (m) *oopravlyáyooschi diryéktar* managing director
упражне́ние (n) *ooprazhnyéniye* exercise

у́ровень (m) *óoravyen* level (height, standard)
уро́к (m) *oorók* lesson
успоко́йтесь! *oospakóityes* calm down!
уста́лый *oostály* tired
устра́ивать/устро́ить *oostráivat/ oostróit* to arrange
усы́ (m) *oosý* moustache
у́тка (f) *ootka* duck
у́тро (n) *óotra* morning
у́тренний *óotrinni* morning (adj.)
утю́г (m) *ootyóok* iron (for clothes)
учёный *oochóny* scientist, academic
учи́тель (m) *oochítil* teacher
учи́ть/научи́ть *oochít/naoochít* to teach
учи́ться *oochítsa* to study
уще́рб (m) *ooschérb* damage, loss
Уэ́льс (m) *ooéls* Wales
уэ́льский *ooélski* Welsh (adj.)

ф

фа́брика (f) *fábrika* factory
файл (m) *fail* file (computer)
фами́лия (f) *famíliya* surname
фана́т (m) *fanát* fan (supporter)
фейерве́рк (m) *fiyirvyérk* fireworks
фемини́ст/ка (m/f) *fiminíst/ka* feminist
фен (m) *fyen* hairdryer
фе́рма (f) *fyérma* farm
фе́рмер (m) *fyérmir* farmer
фестива́ль (m) *fistivál* festival
фигу́рное ката́ние (n) *figóornaye katániye* figure skating
фильм (m) *film* film
» фильм без перево́да *film byes pirivóda* original language film
фи́ниш (m) *fínish* finish
фи́рма (f) *fírma* firm (company)
флаг (m) *flak* flag
фона́рь (m) *fanár* torch

фона́рный столб (m) *fanárny stolp*
  lamp post
фонта́н (m) *fantán* **fountain**
фортепиа́но (n) *fartepiána* **piano**
фотоаппара́т (m) *fataparát* **camera**
фотогра́фия (f), фо́то (n) *fatagráfiya,*
  fóta **photo**
францу́зский *frantsóoski* **French**
фрукт (m) *frookt* **fruit**
фунт (m) *foont* **pound** (*sterling*)
фурго́н (m) *foorgón* **van**
футбо́л (m) *footból* **football**
футбо́лка (f) *footbólka* **T-shirt**

Х

химчи́стка (f) *khimchístka* **dry-**
  cleaner's
хлеб (m) *khlyep* **bread**
» бе́лый хлеб *byély khlyep* **white**
  bread
» се́рый хлеб *syéry khlyep* **brown**
  bread
» ржано́й хлеб *rzhanóï klyep* **rye**
  bread
» цельнозерново́й хлеб
  tselnazirnovóï khlyeb **wholemeal**
  bread
хло́пок (m) *khlópak* **cotton** (*material*)
хо́бби (n) *khóbi* **hobby**
холм (m) *kholm* **hill**
холоди́льник (m) *khaladílnik* **fridge**
холо́дный *khalódny* **cold**
» хо́лодно *khólodna* (*it's*) **cold**
хоро́ший *kharóshi* **good**
хорошо́! *kharashó* **OK**
хоте́ть/захоте́ть *khatyét/zakhatyét*
  to want
» я бы хоте́л/а (m/f) *ya by khatyél/a*
  I would like
» хоте́ть/захоте́ть есть *khatyét/*
  zakhatyét yest **to be hungry**
» хоте́ть/захоте́ть пить *khatyét/*
  zakhatyét pit **to be thirsty**

христиани́н/христиа́нка (m/f)
  khristianín/khristiánka **Christian**
  (*people*)
христиа́нский *khristiánski* **Christian**
  (*adj.*)
хру́пкий *khróopki* **fragile**
хрустя́щий карто́фель (m)
  khroostyáschy kartófyel **crisps**
худо́й *khoodóï* **thin**
ху́же *khóozhi* **worse**

Ц

царь (m) *tsar* **tzar**
цветно́й *tsvitnóï* **colour** (*adj.*)
цвето́к (m), цветы́ (pl) *tsvitók, tsvitý*
  flower(s)
целова́ть/поцелова́ть *tsilavát/*
  patsilavát **to kiss**
цена́ (f) *tsiná* **price**
це́нности (pl) *tsénnasti* **valuables**
це́нный *tsénny* **valuable**
центр (m) *tsentr* **centre**
» центр го́рода *tsentr górada* **town**
  centre
центра́льный *tsintrálny* **central**
» центра́льное отопле́ние(n)
  tsintrálnaye ataplyéniye **central**
  heating
це́рковь (f) *tsérkaf* **church**
цирк (m) *tsirk* **circus**
цифрово́й *tsifravóï* **digital**
» цифрово́й фотоаппара́т (m)
  tsifravóï fataparát **digital camera**

Ч

чаевы́е (pl) *chiyivýye* **tip** (*in*
  restaurant)
чай (m) *chaï* **tea**
ча́йная ло́жка (f) *cháinaya lóshka*
  teaspoon
ча́йник (m) *cháinik* **kettle, teapot**
ча́йный паке́тик (m) *cháiny pakyétik*
  teabag
час (m) *chas* **hour**

часы́ рабо́ты *chisý rabóty* opening hours
часо́вня (f) *chasóvnya* chapel
час-пик (m) *chas-pik* rush hour
ча́стный *chásny* private
ча́сто *chásta* often
ча́стый *chásty* frequent
часть (f) *chast* part
часы́ (pl) *chisý* watch, clock *(time)*
ча́шка (f) *cháshka* cup
чем *chem* than
чемода́н (m) *chimadán* suitcase
чемпиона́т (m) *chimpianát* championship
че́рез *chyéris* via, through
че́стный *chésny* honest
чётный *chótny* even *(not odd)*
чини́ть/почини́ть *chinít/pachinít* to mend
чи́псы (pl) *chípsy* crisps
число́ (n) *chisló* number, date
чиха́ть/чихну́ть *chikhát/chikhnóot* to sneeze
что? *shto* what?
что́бы *shtóby* in order to
что́-нибудь *shtó-niboоd* anything
» что́-нибудь ещё *shtó-niboоd yischó* anything else
что́-то *shtó-ta* something

Ш

шампа́нское (n) *shampánskaye* champagne
шампу́нь (m) *shampóon* shampoo
ша́риковая ру́чка (f) *shárikavaya róochka* ballpoint pen
шарф (m) *sharf* scarf
шёлк (m) *sholk* silk
» шёлковый *shólkavy* silk *(adj.)*
шерсть (f) *sherst* wool
» шерстяно́й *shirstinói* woollen
шипу́чий *shipóochi, z gázam* fizzy
широ́кий *shiróki* wide

широкополо́сный интерне́т (m) *shirakapalósny internét* broadband
шить/сшить *shit/s-shit* to sew
шко́ла (f) *shkóla* school
шлем (m) *shlyem* helmet
шокола́д (m) *shikalát* chocolate
шоссе́ (n) *shassé* motorway
Шотла́ндия (f) *shatlándiya* Scotland
шотла́ндский *shatlánski* Scottish *(adj.)*
штéпсельная ви́лка (f) *shtépsilnaya vílka* plug *(electric)*
што́пор (m) *shtópar* corkscrew
што́ра (f) *shtóra* curtain
штраф (m) *shtraf* fine *(penalty)*
шу́ба (f) *shóoba* fur coat
шу́мный *shóomny* noisy
шу́тка (f) *shóotka* joke

Щ

ще́дрый *schédry* generous
щётка (f) *schótka* brush
» зубна́я щётка *zoobnáya* toothbrush
» щётка для воло́с *dlya valós* hairbrush

Э

экза́мены (pl) *ekzáminy* exams
экологи́чески чи́стые проду́кты (pl) *ekalagíchiski chístyye pradóokty* organic food
эконо́мика (f) *ekanómika* economics
экску́рсия (f) *ekskóorsiya* guided tour
экскурсово́д (m) *ekskoorsavót* guide *(person)*
эксперимéнт (m) *ekspirimyént* experiment
экспéрт (m) *ekspyért* expert
экспорти́ровать *ekspartírovat* to export
элéктрик (m) *elyéktrik* electrician
электри́чество (n) *eliktríchistva* electricity

эпилéптик (m) *epilyéptik* epileptic
эскалáтор (m) *eskalátar* escalator
этáж (m) *etásh* floor (level)
» пéрвый этаж *pyérvy etásh* ground
    floor
э́ти *éti* these
э́то *éta* this is/these are
э́тот *état* this (one)

Ю

ю́бка (f) *yóopka* skirt
ювели́рные изде́лия (pl) *yoovilírnyye
    izdyéliya* jewellery
ювели́рный магази́н (m) *yoovilírny
    magazín* jeweller's
юг (m) *yook* south
» ю́жный *yóozhny* southern
юри́ст (m) *yoorist* lawyer

Я

я *ya* I
ядови́тый *yidavíty* poisonous
я́зва (f) (желýдка) *yázva (zhilóotka)*
    ulcer
язы́к (m) *yizýk* language, tongue
прлы́к *yirlýk* label
я́щик (m) *yáschik* drawer

Now you're talking!

BBC Active offers a wide range of innovative resources, from short courses and grammars, to more in-depth courses for beginners or intermediates. Designed by language-teaching experts, our courses make the best use of today's technology, with book and audio, audio-only and multi-media products on offer. Many of these courses are accompanied by free online activities and television series, which are regularly repeated on BBC TWO Learning Zone.

Independent, interactive study course
2 x PC CD-ROM; 144pp course book; 60-min audio CD; free online activities and resources www.getinto.com

Short independent study course
128pp book; 2 x 60-minute CDs.

Long independent study course
192pp book; 2 x 70-minute CDs.